THE
CIVIL SERVICE

Vol. 1
Report of the Committee
1966-68

Chairman: Lord Fulton

Presented to Parliament by the Prime Minister
and the Chancellor of the Exchequer
by Command of Her Majesty
June 1968

LONDON
HER MAJESTY'S STATIONERY OFFICE
17s. 6d. net

Cmnd. 3638

Note: The estimated cost of preparing and publishing this Report is £51,854 of which £6,854 represents the estimated cost of printing and publication.

MEMBERS OF THE COMMITTEE

LORD FULTON (*Chairman*)

SIR NORMAN KIPPING, G.C.M.G., K.B.E., J.P.[1]

SIR PHILIP ALLEN, K.C.B.

MR. W. C. ANDERSON, C.B.E.

RT. HON. SIR EDWARD BOYLE, BART, M.P.

SIR WILLIAM COOK, C.B., F.R.S.

SIR JAMES DUNNETT, K.C.B., C.M.G.

DR. NORMAN HUNT

MR. R. R. NEILD

MR. R. SHELDON, M.P.[2]

PROFESSOR LORD SIMEY

SIR JOHN WALL, O.B.E.

---

[1]The Committee appointed Sir Norman Kipping to be their Vice-Chairman.

[2]Mr. Sheldon succeeded Mrs. Shirley Williams, M.P., on her appointment as Parliamentary Secretary, Ministry of Labour, in April, 1966.

1

PREFACE

1.   We were appointed on 8th February, 1966, to "examine the structure, recruitment and management, including training, of the Home Civil Service, and to make recommendations". We describe the scope of our inquiry at Appendix A.

2.   In producing our report we are greatly indebted to a large number of people—for their evidence, both written and oral, and for the research they have done on our behalf. We have thought it best to reserve most of our very many acknowledgements for Appendix L, where we also indicate the methods and procedures we have followed in the course of our inquiry.

3.   In order to keep the main body of our report short and, we hope, readable, we have confined it to a statement of our main proposals and the reasons for them. We have thus, with very few exceptions, deliberately refrained from summarising, debating or even referring in the course of the argument to the many points that have been put to us, both orally and in writing. The evidence has been so voluminous that we could not have done justice to it without multiplying the length of our report many times. We decided that we must avoid this. We hope that this will not lead those who gave evidence to us to feel that what they said has been ignored; it should be clear from what we have written how greatly we have been influenced by it.

4.   Some of the appendices, printed in this volume, deal more fully with certain topics than was practicable in the main body of our report, and make further, more detailed recommendations. In these we discuss some of the evidence that has mainly influenced our thinking on these topics; and Appendix K gives a more general account of the evidence that has made an especially positive contribution to our work.

5.   Our main findings are summarised at the end of the report and before the appendices. A detailed list of our recommendations is at the end of this volume.

6.   We are publishing four further volumes containing the written evidence that has been put before us and the reports of various investigations and surveys. These are listed in the table of contents and briefly described in Appendix L.

7.   We have reached a very wide measure of agreement. Some of us have reservations on certain points, which are indicated in the text. For the rest, we would not all put the same emphasis on every statement; some of us would have wished to go further, and others less far. But except where explicit reservations are made, this is the report of us all.

8.   In addition to the many acknowledgements of help that we make in Appendix L, we wish to record here two special debts. The first is to our staff. Our secretary, Mr. R. W. L. Wilding, has been throughout our task invariably indefatigable, firm, patient and resourceful. He takes with him, on

his return to more normal duties in the Civil Service, the warm thanks and good wishes of us all. We also wish to express our appreciation of all the help we have had from our assistant secretary, Mr. M. A. Simons, and from their staff, Mr. J. A. Lewry, Miss B. J. Fearn and Mrs. E. J. Baker. Individually and collectively, we have received from them constant support and unfailing kindness and courtesy. Secondly, his colleagues wish to acknowledge how much they owe to Dr. Norman Hunt. He led the Management Consultancy Group whose report illuminated so much of our discussions; he also, together with Mr. Wilding, bore the heavy burden of preparing the successive drafts of our report. He brought to bear on this task not only his own great knowledge and enthusiasm but also a sensitive awareness of the views of his colleagues, for which they are very grateful.

TABLE OF CONTENTS

VOLUME 1: REPORT AND APPENDICES

REPORT

CHAPTER 6

CHAPTER 7

CHAPTER 8

APPENDICES

APPENDIX I

APPENDIX J

APPENDIX K

APPENDIX L

OTHER VOLUMES

Volume 2: Report of a Management Consultancy Group
(published with the Report)

Volume 3: Surveys and investigations
(to be published later)
1. Social Survey of the Civil Service
2. Profile of a Profession: the Administrative Class of the Civil Service
3. Civil Service Unsuccessfuls: fifteen years later
4. Administrative Class Follow-up Survey
5. Executive Class Follow-up Survey
6. School Background of Members of the Administrative Class
7. Interim Report on a Survey of Wastage of Executive and Clerical Officers
8. Study of Ability, Efficiency and Job Satisfaction among Executive and Clerical Officers
9. Recruitment of Graduates to the Civil Service: Survey of Student Attitudes
10. Reports on the Civil Service since the Northcote-Trevelyan Report

Volume 4: Factual, statistical and explanatory papers
(published with the Report)

Section I	Introductory Factual Memorandum
Section II	Manpower
Section III	Recruitment
Section IV	Terms of Service
Section V	Structure and Staff Representation
Section VI	Training
Section VII	Careers and Career Management
Section VIII	Management Services

Volume 5: Proposals and opinions
(published with the Report)

Part I	Government Departments
Part II	Staff Associations (with some comments from H.M. Treasury)
Part III	Organisations outside the Civil Service
Part IV	Individuals

CHAPTER 1

THE CIVIL SERVICE TODAY

1. The Home Civil Service today is still fundamentally the product of the nineteenth-century philosophy of the Northcote-Trevelyan Report. The tasks it faces are those of the second half of the twentieth century. This is what we have found; it is what we seek to remedy.*

2. The foundations were laid by Northcote and Trevelyan in their report of 1854. Northcote and Trevelyan were much influenced by Macaulay whose Committee reported in the same year on the reform of the India Service. The two reports, so remarkable for their bluntness and brevity (together they run to about twenty pages in the original printing), have had such a far-reaching influence that we reproduce them in full in Appendix B.

3. These reports condemned the nepotism, the incompetence and other defects of the system inherited from the eighteenth century. Both proposed the introduction of competitive entry examinations. The Macaulay Report extolled the merits of the young men from Oxford and Cambridge who had read nothing but subjects unrelated to their future careers. The Northcote-Trevelyan Report pointed to the possible advantages of reading newer, more relevant subjects, such as geography or political economy, rather than the classics. But as the two services grew, this difference between the two reports seems to have been lost. There emerged the tradition of the " all-rounder " as he has been called by his champions, or " amateur " as he has been called by his critics.

4. Both reports concentrated on the graduates who thereafter came to form the top of each service. They took much less notice of the rest. In India, the supporting echelons were native, and the technical services, such as railways and engineering, were the business of specialists who stood lower than the ruling administrators. At home, the all-round administrators were to be supported by non-graduates to do executive and clerical work and by specialists (e.g. Inspectors of Schools) in those departments where they were needed. A man had to enter the Service on completing his education; once in, he was in for life. The outcome was a career service, immune from nepotism and political jobbery and, by the same token, attractive for its total security as well as for the intellectual achievement and social status that success in the entry examination implied.

5. Carrying out the Northcote-Trevelyan Report took time; there was long debate. Over the years other committees and commissions have considered various aspects of the Civil Service. Many new specialist classes have been added to the system, notably the scientists, engineers and their supporting classes. There is now an impressive amount of detailed training. Many other modifications have been made. The reports of the main committees and commissions are summarised and discussed in a note published in Volume 3.

---

*Lord Simey enters a reservation on this chapter. It is printed on page 101.

6. Nevertheless, the basic principles and philosophy of the Northcote-Trevelyan Report have prevailed: the essential features of their structure have remained.

7. Meanwhile, the role of government has greatly changed. Its traditional regulatory functions have multiplied in size and greatly broadened in scope. It has taken on vast new responsibilities. It is expected to achieve such general economic aims as full employment, a satisfactory rate of growth, stable prices and a healthy balance of payments. Through these and other policies (e.g. public purchasing, investment grants, financial regulators) it profoundly influences the output, costs and profitability of industry generally in both the home and overseas markets. Through nationalisation it more directly controls a number of basic industries. It has responsibilities for the location of industry and for town and country planning. It engages in research and development both for civil and military purposes. It provides comprehensive social services and is now expected to promote the fullest possible development of individual human potential. All these changes have made for a massive growth in public expenditure. Public spending means public control. A century ago the tasks of government were mainly passive and regulatory. Now they amount to a much more active and positive engagement in our affairs.

8. Technological progress and the vast amount of new knowledge have made a major impact on these tasks and on the process of taking decisions; the change goes on. Siting a new airport, buying military supplies, striking the right balance between coal, gas, oil and nuclear-powered electricity in a new energy policy—all these problems compel civil servants to use new techniques of analysis, management and co-ordination which are beyond those not specially trained in them.

9. The increase in the positive activities of government has not been solely an extension of the powers and functions of the State in an era of technological change. There has also been a complex intermingling of the public and private sectors. This has led to a proliferation of para-state organisations: public corporations, nationalised industries, negotiating bodies with varying degrees of public and private participation, public participation in private enterprises, voluntary bodies financed from public funds. Between the operations of the public and the private sectors there is often no clear boundary. Central and local government stand in a similarly intricate relationship; central government is generally held responsible for services that it partly or mainly finances but local authorities actually provide. As the tasks of government have grown and become more complex, so the need to consult and co-ordinate has grown as well.

10. The time it takes to reach a decision and carry it out has often lengthened. This is partly because of technological advance and the resulting complexity e.g. of defence equipment. Another reason is that the public and Parliament demand greater foresight and order in, for example, the development of land, the transport system and other resources, than they did in the past.

11. Governments also work more and more in an international setting. The improvement in communications and the greater interdependence of nations enlarges the difficulties as well as the opportunities of government.

12. To meet these new tasks of government the modern Civil Service must be able to handle the social, economic, scientific and technical problems of our time, in an international setting. Because the solutions to complex problems need long preparation, the Service must be far-sighted; from its accumulated knowledge and experience, it must show initiative in working out what are the needs of the future and how they might be met. A special responsibility now rests upon the Civil Service because one Parliament or even one Government often cannot see the process through.

13. At the same time, the Civil Service works under political direction and under the obligation of political accountability. This is the setting in which the daily work of many civil servants is carried out; thus they need to have a lively awareness of the political implications of what they are doing or advising. The Civil Service has also to be flexible enough to serve governments of any political complexion—whether they are committed to extend or in certain respects to reduce the role of the State. Throughout, it has to remember that it exists to serve the whole community, and that imaginative humanity sometimes matters more than tidy efficiency and administrative uniformity.

14. In our view the structure and practices of the Service have not kept up with the changing tasks. The defects we have found can nearly all be attributed to this. We have found no instance where reform has run ahead too rapidly. So, today, the Service is in need of fundamental change. It is inadequate in six main respects for the most efficient discharge of the present and prospective responsibilities of government.

15. First, the Service is still essentially based on the philosophy of the amateur (or " generalist " or " all-rounder "). This is most evident in the Administrative Class which holds the dominant position in the Service. The ideal administrator is still too often seen as the gifted layman who, moving frequently from job to job within the Service, can take a practical view of any problem, irrespective of its subject-matter, in the light of his knowledge and experience of the government machine. Today, as the report of our Management Consultancy Group* illustrates, this concept has most damaging consequences. It cannot make for the efficient despatch of public business when key men rarely stay in one job longer than two or three years before being moved to some other post, often in a very different area of government activity. A similar cult of the generalist is found in that part of the Executive Class that works in support of the Administrative Class and also even in some of the specialist classes. The cult is obsolete at all levels and in all parts of the Service.

16. Secondly, the present system of classes in the Service seriously impedes its work. The Service is divided into classes both horizontally (between higher and lower in the same broad area of work) and vertically (between different skills, professions or disciplines). There are 47 general classes whose members work in most government departments and over 1,400 departmental classes†. Each civil servant is recruited to a particular class; his membership of that class determines his prospects (most classes have their

---

*See Chapter 2, paragraph 26.

†These figures, and those quoted throughout our report, relate except where otherwise stated to non-industrial staff excluding the Post Office (see Appendix A).

11

own career structures) and the range of jobs on which he may be employed. It is true that there is some subsequent movement between classes; but such rigid and prolific compartmentalism in the Service leads to the setting up of cumbersome organisational forms, seriously hampers the Service in adapting itself to new tasks, prevents the best use of individual talent, contributes to the inequality of promotion prospects, causes frustration and resentment, and impedes the entry into wider management of those well fitted for it.

17. Thirdly, many scientists, engineers and members of other specialist classes get neither the full responsibilities and corresponding authority, nor the opportunities they ought to have. Too often they are organised in a separate hierarchy, while the policy and financial aspects of the work are reserved to a parallel group of " generalist " administrators; and their access to higher management and policy-making is restricted. Partly this is because many of them are equipped only to practise their own specialism; a body of men with the qualities of the French *polytechnicien*—skilled in his craft, but skilled, too, as an administrator—has so far not been developed in Britain. In the new Civil Service a wider and more important role must be opened up for specialists trained and equipped for it.

18. Fourthly, too few civil servants are skilled managers. Since the major managerial role in the Service is specifically allocated to members of the Administrative Class it follows that this criticism applies particularly to them. Few members of the class actually see themselves as managers, i.e. as responsible for organisation, directing staff, planning the progress of work, setting standards of attainment and measuring results, reviewing procedures and quantifying different courses of action. One reason for this is that they are not adequately trained in management. Another is that much of their work is not managerial in this sense; so they tend to think of themselves as advisers on policy to people above them, rather than as managers of the administrative machine below them. Scientists and other specialists are also open to criticism here: not enough have been trained in management, particularly in personnel management, project management, accounting and control.

19. Fifthly, there is not enough contact between the Service and the rest of the community. There is not enough awareness of how the world outside Whitehall works, how government policies will affect it, and the new ideas and methods which are developing in the universities, in business and in other walks of life. Partly this is a consequence of a career service. Since we expect most civil servants to spend their entire working lives in the Service, we can hardly wonder if they have little direct and systematic experience of the daily life and thought of other people. Another element in this is the social and educational composition of the Civil Service; the Social Survey of the Service which we commissioned suggests that direct recruitment to the Administrative Class since the war has not produced the widening of its social and educational base that might have been expected.* The public interest

*We commissioned a survey of the social and educational background of the main general-service classes. It was carried out by Dr. A. H. Halsey, Head of the Department of Social and Administrative Studies at the University of Oxford, and Mr. I. M. Crewe, Assistant Lecturer in Politics at the University of Lancaster. Their report which will be published in Volume 3 in a few months' time, will contain a full discussion of this subject.

must suffer from any exclusiveness or isolation which hinders a full understanding of contemporary problems or unduly restricts the free flow of men, knowledge and ideas between the Service and the outside world.

20. Finally, we have serious criticisms of personnel management. Career-planning covers too small a section of the Service—mainly the Administrative Class—and is not sufficiently purposive or properly conceived; civil servants are moved too frequently between unrelated jobs, often with scant regard to personal preference or aptitude. Nor is there enough encouragement and reward for individual initiative and objectively measured performance; for many civil servants, especially in the lower grades, promotion depends too much on seniority.

21. For these and other defects the central management of the Service, the Treasury, must accept its share of responsibility. It is unfortunate that there was not a major reform in the post-war years when the government took on so many new tasks and the Service had been loosened by war-time temporary recruitment and improvisation. There was then a great opportunity to preserve and adapt to peace-time conditions the flexibility which war had imposed. For a number of reasons, not all of them internal to the Service, this opportunity was not taken. In the 1950s the old ways reasserted themselves. The nature of the task was changing and the Service was left behind. Only recently has any attempt been made to introduce significant reforms. Despite the recent improvement in its management services the Treasury has failed to keep the Service up to date.

22. To some extent the urgent need for fundamental reform has been obscured by the Service's very considerable strengths, notably its capacity for improvisation—aptly demonstrated by the speed with which new departments have been set up in the last four years. There are exceptionally able men and women at all levels. There is a strong sense of public service. Its integrity and impartiality are unquestioned. We believe that the country does not recognise enough how impressively conscientious many civil servants are in the personal service they give to the public. It is of high importance that these and other qualities should be preserved.

23. In making our proposals for reform we have been influenced by what we have seen of foreign civil services—the emphasis on training and professionalism in France, the way young men of thrust and vigour in France and Sweden quickly reach posts of high responsibility where they are directly advising Ministers, the contributions the " in-and-outers " make to government in the United States and the role played by specialists in both the United States and France. Our impressions of the visits we paid to these three countries are recorded in Appendix C.

24. One basic guiding principle should in our view govern the future development of the Civil Service. It applies to any organisation and is simple to the point of banality, but the root of much of our criticism is that it has not been observed. The principle is: look at the job first. The Civil Service must continuously review the tasks it is called upon to perform and the possible ways in which it might perform them; it should then think out what new skills and kinds of men are needed, and how these men can be found, trained and deployed. The Service must avoid a static view of a new ideal

man and structure which in its turn could become as much of an obstacle to change as the present inheritance.

25. We have sought to devise a form of management for the Civil Service that will ensure that it is better run and able to generate its own self-criticism and forward drive. One of the main troubles of the Service has been that, in achieving immunity from political intervention, a system was evolved which until recently was virtually immune from outside pressures for change. Since it was not immune from inside resistance to change, inertia was perhaps predictable.

14

CHAPTER 2

THE TASKS OF THE MODERN CIVIL SERVICE
AND THE MEN AND WOMEN THEY NEED

26. The tasks of modern government make heavy demands on civil servants at every level. Their jobs are immensely various. We thought it necessary, both for our own guidance and to help general understanding, to investigate and report in detail on the work that civil servants do. We therefore commissioned a special investigation of the work of the Service. It was carried out by a group led by a member of the Committee, Dr. Norman Hunt, and including management consultants, an executive from a business firm and a civil servant from the Organisation and Methods Division of the Treasury. Their report, which we publish as Volume 2, contains a description of the work of those areas of the Service that they studied. We do not propose to summarise it here. But it is important at least to outline the general scope of the work of civil servants before considering what skills and kinds of men and women are needed.

27. Civil servants work in support of Ministers in their public and parliamentary duties. Some of them prepare plans and advise on policy, assembling and interpreting all the data required, e.g. for a decision on a new social security policy, a change in defence policy, a new national transport policy or a new international joint project in the technical field—whether Ministers, individually or collectively, place greater or lesser reliance on direct government intervention. They prepare legislation and assist Ministers with its passage through Parliament. They draft regulations and answers to Parliamentary Questions. They produce briefs for debates and the mass of information which the constitutional principle of parliamentary and public accountability requires. Increasingly, senior civil servants now appear before Parliamentary Committees. Some of this varied work has no counterpart in business or, indeed, anywhere outside the government service.

28. Operating policies embodied in existing legislation and implementing policy decisions take up most of the time of most civil servants. There are taxes to be collected, employment and social security offices to be run. There is a mass of individual case-work both in local offices and in the central departments of state. New policy may require the creation of a new administrative framework. There are major programmes to be managed and controlled, such as the planning and engineering of motorways from their initial location and design to the finished construction; the design of Polaris installations and other military works; the management of international programmes like Concorde; the vast range of scientific research and development and of government procurement; the central responsibility for the nationalised industries and for the state of the economy.

15

29.   Some of the work involves the Civil Service in complex relationships with other bodies which are partners in the execution of government policy or are directly affected by it.   They include local authorities and nationalised industries in the first category and a multitude of organised interests in the second.   This work calls for practical judgement and negotiating skill.   It also calls for a thorough knowledge of the subject under negotiation and of the problems and interests of the bodies concerned.   In the economic field, for example, many civil servants need a knowledge of industry and an understanding of market forces.

30.   Technical progress has a major impact on both the making and the implementation of policy, whether the tasks are traditional or new to government.   Computers are a good example of this; they offer prospects of sophisticated administration hitherto impossible by permitting much more comprehensive approaches to problems and the use of more, and vastly more complex, data.   This trend greatly enhances the importance of numeracy.   Skill in the use of numbers is needed in addition to the qualities of judgement and foresight.

31.   Even this brief and impressionistic description is perhaps enough to make it clear that, as a body, civil servants today have to be equipped to tackle the political, scientific, social, economic and technical problems of our time.   They have to be aware of interests and opinions throughout the country and of many developments abroad.   They have to keep up with the rapid growth of new knowledge and acquire new techniques to apply it.   In short the Civil Service is no place for the amateur.   It must be staffed by men and women who are truly professional.

32.   We use the word " professional " in this context to include two main attributes which in our view are essential in varying combinations for work in the government service.   One is being skilled in one's job—skill which comes from training and sustained experience.   The other is having the fundamental knowledge of and deep familiarity with a subject that enable a man to move with ease among its concepts.   Both spring from and reinforce a constant striving for higher standards.   The work of government demands these qualities not only in the members of the generally recognised professions, but at all levels and in all parts of the Service.   We use " professional " in this comprehensive sense.

33.   These attributes of professionalism are already present in the Civil Service in some measure.   But today's tasks require them to be much further developed than hitherto.   The Service must also be quicker to recognise the contribution new professional skills can make to its work.

34.   There are two broad types of professionalism that we believe the Service needs.

35.   The first is the professionalism of those whose work in government is just one of a number of career opportunities for the exercise of their qualifications and skills.   In this category are the architects, lawyers, doctors, engineers, scientists, accountants, economists, draughtsmen, technicians and so on.   Some of these, like doctors and scientists, have acquired their professionalism or specialism by recognised training outside the Service.   Others, like some draughtsmen and technicians, may acquire and develop their skills after joining the Service.   In either event in their early years they do much

16

the same type of work in the public service as if they had gone into private practice, business, the universities or local government. In the rest of this report we shall normally refer to these men and women as "specialists", not to denote any narrow sub-division of some professional field, but solely as a convenient label for this broad category of Civil Service staff.

36. The Civil Service already employs large numbers of men and women of this type. But it has not always recognised the need for new kinds of specialism quickly enough or recruited enough specialists of the high quality that the public interest demands. In particular, it has been slow to recognise the benefits that would flow from a much larger recruitment of particular categories such as accountants, statisticians, economists and Research Officers and their employment in positions of greater responsibility. For example, while there were 106 economists in the Civil Service in 1967, there were only 19 in 1963. We discuss the specific problems of accountants and Research Officers* in Appendix D. Here we think it right to draw special attention to the position of accountants.

37. Present practice in the Civil Service severely restricts the role of the Accountant Class and excludes its members from responsibility for financial control. They are limited to the relatively narrow field in which departments themselves keep commercial accounts or are concerned with the financial operations of commercial organisations. Their outlets into other kinds of work and into posts of higher management are severely limited. At present the Service employs only 309 accountants of whom 64 are temporary; no post carries a salary of more than £4,500 and there are only six accountants' posts with salaries above £3,650. In our view, qualified accountants could make a valuable contribution to the management of several areas of civil service work: for example, in financial forecasting and control, in the whole field of government procurement and in reviewing the financial performance of nationalised industries. These are areas of work similar to those in which accountants are prominent in industry; but they are generally excluded from them in the Civil Service. Further, the skills of the modern management accountant appear to us to be increasingly needed at high levels of policy-making and management. He is trained to evaluate policy options in financial terms, to compare the costs and benefits arising from different uses of resources, and to apply quantitative techniques to the control of expenditure and the measurement of efficiency.

38. In addition to employing specialists in the right numbers and of the right type and quality, the Service should also allow them to carry more responsibility. Their organisation in separate hierarchies, with the policy and financial aspects of their work reserved to a parallel group of "generalist" administrators, has manifest disadvantages. It slows down the processes of decision and management, leads to inefficiency, frequently means that no individual has clear managerial authority, and prevents the specialists from exercising the full range of responsibilities normally associated with their professions and exercised by their counterparts outside the Service. In addition, the obstacles at present preventing them from reaching top management must be removed. The need for wider outlets also generally applies

*A class engaged on research mainly in the field of the social sciences. A fuller description is given in Appendix D.

to specialists whose work is peculiar to government, such as Tax Inspectors. For specialists who are to carry these greater responsibilities there will need to be a deliberate policy of training in administration and management. Our proposals to achieve these ends are contained in later chapters.

39. The second kind of professionalism which needs to be much more fully developed is the professionalism of those members of the Administrative and Executive Classes who are now treated, and regard themselves, as " generalists ". In the rest of this report we shall refer to members of both these classes and their future counterparts as " administrators ". Parts of their work closely resemble management in industry and commerce; other parts do not. We use " administrator ", like " specialist ", as the most generally convenient label.

40. Frequent moves from job to job within the Service or within a department give " generalist " administrators proficiency in operating the government machine, and in serving Ministers and Parliament. But many lack the fully developed professionalism that their work now demands. They do not develop adequate knowledge in depth in any one aspect of the department's work and frequently not even in the general area of activity in which the department operates. Often they are required to give advice on subjects they do not sufficiently understand or to take decisions whose significance they do not fully grasp. This has serious consequences. It can lead to bad policy-making; it prevents a fundamental evaluation of the policies being administered; it often leads to the adoption of inefficient methods for implementing these policies—methods which are sometimes baffling to those outside the Service who are affected by them; and it obstructs the establishment of fruitful contacts with sources of expert advice both inside and outside the Service.

41. The fuller professionalism now required from all administrators (including by our definition those now classified as " Executive ") in turn calls for new principles to be applied to their selection, training and deployment. It must be accepted that for the administrator to be expert in running the government machine is not in itself enough. He must in future also have or acquire the basic concepts and knowledge, whether social, economic, industrial or financial, relevant to his area of administration and appropriate to his level of responsibility. He must have a real understanding of, and familiarity with, the principles, techniques and trends of development in the subject-matter of the field in which he is operating.

42. As we see it, the application of this principle means that an administrator must specialise, particularly in his early years, in one of the various areas of administration. At the same time, since modern administration requires men to have breadth as well as depth, and since civil servants operate in a political environment, it seems to us important that such specialisation should not be too narrowly conceived. We considered two possible ways of achieving these objectives.

43. We considered whether we should recommend a grouping of departments on the basis of their main areas of activity. Thus, some departments are mainly concerned with social problems, others with economic, financial, commercial and industrial problems and others with scientific or technical problems. It seemed attractive to believe that if departments were broadly

18

grouped in this way an administrator might best develop his professionalism, and in particular his knowledge of the subject-matter of his area of administration, by spending most of his career within one group of departments. We rejected this solution. It is possible broadly to group departments in this way, yet almost every department has its own mixture of social, scientific, economic and financial work. The Department of Education and Science is a good example. While predominantly a social department, with branches dealing with schools, teachers, further education and so on, nevertheless:—

(a) administrators also staff the Accountant General's Branch which deals mainly with financial and economic questions;

(b) there are administrators in its Architects and Buildings Branch concerned largely with the technical and financial aspects of school building programmes and projects;

(c) administrators staff its Establishment and Organisation Branch which is concerned with individual career management and the promotion of efficiency and economy in the organisation of the department;

(d) there is a large proportion of administrators among the staff of the General Science Branch and of the Council for Scientific Policy.

Today the pattern in the Department of Education and Science, as in any other department, is for an administrator to move from job to job between these widely differing branches within the department. It is this pattern of movement that we have criticised as an obstacle to the development of the required professionalism. If the Department of Education and Science were simply grouped with other social departments, this would only multiply the number of different kinds of job to which a man would be liable to be moved. This would defeat our aims rather than promote them. We recommend, therefore, a different solution.

44. Although the tasks that fall to administrators are immensely varied, we believe that they fall into broad categories which are identifiable on the basis of the subject-matter of the work rather than on the basis of the particular department in which the work is done. It is on this categorisation by subject-matter that administrative specialisation should be based.

45. We have not been able to survey all the administrative jobs in the Service. It is for the Civil Service Department* to analyse them and to identify groups of jobs which provide a field for specialisation on the basis of their common subject-matter. We believe, however, that we can identify two such groups at present.

46. First, we think that a broad group of administrative jobs in different departments is concerned with a subject-matter that is primarily economic and financial. Within this broad group the emphasis in some areas of government may be on general economic planning and control; in others, on the problems of international trade or of particular industries; in others, on the financial control of major programmes of capital and current expenditure;

*We recommend in Chapter 7 that the central management of the Civil Service should be transferred from the Treasury to a new Civil Service Department. From this point onwards in our report we refer to this new department by name when we discuss the part to be played by central management in running the Service.

in others (mainly in technical and scientific departments) on the economic and financial aspects of large technological projects. Thus, from a general economic and financial basis, the work develops its own internal specialisms. We think that this pattern should be reflected in the training and deployment of individual administrators for this work.

47. There is a second broad group of administrative jobs where the basis is essentially social; for example, housing, town and country planning, education, race relations, social security, industrial relations, personnel management, crime and delinquency. Again, within a common framework of knowledge and experience, the work develops its own specialisms. Here too the training and deployment of individual administrators should reflect this pattern.

48. Each of these two main categories of work has its own substantial and broadly based body of knowledge. We believe that a civil servant needs to draw on this to supplement his skills as an administrator if he is to develop the professionalism now needed. So the Service must ensure that its administrators acquire and develop the appropriate body of knowledge together with its associated conceptual framework and analytical tools. This means that an administrator, at least in his early years, should specialise in one or other of these main categories of work—the economic, industrial and financial, or the social. In consequence, for basic training and career management administrators should be distinguished into these two broad groups. We emphasise that this should not preclude further groupings if these are found necessary or desirable.

49. The economic and financial administrators should be men and women who, in addition to their skill in administration, also have appropriate qualifications, experience and training in such subjects as economics, finance, business administration and statistics, especially as applied to government work. Their deployment should not be limited only to the main economic departments of government. They should be employed in any department in posts that are mainly financial or concerned with economic administration and management. They should, as we have said, add to their basic knowledge of their field any further specialisation that particular areas of government work require. Thus, the career pattern of the economic and financial administrator may involve moment between departments; it should involve a steady broadening of an individual's responsibility as he moves upwards, but he should normally move between posts appropriate to members of the group. These administrators will not replace specialist economists; we discuss their relationship below.

50. We have proposed that within the economic and financial group of administrators there should be different branches of further specialisation. One of these to which we wish to draw special attention is work in the predominantly scientific and technical areas of the Service. These areas will be largely staffed by specialists, for example, scientists and engineers. Some of these—we hope an increasing number—will eventually come to be managers or administrators in the field of their specialism. But we see a continuing need in some departments for economic and financial administrators who have been specially trained to apply their skills to work of a high scientific and technological content, for example to the economic aspects of research and to the financial control of advanced technological projects. Some of them,

and we hope their number will grow, will have had scientific or technical training before they enter the Service; and this will be of value to their understanding of the language and problems of their specialist colleagues. However, the primary function of the administrator in this field is not to duplicate the specialist knowledge of the scientist or engineer, but to apply his economic and financial skills in a scientific and technological context.

51. The group of social administrators would be broader and more heterogeneous than its economic and financial counterpart. In addition to their administrative skills, social administrators should also have training and experience in the social studies relevant to modern government. These include a knowledge of the social structure, organisation and planning of communities and regions; methods of social investigation and the techniques of collecting and analysing information commonly used in public and private inquiries into social problems; and of social administration, especially the structure of the publicly provided social services and the policy problems which arise from their development. The emphasis in this training should vary, depending very much on the particular social area of government concerned. Clearly, most social administrators will be concentrated in the main social departments of government. But many will also be employed throughout the Service. For example, we would expect the personnel and organisation divisions of all departments to contain a proportion of social administrators. There will also be jobs in the economic departments for which social administrators will be needed. As with the economic and financial administrators, the career pattern may involve service in more than one department, but normally within the area of the social administrator's expertise.

52. Though in each department there should be a suitable blend of administrators from both groups, they should not replace those specialists in their departments (e.g. engineers, accountants, economists, sociologists) whose primary concern is the practice of their specialism. Thus the economic administrators in an economic department would not, for example, generally replace those who are economists by profession. The economic administrators will not have the same depth of expertise, and will be immersed in the day-to-day operations of the department in a way that would be inappropriate for the specialist economist. On the other hand, the employment of specialist economists in a department will not duplicate or make unnecessary the work of economic administrators. Besides making their contribution to policy-making, the economic administrators will be providing a great deal of explanatory information for Ministers, Parliament and the public; they will also be engaged in negotiation with outside interests; many will be involved in the administration of existing economic policies, for example, policies for the distribution of industry. Jobs of this kind do not need to be, nor should they be, handed over to specialist economists. Indeed, a specialist economist who became immersed in these day-to-day problems of administration could not maintain the high degree of economic expertise his work demands. Similar considerations apply to the relationships between social administrators and the specialists with whom they work. Our aim is not to replace specialists by administrators, or vice versa. They should be complementary to one another. It is, rather, that the administrator, trained and experienced in his subject-matter, should enjoy a more fruitful relation-

21

ship with the specialist than in the past, and that the Service should harness the best contribution from each.

53. The policy of grouping administrators which we have proposed is necessary to enable them to gain the knowledge and experience their work requires. Within each group the depth of understanding, skill, knowledge and experience demanded will vary with the level of responsibility. The higher the responsibility of the post, the greater the understanding required of its occupant. It is therefore important that those who have entered the Service direct from school and have the ability to rise to positions of high responsibility should be given the kind of experience, and encouraged to gain the qualifications, that they will need for this purpose. We are convinced however that professionalism, as we have described it, is not limited in its conception to work at senior levels. It means the ability and the sustained effort needed to ensure that each job, whatever its level, is performed to a constantly improving standard. The principle that every civil servant should be equipped to pursue this aim applies throughout.

54. This grouping will also provide the necessary basis of knowledge for a dynamic Service. Civil servants who are more at home with the machinery of administration than with its content tend to be cautious—sometimes, even negative; a few, reacting the other way to what they do not fully understand, may well be rash. Either because they lack training or have moved too frequently between jobs, they are often not equipped to conduct a fruitful dialogue with experts both inside and outside the Service. Well-prepared innovation is more likely to come from those whose grasp of their subject gives them a sure awareness of its possibilities as well as its limitations and from those able to talk with experts in their own language. This is what our proposed grouping of administrators is designed to produce.

55. We do not wish that these two groups of administrators should be frozen into a rigid pattern for the rest of the century. They represent what we see as the present application of the guiding principle set out in paragraph 41: that those engaged in administration and management must not only be skilled in running the government machine, but must also have the basic concepts and knowledge relevant to their area of administration. We propose these groups as a starting-point. It should be the task of the central management of the Service to develop and refine them and to keep them up to date as the tasks of the Service change and develop. But we are confident that the continuous application of this principle will provide for the Service the necessary reservoir of trained talent and expertise.

56. From these groups and from the specialists (as defined in paragraph 35) will also come men and women to specialise in the kinds of government work for which many different kinds of background and experience can be appropriate. Examples are contracts work, computers, O and M, personnel work and so on. Such further specialisation should be encouraged and it should be possible where appropriate for some people to make their careers in one or other of these areas of further specialisation. For example, a social administrator or an accountant might go on to specialise in O and M work, moving in this field between departments to jobs of higher responsibility and eventually, perhaps after appropriate experience outside government, rising to the most responsible jobs in this field in the Service.

57. From all these professionals, administrators and specialists alike, will come the future top management of the Service. They will be men and women experienced in running the government machine; they will have a basic expertise in one or more aspects of a department's work; and they will have been broadened by increasing responsibilities and experience to become the fully professional advisers of Ministers and managers of their policies.

58. The pattern of professionalism which we propose for the future will thus be based upon training and specialisation in the early years of a civil servant's career. Some twenty years will pass before the Service is predominantly staffed by men and women whose careers have been formed in this way. We believe, however, that greatly improved standards of professionalism can be achieved in a much shorter time by the present generation of civil servants. This will need carefully planned posting and specially devised training courses. We revert to this in the section on training in the next chapter.

CHAPTER 3

RECRUITMENT, TRAINING AND CAREER MANAGEMENT

59. We have so far discussed the tasks of the Service and the professional skills they call for in its members. We turn now to the problems of recruitment, training and career development.

60. We begin by considering where the main responsibility for recruitment to the Service should lie and how far it should be delegated to individual departments or establishments. In this context we make general recommendations designed to reduce the present length of the recruitment process. We go on to the principles and methods that should apply to the recruitment of the various types of men and women the Service needs. Finally, we turn to the question of post-entry training and career management.

THE RESPONSIBILITY FOR RECRUITMENT

61. The central responsibility for recruitment is at present divided. The Treasury is responsible for recruitment policy. The running of competitions, the selection of successful candidates and (in large part) their initial allocation to departments is in the hands of an independent body, the Civil Service Commission. In addition, some very large categories of staff are recruited initially by departments. But in all cases the Commissioners must issue a certificate for a civil servant to achieve permanent status*. The Commissioners hold their appointments directly from the Crown and are appointed by Order in Council. The justification for this independence has been the need to ensure that all appointments to the Service are made strictly on merit and are clear of political or other patronage. We consider, however, that the present arrangement is in need of fundamental revision.

62. We regard recruitment, training and subsequent career development as parts of a single process to be as closely integrated as possible. We believe accordingly that recruitment should be in the hands of those who also share a direct responsibility for the individual's subsequent training, deployment and development. As a consequence, assessments of performance will be much more fully and directly fed back to those responsible for recruitment. These in turn will be better placed to adjust their criteria and methods as necessary; they will also have a much closer knowledge of the changing work and needs of departments. In our view the Service suffers now from the separateness and consequent remoteness of the Civil Service Commission, which under the existing arrangements cannot know enough of the needs of individual departments and is too little connected with the training and early management of those whom it appoints.

63. We recommend, therefore, that the Civil Service Commission should

---

*i.e. to be established. Where recruitment is central, establishment is a part of initial recruitment. Where it is departmental, establishment comes later.

cease to be a separate and independent organisation*. It should become part of the new Civil Service Department, and its staff should be integrated with it. Some of its functions should be shared with the various employing departments in ways we discuss below.

64. The selection of recruits should be, and should be seen to be, independent of any form of patronage. But this is not incompatible with a much closer association between the selectors and both the central management of the Service and the employing departments. We believe that the tradition of making appointments solely on merit is now well enough established to survive without keeping the Civil Service Commission as a separate organisation; independence in selection can be assured by other means. We do not wish to make a detailed recommendation; one such means, however, might be to designate an individual senior officer in the Civil Service Department as First Civil Service Commissioner, and to give him the formal responsibility for final decisions on the selection of recruits. It should be accepted no less clearly than in the past that the First Commissioner would not be subjected to ministerial or parliamentary questioning over individual appointments.

65. We have expressed the view that some of the Civil Service Commission's present functions should be shared with the various employing departments. This is desirable because recruitment should be directly related to the needs of individual departments. They know the tasks they have to perform and are best placed to indicate the qualifications, training and experience needed. Therefore, we wish to see departments play a larger part in the recruitment process in two ways.

66. First, in drawing up the annual manpower budget for discussion with the Civil Service Department, each department should indicate as exactly as possible its needs at all levels, both for the various kinds of specialist staff and also for the different types and groups of administrative staff referred to in Chapter 2. These needs (allowing for the necessary interdepartmental movement) would determine the pattern of recruitment. Essentially this would be recruitment for specific ranges of jobs.

67. Secondly, we think departments should have a greater influence on the selection of individuals. We considered the case for handing all recruitment over to the departments; but we rejected this on the grounds that it would encourage wasteful competition, place the less glamorous departments at too great a disadvantage and break up a Service which, in our view, should remain unified. We think, however, that a higher proportion than at present should be recruited directly by departments, and that the employing departments should be better represented in the recruitment process where it continues to be central. We return to these proposals in more detail later in this chapter.

RECRUITMENT PROCEDURES AND THE PROBLEMS OF DELAY

68. Another serious criticism of the present methods of recruitment is that they are too slow in operation. This criticism has arisen partly because the

---

*The Commission now also recruit staff for the Diplomatic Service, the House of Commons, the Government of Northern Ireland and a number of " fringe " bodies whose staff do not form part of the Civil Service. The Civil Service Department could, perhaps, continue to act for them on an agency basis.

Civil Service Commission has until recently interpreted the principle of competitive examination as obliging it to wait until the whole of a very large field has been examined and put in order of merit, no matter how outstanding a particular applicant may be. Various modifications made in recent years have led to considerable improvements. These have included " continuous competitions " for a number of important groups, e.g. Tax Inspectors and the relatively small number of Experimental Officers who are recruited centrally. But the process is still apt to take too long. It takes too long between application and the announcement of the result of the examination; and between the result of the examination and the time when successful candidates are able to start work*. Lengthy periods of waiting and suspense are undesirable for those still attending school or university. For those who have left and who feel under pressure to start earning, they may be decisive in causing them to turn to other employment. For those already in jobs who are candidates for late entry (often scarce specialists), they cause serious embarrassment, because of obligations to existing employers.

69. The Service will continue to face severe competition for talent. It cannot allow the survival of traditional procedures to place it at a disadvantage with industry and commerce, the nationalised industries and local government. We recognise that when there are many well-qualified applicants for a small number of posts, competitions must continue. But we think that the procedures of formal competition should be restricted to posts for which they are indispensable; even then it should be made possible to offer outstanding candidates rapid appointment. Wherever qualified applicants are relatively scarce, and it is in practice certain that there will be posts for all suitable candidates, these should be brought in without delay, once it is clear that they are up to the required standard; this is especially important in regard to the recruitment of those with scarce specialist skills.

70. We hope that the absorption of the Civil Service Commission within the Civil Service Department will assist in bringing about these improvements. The need to reduce to the minimum the interval between the results of competitions and the time when those who have been declared successful actually start work will partly be met by the proposals about establishment that we make in the next chapter. In addition, we recommend that a review of the processes of recruitment should be put in hand; besides seeking ways of reducing the time they take, it should examine the problems of methods of selection to which we refer in paragraph 82 below and Appendix E.

---

*The following examples have been provided by the Civil Service Commission:—

(a) Candidates for the Method II competition for the Administrative Class, applying by the end of November, get their results between early March and May, depending on when they go to the Civil Service Selection Board. (Most must then wait for their degree results in June or July before the offer of an appointment becomes certain.)

(b) Candidates for the competition for direct entrant Principals (age limits 30-35) know their results between 9 and 19 weeks after the closing date for applications. The average period between the notification of results and being able to start work is 5½ weeks, ranging from 2½ to 9 weeks.

(c) For recruits to the Executive Class the average total period (on the basis of a sample taken in 1966) between application and being able to start work is 69 days, ranging from 30 to 88 days. Within this the average period between the notification of results and being able to start work is 23 days, ranging from 11 to 43 days.

THE RECRUITMENT OF GRADUATES, POST-GRADUATES AND THEIR EQUIVALENTS

71. Our proposals in Chapter 2 mean that graduates, post-graduates and their equivalents should be employed, in their early years at any rate, either as specialists (architects, scientists, engineers, etc.) or in one of the new groups of administrators. In either case, men and women should be recruited for a specified range of jobs.

72. This does not involve any basic change in the recruitment policy for specialists. They are at present recruited for a clearly defined range of jobs, and clearly defined, relevant qualifications are therefore demanded. It would be an advantage if more of them were already grounded in management and administration and could be equipped with the confidence and prestige of the French *polytechniciens*. Some university courses are now beginning to recognise this need. In this connection we have noted the development of courses that combine engineering with economics, and science with economics; and we welcome the sandwich courses at some universities that give scientists and engineers experience in industry and a grounding in economics and business administration as well as a purely scientific or specialist qualification. This however is only a start; and for the time being it must be the task of the Service to equip its specialists with the additional administrative, managerial and other skills they need; we discuss this in our later paragraphs on training.

73. Many specialist staff are now recruited direct by the department or establishment that is to employ them. We think that this should become the normal rule. Recruitment should be by interview before a board. The board should normally include a kindred specialist from outside the Service and a representative of the Civil Service Department. But the majority should be from the " user " department or establishment. For certain specialists, recruitment may conveniently be done by departments acting together in groups or by the Civil Service Department on their behalf. This is matter for decision from time to time between the Civil Service Department and the other departments. But the essential need where scarce specialist skills are concerned is for speed; grouping and co-ordination should not be allowed to lead to time-consuming formality.

74. Our proposals in Chapter 2 for grouping administrators have important implications for the direct recruitment of graduates, post-graduates and their equivalents for administrative work. They mean that in future men and women should not be recruited for employment as " generalist " administrators and intelligent all-rounders—to do any of, and a succession of, the widely differing jobs covered by the " generalist " concept. Instead, they should be recruited to do a specified range of jobs in a particular area of work, at any rate during their early years. In Chapter 2 we distinguish two broad categories of administration—the economic and financial, and the social. It follows that the Service should aim to recruit those with the best qualifications, aptitudes and qualities for the jobs falling within one of these broad groups; for the later entrants relevant experience will also be an important consideration.

75. Clearly, most recruits who come straight from their university will not on entry have the full range of knowledge and skills required for work in one or other of the administrative groups. They will require in-service train-

ing and experience. But a majority of us* consider that the relevance to their future work of the subject-matter of their university or other pre-Service studies should be an important qualification for appointment.

76. To give preference for relevance is to adapt to the needs of today the old principle that the Service should seek to recruit those it believes best equipped for work in government. When the aim was to recruit men and women to be intelligent all-rounders, the Service naturally drew heavily on courses like classics and history at Oxford and Cambridge, which by their prestige have always attracted young people of the highest abilities. These courses give an insight into the conditions of historical change and because for the most part the material they use is remote from the here and now they provide a " disinterested " intellectual training. Today, when the tasks or government have changed, the Service should seek to recruit those equipped for the new tasks. First-degree courses based on the study of modern subjects especially attract many young people with a positive and practical interest in contemporary problems, political, social, economic, scientific and technological. These problems will yield their solutions only to the most concentrated assaults of minds equipped through rigorous and sustained intellectual discipline wth the necessary apparatus of relevant ideas, knowledge, methods and techniques. We therefore wish the Civil Service to attract its full share of young people motivated in this way, with minds disciplined by undergraduate (and post-graduate) work in the social studies, the mathematical and physical sciences, the biological sciences or in the applied and engineering sciences.

77. There is also evidence that most undergraduates want jobs in which they can make direct use of their university studies†. In recent years the Service has not properly recognised this, giving the general impression that it is more concerned with the quality of a man's degree than its relevance to the work of government. This, in our view, has discouraged applications from graduates whose interest and studies are focused on modern problems. Thus post-war recruitment to the Administrative Class has run counter to the increased trend in the universities towards the study of the problems of the modern world. Therefore, to be attractive to this growing number of graduates, the Service should declare its special interest in the relevance of their studies. In this way, too, the Service would be attracting its recruits from a wider range of degree subjects than those from which administrators have traditionally been drawn.

78. Though the ancient universities of Oxford and Cambridge have played their part in this growth in the academic study of the problems of contemporary society, it has been most characteristic of the universities founded in this century. The date and circumstances of their foundation have ensured that their courses have been mainly designed to prepare their undergraduates for work in a modern industrial society. To draw more fully on this source of manpower, trained in these subjects, would have many advantages for the Civil Service. Our suggestions about possible ways in which this principle of preference might work are set out in paragraphs 24-25 of Appendix E.

---

*Lord Fulton, Mr. W. C. Anderson, Sir Edward Boyle, Sir William Cook, Dr. Norman Hunt, Mr. Robert Neild, Mr. Robert Sheldon and Sir John Wall.

†See Section 1.2 of the survey of undergraduate attitudes by the Psychological Research Centre, entitled " The Recruitment of Graduates to the Civil Service ", which we publish in Volume 3.

79. We do not intend that our emphasis on " preference for relevance " should be read as a sign that we wish to discourage applications from those men and women of outstanding ability who have studied " irrelevant " disciplines. The Service needs to recruit outstandingly able men and women whatever the subject of their university degree. Our fundamental aim is to secure for the Service the best man or woman for the job, with the education, training and attitudes appropriate to it. It follows that those appointed to the Service without a " relevant " qualification should be required either to: —

(a) take a special training course at the new Civil Service College* in addition to that provided for all graduate direct-entrants to one of the two main groups of administrators;

or (b) take a relevant post-graduate degree or course of study at the Service's expense at some university or other appropriate institution.

The choice between (a) and (b) should be determined by what is most suitable for the individual concerned in the light of the various courses available.

80. A minority of us† take a rather different view. We fully agree that all administrators at the graduate level need a thorough grounding in the subject-matter of their work—whether they enter direct from university or are promoted within the Service. But we do not place the same emphasis on the relevance of studies taken before entry. On practical grounds, three of us support the proposals made in paragraph 82 below for a revised Method I competition based on examination in relevant university studies. All four think however that the alternative selection procedure (Method II) should be impartial as between different academic backgrounds. It is essential that the Service should attract to administrative work a large number of young men and women of outstanding ability and character. Such people are naturally in short supply. We believe that if both methods of entry give preference to those with relevant studies, the field of selection will in practice be unnecessarily narrowed, and that this will involve a serious risk of defeating the essential aim. Our reasons for this are:—

(a) We believe that many able young men and women start their university course without having decided upon their future career, or change their minds in the course of it; and that many select their subject not for career reasons but because they like it and are good at it‡. We do not think that the attractions of the Civil Service as a career are so outstanding by comparison with the other employments open to graduates that the Service can afford to discourage any source of supply.

(b) At the moment, it is often necessary, in practice, for a grammar-school boy or girl to decide as early as 13 years of age which subjects he or she wishes to specialise in at the university. A decision to give a preference to graduates with " relevant " university subjects could therefore tend to narrow still further the range of educational courses at a time when efforts are being made to postpone final and irrevocable choices between them.

(c) Many of the Service's main competitors for graduate talent in this country recruit graduates on grounds of general ability and reckon to give them the necessary training after entry. Apart from not wishing to improve their competitive position at the expense of the Service, we find it hard to believe that they are mistaken or that different considerations should apply to the Civil Service.

(d) We do not at all decry the advantage of a previous grounding in a relevant subject. But we think that it can be overrated. A rigorous and disciplined habit of mind, which can be imparted by " irrelevant " as well as by " relevant " studies, is no less important. At the same time, we are impressed by the evidence that the best of the Assistant Principals who have not read economics at the university show up very well by the end of the course at the Centre for Administrative Studies as compared with those who have. We believe that administrators can achieve professionalism in their chosen field of work (the need for which we wholly accept) by means of the grouping we have recommended in Chapter 2 and the thorough post-entry training courses recommended later in this chapter.

(e) We are doubtful both about the proposals for the special training of those with " irrelevant " studies made in paragraph 79 and about the method of giving preference for relevance set out in Appendix E. Both, in our view, will puzzle and may well discourage potential recruits.

81. We are all agreed, however, that there is an increasing need for administrators handling the problems of modern government and the techniques associated with their solution to be numerate. Senior managers in departments will have to be able to handle problems with variables that can be expressed only in numerical terms. This need is general in all kinds of management throughout the country. We recommend that over the years an increasing importance should be attached to the requirement that graduates seeking appointments to administrative posts should understand the use of numerical techniques and be able to apply quantitative methods to the solution of their problems. We hope that curricula in schools and universities will gradually be modified to make this possible. We also wish to emphasise the value of familiarity with major modern languages. An increasing number of civil servants are employed in work in which their effectiveness and understanding are hampered if they are confined in practice to English.

82. In general we think that all non-specialist graduates and their equivalents should be recruited centrally by the appropriate section of the new Civil Service Department. A majority of us* consider that there should be two main methods of entry:—

(a) Method I should, as at present, be primarily a written examination. The papers candidates can offer, however, should be restricted entirely to those with a direct relevance to the problems of modern government. In any event, as we show in Appendix E, it is not practicable to maintain Method I in its present form. We think it important to maintain a method of entry by written examination

---

*Lord Fulton, Sir Philip Allen, Mr. W. C. Anderson, Sir Edward Boyle, Sir James Dunnett, Dr. Norman Hunt, Lord Simey.

because we think it likely that some good candidates will come forward to compete by such a method who would not choose to enter if the only method open to them were the extended interview procedure (Method II) which we discuss below; and that the former will offer some of them a way of showing their real merit more effectively. We recommend however that Method I should be retained, in the modified form we propose, on a trial basis only. If it fails to attract a sufficient number of good candidates, we would expect the Civil Service Department to abandon it.

(b) Method II should involve a procedure based on that of the present Civil Service Selection Board. We make recommendations in Appendix E however for changes in the procedure and staffing of the selection process. Briefly, those of us who recommend preference for relevance offer suggestions about how this might be done. We all propose in addition that there should be a larger representation of employing departments among the selectors; and that their age-distribution should be changed to increase the proportion of younger people. We also recommend an inquiry into the methods of selection, to include such matters as the part played by the Final Selection Board and possible ways of making the process of selection more objective in character.

83. These proposals should not be taken to imply that separate entry competitions should not in future be held for appointments to such groups as Tax Inspectors and Ministry of Labour Cadets. These should continue wherever they are found to be most appropriate, selection being made either by the department concerned or by the Civil Service Department on its behalf.

84. A minority* of us consider that Method I should cease to exist altogether, for the following reasons:—

(a) A written examination in the subjects studied by the candidate will be a repetition of the testing by his university.

(b) Many candidates will be reluctant to sit two examinations of the same kind.

(c) It is hard to see how the Civil Service Department would be able to examine better than the university the wide range of subjects we consider relevant.

(d) Advances in recruitment procedures are likely to bring steady improvements in Method II. It is here that techniques of selection should improve fastest.

(e) To retain Method I would be to keep a separate system of entry which in 1967 produced 18 successful applicants from 54 candidates. These numbers are likely to decline still further.

(f) If a certain number of entrants with very high academic attainments are required, Method II can provide for this by weighting the university record of the candidate. Method I provides no adequate test of other qualities.

(g) The new Method I, because it is designed to cover in a few papers

---

*Sir William Cook, Sir Norman Kipping, Mr. Robert Neild, Mr. Robert Sheldon, Sir John Wall.

a very heterogeneous field, cannot hope to examine candidates in depth and is bound to come close to the broad test of knowledge of the modern world which the written papers of Method II, proposed in Appendix E, are intended to provide. We can see no purpose in keeping both.

(h) The argument for Method I is that Method II will deter applicants who lack confidence in their ability to compete in the social atmosphere of Method II. If this argument is sound, Method II should be revised.

85. We have said that each department should assess in detail the numbers and types of staff it needs. This poses a special problem in the recruitment of graduates, both specialist and non-specialist. We think it likely, for reasons we discuss in Chapter 8 and Appendix F, that the Service will employ more graduates than at present, although the number of top posts in the Service may not show a proportionate increase. It would be wrong for a large employer like the Civil Service to seek to recruit more of the best graduate talent than it can make proper use of now or in the future. Matching graduates to jobs and prospects requires that departments should decide, in consultation with the Civil Service Department, on the level and kind of ability they require for particular types of appointment; the intake should be adjusted accordingly. All however should enter the same training grade (see paragraph 95 below), so that their fitness for different kinds of work can be fully tested after they have entered the Service. We attach great importance to ensuring that the early decisions which may shape a man's career in the Service (e.g. about different kinds of post-entry training or allocation to differently graded jobs at the end of the training period) should be based on post-entry performance rather than pre-entry promise. We discuss this in more detail in Appendix F.

86. To underline the concern of the Service to recruit men and women of the highest calibre, we consider that those judged outstandingly able and well-qualified on entry should be given a starting salary two or three increments above the basic for the entry grade. This should apply to specialists as well as to the different groups of administrators. This should not, however, carry the implication that senior posts should be reserved for those who start their careers with additional increments. The careers of all entrants to the Service should be determined by performance on the job.

RECRUITMENT OF NON-GRADUATES

87. For most specialist posts, relevant educational and technical qualifications will also be needed by those who are not graduates. Men and women with such qualifications as the H.N.C. (which may have been gained after entry to the Service) or with "A levels" in scientific or technical subjects should normally be posted to jobs for which their qualifications are relevant, whether those jobs are purely specialist or in a related area of management. For administrative staff recruited at this level, specific qualifications and the relevance of the subjects they have studied are clearly less important. Their "A level" qualifications may be pointers to the direction in which they should specialise. More important, however, for all those recruited at this age (specialist and non-specialist) is that they should be given jobs that match

and stretch their abilities; they should also be given the opportunity of developing the skills and specialisms the Service needs, including the ability to use quantitative methods. Departments have a special responsibility for ensuring that the best of this age-group are picked out for early advancement and for appropriate further training. We make proposals for this in later paragraphs of this chapter.

88. We recommend that non-graduate specialists should be recruited by similar procedures to those recommended for graduate specialists in paragraph 73. For the non-specialist entry, we recommend different procedures depending on their age and educational level:—

    (a) The 18-year-old entry (school-leavers with "A levels"), corresponding to the present entry to the Executive Officer grade, should continue for the most part to be recruited centrally by the new Civil Service Department on the basis of "A level" results and interviews —though there is scope for decentralisation on a regional basis. We do not think that direct recruitment by departments is at present desirable at this level because:—

        (i) The non-specialist 18-year-old can have only a vague idea of the work that different departments do and of the various career opportunities open to him in the various administrative groups. He will need general guidance and advice on a wider basis than could be available to him at departmental level.

        (ii) To ensure a fair distribution of talent over all departments, the Civil Service Department must play a major role in the allocation of these new recruits.

    Individual departments should, however, be as closely associated as possible with the recruitment process.

    (b) The 16-year-old entry (school-leavers with "O levels") should continue as at present to be recruited by individual departments, though *ad hoc* grouping arrangements, particularly on a regional basis, have obvious advantages.

LATE ENTRANTS AND RECRUITMENT FOR SHORT-TERM APPOINTMENTS

89. So far in this chapter we have been outlining a recruitment policy for young people entering a career service; as we recommend in Chapter 4, most of its members should enter the Service when young with the expectation, though not the guarantee, of making the Service their life-time career. But the Service should look for and encourage a considerably larger number of late entrants and temporary appointments for fixed periods than in the past. For late entrants of all kinds the prime factor in their appointments must clearly be the relevance of the skills, qualifications and experience they already possess for the job or range of jobs in which it is proposed to employ them. We envisage that some would be appointed by one or other of the processes recommended in paragraphs 73 and 82 above; but it will be for the Civil Service Department to authorise special procedures where these are needed to attract recruits of high standing or with scarce skills.

THE MANAGEMENT OF NEW ENTRANTS

90. Those who enter the Service at young ages should be properly looked

after and their development carefully planned. In our view, the present arrangements are unsatisfactory, especially at Executive Officer and Clerical Officer levels.

91. Our Management Consultancy Group found that young Executive Officers were sometimes confined to routine, undemanding work of a lower quality than their educational qualifications justified. A Treasury study has found that 46 per cent of Executive Officers under the age of 40 believe that their work does not fully use their capabilities or enable them to develop their potential (Volume 3, No. 8). Not surprisingly, therefore, there is a comparatively high wastage rate among newly-recruited Executive Officers. A similar situation is to be found among young Clerical Officers. The Management Consultancy Group drew attention to the fact that many young Clerical Officers and Clerical Assistants are grossly under-utilised at present in jobs scarcely demanding the minimum educational qualifications for their grades. The same Treasury study has shown that 53 per cent of Clerical Officers under the age of 40 consider that their work does not fully employ their capabilities or enable them to develop their potential. We have seen no evidence on the extent to which similar problems may afflict young people in comparable employments outside the Service. But the evidence that the Service is seriously mis-using and stultifying potential talent at these levels is disturbing, and urgent steps should be taken to find remedies.

92. At both these levels, the Service faces the problem of a wide age-spread. The young Clerical Assistant or Clerical Officer entering at about 16 finds himself a member of a grade that contains many older men and women, many of whom have entered the Service in middle age. Similarly the young Executive Officer entering at 18 enters a grade that consists as to 60 per cent of promoted Clerical Officers. The numbers involved in a large department are very considerable, and it is a major problem of management to make sure that the very different types of Clerical and Executive Officer are posted to the right kinds of job, and that young entrants are kept interested and their potential developed. The Service has in our view failed to solve this problem.

93. A necessary step seems to us to be a complete review of grading at these levels designed to separate the jobs that are appropriate to the older civil servant whose aptitudes and experience fit him for the supervision of clerical and similar work, from those appropriate to the young entrant who with training and experience should be capable of rising in the Service. We believe that there are at present too few grades for this purpose, and that an increase in their number (which need not be great) should also help to reduce the length of the Clerical Officer and Executive Officer pay-scales—at present a deterrent to the recruitment and retention of capable young men and women. The proposal we make in Chapter 6 for a common grading system based on more rigorous methods of job evaluation should be a major factor in bringing about this necessary change.

94. In addition, however, we think that departments will need to put much greater effort into personnel management at these levels. New entrants should be regarded as being under training for their first three or four years. They should receive more substantial induction training. It should be the duty of the personnel management of the department to watch them all, assess

34

their progress, encourage the good ones and admonish the indifferent. They should be guided to take additional qualifications appropriate to their field. More specialised training should be provided as aptitudes and potential begin to emerge; the best of them should join the training grade we propose in the next paragraph by the time they reach their mid-twenties.

95. For the graduate entry, and for those who have shown the highest ability among non-graduate entrants, we propose the introduction of a training grade. Its object should be to create a fast promotion route for the most promising young men and women; to test these young civil servants in jobs at different levels of responsibility; and to provide a sufficiently extended period for their training. The time spent in the training grade would be variable; it might well differ as between a non-graduate entrant promoted from below, a direct entrant to one of the groups of administrators referred to in Chapter 2, and a directly recruited specialist; depending on individual circumstances, it could be anything from two to five years. We give further details in paragraphs 106 to 108 below.

96. In each case the destination of the trainee when he leaves the training grade should be determined by his ability and performance without regard to the claims of seniority; it is essential to the concept of a training grade distinct from the general grading structure that trainees should go straight from it to the level justified by their preformance. Our proposal for a training grade does not however imply that a recruit should not have a fully responsible job while he remains in the grade. On the contrary, it is partly intended as a device to enable him to be given the maximum responsibility he can shoulder, to try him out in different jobs, and at the same time to see that he gets the training and opportunities appropriate to his case. We see it and the proposals we have made in paragraphs 93 and 94 as an explicit affirmation of the Service's intention to give special care and early training to those young men and women who are capable of rapid advancement.

TRAINING

97. Great efforts have been made in recent years to increase the amount of training that civil servants receive. The total training effort is now, therefore, impressive—particularly vocational training. There are very thorough courses, for example, for those who have to be schooled in the intricacies of the social security regulations or for those who have to be taught particular skills such as contract procedures or computer programming. But, these apart, there is little certainty that the subjects and techniques people are taught on training courses will actually be relevant or applicable to their work. This is hardly surprising when, as we have pointed out, the practice of the Service hitherto has been to move staff at frequent intervals from one field of activity to another. Moreover as our Management Consultancy Group makes clear, many administrators and specialists have received inadequate training (or none at all) in techniques of modern management.

98. We have said that in the more professional Civil Service of the future it will not be enough for civil servants to be skilled in the techniques of administration: they must also have a thorough knowledge of the subject-matter of their field of administration and keep up to date in it. Thus training should be designed to equip administrators to operate in one or other of

the broad groups we have referred to in Chapter 2. Similarly, specialists need to be equipped to an appropriate degree for administration and management in addition to their normal skills in their specialism.

99. In order to achieve this objective, we propose the creation of a Civil Service College. We see the College as fulfilling three main functions.

100. First, the College should provide major training courses in administration and management. These should include:—

(a) courses for specialists (e.g. scientists, engineers, architects) who need training in administration and management both early in their careers and later;

(b) post-entry training for graduates directly recruited for administrative work in the economic and financial or social areas of government;

(c) additional courses in management for those in their 30's and 40's moving into top management;

(d) refresher courses in the latest management techniques;

(e) courses for the best of the younger entry to help them to compete with the graduates.

Some of the courses should be wholly or partly residential.

101. Secondly, the College should provide a wide range of shorter training courses for a much larger body of staff. These shorter courses should be in both general management and vocational subjects; they should be designed for all levels of staff and particularly for the more junior. We think it likely that such central courses could train civil servants more economically and to a higher standard in some fields than can be achieved by separate departmental training; we recommend, therefore, a review of the balance between central and departmental training to assess the possible extent of such a change.

102. Thirdly, we think that the College should also have two important research functions. It will be uniquely placed to conduct research into problems of administration and those of machinery of government. In addition, however, we hope that the Planning Units in departments, which we recommend in Chapter 5, will commission the College to undertake specific research into problems of present or future policy on which they need assistance. Publication and open discussion are important to research; the College should encourage this to the greatest possible extent.

103. This combination of major teaching and research functions should enable the College to fulfil a role that we believe is greatly needed. It should become a focus for the discussion of many of the most important problems facing the Civil Service as a whole—discussion in which we hope that many outside the Service will share.

104. We do not attempt to prescribe exactly where the two kinds of training courses should be provided. We think it important however that the major courses, including those that are residential, should be concentrated in a single establishment large enough to be the natural centre of training and research within the Service. It need not necessarily, as we see it, be in London—indeed, there would be some advantage in its being outside. But it should be close enough to London to be accessible without difficulty for

36

leaders in many walks of life. The shorter courses for the larger student body on the other hand will need to be provided in London within easy reach of Whitehall and the main range of government offices. A large, non-residential centre will be needed. It may well be that this will have to be physically separate from the main establishment, because of the difficulty of providing teaching accommodation for a very large total student-body in one place; unless the residential establishment is quite near the centre of London, the other should in any case be separate.

105. It would not be appropriate for us to try to lay down the exact scope and content of the courses to be provided by the Civil Service College. In the next three paragraphs, however, we give a broad outline of the way training in the future should in our view assist, both in providing the new professionalism we have sought to prescribe and in giving ample opportunity for every civil servant fully to develop his talent.

106. Young graduates recruited into the training grade for one of the administrative groups referred to in Chapter 2 should, after an appropriate induction course, spend an initial period of up to two years in their departments, either at headquarters or, wherever possible, for some of the time in local or regional offices. During this period they should be placed in one or two different jobs selected to test their ability and aptitudes and develop their capacity to take responsibility. We attach importance to giving as many as possible the experience—more than can be gained from sight-seeing visits—of working in the places and at the levels at which the Civil Service meets and deals with individual members of the public. Once they have passed probation (see Chapter 4, paragraph 143), they should embark upon their main formal training. This should last for up to one year, but it may well be appropriate to divide it into two or three approximately equal parts. We think that the course should contain four main elements:—

(a) Further training in the subject-matter of the various administrative groups, designed to relate the concepts of the fields concerned (economic and financial or social) to the practical problems of government. The course for Assistant Principals at the Centre for Administrative Studies now gives such training in economics; there should also be courses to cover the social field. As far as possible, both should be adapted to the needs of the individual, by taking into account the qualifications he already possesses in his chosen field and by providing in whatever way is most appropriate for special study of subjects handled by his particular department.

(b) The techniques of modern management, including staff organisation and management and the uses of numerate analysis as a tool for dealing with management problems.

(c) More advanced and specialised training in the application of an individual's specialism to his particular field of activity.

(d) The machinery and practice of government and administration including relations with Parliament, public corporations, and local authorities.

We expect that the weighting and timing of these four broad elements will vary between individuals. Not all will be of the type to get most benefit from advanced theoretical training. Equally, not all will need to make the

37

same detailed study of the machinery and practice of government. Some will need training at relatively greater depth in management techniques. We do not wish to lay down any rigid pattern in what should essentially be a flexible process designed to meet the needs of the individual, the administrative group in which he is working, and the requirements of his department. Between the parts of his training course, and after it is over, the graduate should spend some further time in his department, still under training but undertaking more responsible work. During this period also, as many as possible should gain experience of work outside the Service—in local government or private or nationalised industry, as is most appropriate. We discuss this further in Chapter 4 and Appendix G. At some stage, too, all should have practical experience in the supervision and control of staff. For some there may also be a spell in a Private Office. The whole process should take up to 5 years, after which the graduate should be posted to the grade and level of job commensurate with the ability he has demonstrated since joining the Service. The outstandingly able graduate who has entered without a relevant qualification for his administrative group should start the process after one of the additional courses of academic training outlined in paragraph 79 above.

107. We are proposing for the graduate entrant to administrative work a crowded programme of training—on the job, in formal courses, and on attachments designed to broaden his outlook. We recognise that this involves the risk of trying to do too much in too short a time and of preventing young entrants from settling down to a sustained job of work. To counter this, the programme should be flexible. We do not wish to insist that every entrant should go through the whole of the process we have outlined before he leaves the training grade; in some cases it may be appropriate that attachments and loans should take place at a rather later stage. But such variations should not be allowed to upset the general objective of giving the graduate entrant his professional training as soon as possible after he enters the Service, so that he can make a fully effective contribution in the field of his specialisation during the early years of his career.

108. The arrangements for young graduates recruited to the training grade as specialists should not follow any single pattern. Much will depend on their particular field of expertise—whether, for example, they are scientists, engineers, architects or economists. Much will also depend on the requirements of the job they have been recruited to do. In any event, after an initial introduction to the work of the department or establishment, most will be put on the particular job for which they have been recruited. We think that in most cases they will wish to concentrate on their particular line of specialist activity for some time. It may, however, become clear after a period that an individual is more suited to a different type or level of job; the fact that he is in a training grade will facilitate his transfer to this. It may well be, too, that the requirements of a particular profession involved obtaining further qualifications or experience; some may be obtainable in the Service, some not. In any event we envisage that many specialist graduates should, after a few years in the Service, go to appropriate management courses at the Civil Service College. For some the emphasis will be on the organisation and control of staff, for others on the techniques of management

and financial control. After the completion of such courses, and in any case within three of four years, the specialist should be posted to the grade and level of job commensurate with the ability he has demonstrated since joining the Service. Thereafter we think that many should be selected to return to the Civil Service College at the appropriate stage for longer and more general courses in administration and management, to qualify them for the wider role we have proposed they should play.

109. The 18-year-old entry, both administrative and specialist, should be encouraged to take additional qualifications appropriate to their work (diplomas, H.N.C., etc.). Many of the training and further educational facilities needed for this are available in the general educational system of the country. We recommend that bursaries and paid leave should be made available for those attending such courses. These should be supplemented as necessary within the Service through the shorter non-residential courses we have proposed. In addition to this, however, those of them who are engaged on, or are expected to go on to, management work will need training, and we recommend that the best of these should be picked out to join the graduates on the courses proposed in paragraph 100 above. Short central courses could be a useful aid to selection for this purpose.

110. The proposals we have made so far relate to the new entrants of the future. The Civil Service College will also need to provide immediately for the present generation of civil servants, many of whom have had little training since they first entered the Service. This constitutes a major transitional problem which must be energetically tackled if the professionalism the Service needs is to be achieved, and to prevent the older and younger members of the Service from being separated by a damaging gap. Besides building up its courses for new entrants, therefore, the College will need to put in hand a rapid and large-scale programme for the further training of the present generation, and especially of those who entered the Service before recent improvements in the training programme began.

111. The course provided by the Civil Service College should not be restricted to civil servants. Indeed, we hope that on many of its courses a proportion of the places will be set aside for men and women from private industrial and commercial firms, local government and the public corporations. In our view, the College has an important part to play in laying the foundations for a greater understanding between civil servants and the outside world.

112. At the same time, the Civil Service College should not attempt to provide the total amount of training required by civil servants. First, departments should continue to run their own courses, though the College will have a part to play in giving advice and guidance. Secondly, we think it most important that more civil servants should attend courses at universities and business schools, not only because of the intrinsic value of their curricula but also again to help ensure that civil servants are not isolated from their counterparts in other employments. Many courses, especially those designed for the particular needs of the Service, must always be mounted internally. But wherever appropriate courses are to be found outside the Service, we hope that full advantage will be taken of them.

113. A College operating on the large scale we propose will obviously

need its own full-time teaching and lecturing staff. But in our view the College should also use on a part-time or ad hoc basis civil servants and a substantial number of teachers and instructors drawn from a wide range of institutions of higher education (including the new schools of business administration). They should also come from industry and commerce, nationalised industry, and local government. We hope that the Service will associate with the work of the College the widest possible range of interests that can contribute something of value to the training of civil servants.

114. The Civil Service College should be under the general direction of the Civil Service Department which will be responsible for the training policy of the Service as a whole. We consider, however, that the College should have its own governing body, consisting not only of civil servants but also of men and women drawn from a wide range of interests outside the Service—from the universities, polytechnics and business schools, from private and nationalised industry, and from the trade unions and local government. This will help it to remain outward-looking and keep it in touch with the needs of the rest of the country.

CAREER MANAGEMENT

115. During the early years of a man's career we expect him to remain within the specialism or group for which he is trained. This does not mean that he must stay in one job in one department; he should move between jobs and perhaps between departments but usually within the area of his specialism. As far as the administrator is concerned, he should move at much less frequent intervals than he does now. While there will be a great variety of individual career patterns, the basic principle of career management should be a progressive development within a specialism and between fields of activity that are related to each other. While the needs of the Service must come first in this, nevertheless the personal interests and wishes of the individual should be taken into account more positively than appears to be the usual practice at present. This increased attention to personnel management and individual career planning should apply to specialist no less than to administrative staff; in our view much too little of the limited effort that has been put into personnel management in the past has been devoted to the specialists. This will clearly place much greater demands on the personnel and organisation branches of departments, which will need to be expanded to meet them. And, as we explain in Chapter 7, it will also mean that the Civil Service Department must play a much bigger role in this respect than the management side of the Treasury does now.

116. The right promotion at the right time is an essential part of the process of developing to the full the talents of the men and women in the Service. In our view, the present promotion system has serious weaknesses.

117. First, at the middle and lower levels there is too much emphasis on seniority. Seniority is given much less importance at higher levels. But to the extent that this does occur there, it is correspondingly serious. It is in our view of the greatest importance that those who are really able should be appointed to Assistant Secretary and parallel ranks at an early age. There is evidence that there are civil servants, both administrators and specialists, below these ranks who are now frustrated by being given too little responsi-

bility; this is particularly true from the salary level of about £2,500 downwards. Seniority will doubtless always count for promotion in the Civil Service as it does elsewhere; this is right when it reflects experience that will be of value in posts at higher levels. But there should be more opportunity than at present for the exceptionally able to move rapidly up the system. We believe that the pressure to give undue weight to seniority within a given field of work should be relieved by the widening of career opportunities, and that there should be a change of emphasis in the assessment of staff so that more weight is given to performance on the job measured against set objectives. We think that the proposals we make in Chapter 6 for a new structure based on job evaluation will facilitate this change.

118. The second main criticism we make of the present system is that it does not allow promotion to be sufficiently closely linked to the individual's ability, aptitude and qualification to do a particular kind of job at a higher level. The main reason for this is that promotion is based on, and restricted by, the civil servant's membership of his class. We develop this point further in Chapter 6.

119. A system in which promotion is based on past performance and suitability for specific jobs should also help to ensure that undue importance is not attached to the candidate's performance before a promotion board. It should be evident to all that this is not the decisive factor. The primary job of a promotion board should be to produce a fair and uniform judgment of individuals' promise and performance based primarily on the assessment by their different superior officers of their performance in their present jobs.

120. We also recommend a change in promotion procedures. Promotion boards at present deal with promotions up to Chief Executive Officer and equivalent levels, but promotions above these levels are the result of informal consultations. We consider that for promotions to posts at the level of Assistant Secretary, Under Secretary, and their equivalents, the Permanent Secretary of the department should be assisted by a small committee (i.e. a " paper board "). We think that the Committee should always include one of the specialists in the department*. We also recommend in Chapter 7 that a representative of the Civil Service Department should be a member of this committee when promotions to Under Secretary level are being considered, to help to ensure as far as possible that policy and practice are uniform across the Service. In Chapter 6 we distinguish a senior policy and management level for this purpose.

121. Two final points about the status and staffing of the branches responsible for personnel management and organisation. The first is a matter of terminology. These branches are generally called " establishment divisions " and their work is known as " establishment work ". This word now carries implications of stuffiness and we believe it to have bad effects both on the status of the work and on the way it is done. We recommend

*One of us (Dr. Norman Hunt) also recommends that a Minister of State or Parliamentary Secretary should be a member of this committee. His presence is necessary for two reasons. Ministers should be more closely associated with these senior-level promotions which will do much to determine the tone and attitudes of the department. Secondly, it is particularly important that promotions at these levels should not become too much based on " in-bred " Civil Service values and attitudes; the Minister will be able to contribute the " outside " detachment which can do something to check this danger.

that it should be used no longer. In the rest of our report we refer to " personnel and organisation " divisions or branches; the Service may be able to find a better name.

122. Secondly, these branches and those who have served in them have suffered, both because the work has not generally been regarded as an avenue to promotion to the highest posts in the Service, and because the staff have not developed sufficient expertise. Our proposals, if accepted, will enlarge their future responsibilities and thus improve their status. This should help to attract those who are capable of rising to the highest posts. At the same time this work will call for high expertise and thus for greater specialisation. We welcome this prospect. We wish to add two riders. Those specialising in personnel work should from time to time get experience of work in this field outside the Service. They should also have experience of working in " operating " divisions and of the effect of personnel and organisation work upon them.

CHAPTER 4

MOBILITY, PENSIONS AND A CAREER SERVICE

123. In Chapter 1 we criticised the lack of contact between the Civil Service and the rest of the community. This is partly the consequence of a career service; since we expect most civil servants to spend their entire working lives in the Service some degree of isolation is almost inevitable. The concept of a career service has also been criticised because of the sense of almost total security of tenure that it gives to all established civil servants. Thus though there are provisions for dismissal and for premature retirement in the interests of efficiency, both are in practice rare—and, in the middle and senior grades, very rare. In 1967 dismissals and compulsory retirements of permanent staff in the grades of Executive Officer (and equivalents) and above on the grounds of misconduct and inefficiency numbered 22 (0.015 per cent of the permanent staff in these groups). In the previous four years the figures were

1963	1964	1965	1966
24	24	25	20

We find it hard to believe that these figures should not have been higher. On the other hand, there are strong arguments for preserving a mainly career service in the sense that most civil servants should enter when comparatively young with the expectation, but not the guarantee, of a life-time's employment. We consider them in detail later in this chapter and in substance accept them. Nevertheless we are convinced that, both in the public interest and also for the health of the Service itself, effective steps must be taken to ensure a very much larger and freer flow of men and women between the Service and outside employments than there has been in the past. The proposals in this chapter are designed with these ends in view.

LATE ENTRY

124. Late entry should be considerably expanded. There are people in business, the professions, nationalised industry, local government and the universities whose experience would be most valuable to the Service. The need is particularly obvious in the specialist disciplines such as engineering, where men are needed with practical experience of kinds that the Service cannot always provide. In these fields there is already some late entry; there should be more. But more late entry is also needed on the administrative side (which, as we define it, includes the present Executive Class) where at present it is sporadic and unduly restricted. For example, there is no regular late entry into the Service between the ranks of Executive Officer and Principal. Recruitment to the Executive Class is now restricted to the Executive Officer grade; and no starting salary can be higher than the salary point for 25-year-olds. In the Administrative Class late recruitment (leaving aside

43

special provisions for serving and former members of the Armed Forces and Overseas Civil Service) is mainly to the Principal grade, though there is also provision for the late entry of up to three Assistant Secretaries a year. This was started only in 1964, when six Principals were recruited (35 in 1965, 27 in 1966 and 30 in 1967); so far there have been no more than five late-entry Assistant Secretary appointments. (One of the reasons for the small number of Assistant Secretary appointments is that they are made only if the specific qualifications and experience needed cannot be found within the Service.) This is very far from enough. In our view there should be no restriction on the levels to which suitably qualified and experienced people from outside the Service can be directly appointed. A steady inflow of suitably-qualified older entrants with new ideas and relevant experience would, we believe, bring great benefits throughout the Service.

TEMPORARY APPOINTMENTS

125. At middle and higher levels, there should also be more short-term appointments for fixed periods; this would help to maintain regular movement in and out of the Service. It would be particularly valuable in the case of those specialists, for example some engineers and scientists, whose special contribution would be up-to-date knowledge and practical experience of work outside government. It is also often the best way of using the talents of those, again mainly specialists, who are needed in an advisory capacity. For example, the present system by which professional economists come into the Service from the universities for a few years and then return, perhaps to come back again for further spells later, has been of great value. We think that it should be adopted in other specialist fields. In the various administrative groups similar short-term appointments for those with relevant experience in industry, commerce or the universities could also bring advantages.

126. In addition to temporary appointments of this kind, it has been put to us that the Service also needs to employ people whose status is expressly temporary but of indefinite duration. In total the number of temporaries is very large: 124,000 or 29 per cent of the total non-industrial staff. The great majority are in the lower grades (for example, there are 37,500 temporary Clerical Assistants) and there is a rapid rate of turnover. But there are many temporary appointments at higher levels, and temporaries continue to be employed on this basis for long periods—some for over 20 years and until they reach the retiring age. A number of reasons are given why many civil servants are "temporaries". Some prefer for their own reasons to enter on a temporary basis or to become temporaries after a period of established service, e.g. retired persons or married women. Others, recruited when pressure was urgent, have been offered only temporary posts because they did not possess the full qualifications needed for permanent appointments. The largest group are those whose jobs are themselves temporary because the need for them is not expected to last.

127. We doubt if the Service is justified in employing as many as 29 per cent of its staff on a temporary basis. In so far as it remains necessary to employ temporaries for indefinite periods, we make recommendations on the terms of service that should apply in their case in paragraphs 137

and 143 below. We consider, however, that the Service should find means of reducing the proportion of temporary staff, and should in particular examine ways of ensuring that civil servants do not continue to serve on a temporary basis for unduly long periods.

SHORT-TERM LOANS AND SECONDMENTS

128. Determined efforts are needed to bring about the temporary interchange of staff with private industry and commerce, nationalised industry and local government on a much larger scale than hitherto. War-time experience proves beyond doubt the value of such movement in promoting mutual knowledge and understanding. Coming at the right stage, experience in a changed environment can also be of decisive importance in the individual's development. Interchange should be a two-way process (though not necessarily head for head) covering both administrative and specialist staff from the level of Higher Executive Officer and equivalent upwards. Efforts are being made to promote these exchanges at present. We welcome the scheme, started in 1965, under which about 25 nominees from industry, commerce and the universities were loaned to the Service for a two-year spell as Principals. We hope that it can be continued and developed. But it is at least as valuable for civil servants to go out for a spell. No doubt there are real obstacles: no doubt it is extremely difficult to spare good civil servants, especially at the level of Principal and upwards. At 1st December, 1967 only 30 civil servants were away on secondment to industry, commerce and local government. We cannot believe that this is the most that can be managed. We develop this point further in Appendix G.

PERSONAL APPOINTMENTS BY MINISTERS

129. Several times in recent years Ministers have brought in professional experts and advisers of their own. These have been personal appointments in the sense that they have been individuals known to the Ministers concerned, who have judged that their individual qualities and experience could be of special help to them in their departments. We welcome this practice as a means of bringing new men and ideas into the service of the State. We are satisfied that a Minister should be able to employ on a temporary basis such small numbers of experts as he personally considers he needs to help and advise him. They should be men and women of standing and experience. We consider however that this practice should be put on to a regular and clearly understood basis. We think it inappropriate to propose any precise limitation of the numbers of these appointments or any defined procedures. But it should be made clear that such appointments are temporary and that the person concerned has no expectation of remaining when there is a change of Minister.

MOVEMENT OUT OF THE SERVICE

130. The corollary of more late entry into the Service should be a similar flow out of the Service. We think that it should be of three kinds.

131. First, however well the Service is managed, there will always be able men and women who decide for personal or other reasons that they wish to leave the Service for another kind of work. At present the pension

arrangements make voluntary severance difficult. We do not believe that restrictive pension arrangements are the right way to keep staff—even those with scarce skills whose departure is a real loss to the Service. It would be highly regrettable if civil servants did not have valuable contributions to make to other areas of our national life; it should be natural for others to wish to employ them.

132. Secondly, we consider that the Service should take the system of probation much more seriously than it appears to do at present. Out of the Assistant Principals who entered from 1961 to 1965, 221 passed their probation and only four failed. While no doubt the great majority of men and women can be expected to be confirmed in their appointments at the end of probation, the present almost complete certainty of passing success-fully through it is not an adequate spur to effort.

133. Thirdly, the Service should have wider powers to retire on pension those who have ceased to earn their keep, and should use them with more determination. Where culpable inefficiency is in question, the present powers seem adequate, though we suspect that they are not always used as fully as they should be. But wider powers are also needed to deal with the small minority who, perhaps through no fault of their own, have unforeseeably ceased to be able to give a satisfactory performance and ought to be retired early in the interests of the Service—on fair terms (see Appendix H).

THE CIVIL SERVICE AS A CAREER

134. We have recommended a much greater flexibility of movement between the Civil Service and other employments. We think however that it should remain a career service in the sense that most civil servants should enter at young ages with the expectation, but not the guarantee, of a life-time's employment; and that the great majority of those who come to occupy top jobs will in practice be career civil servants. There are in our view substantial reasons why this should continue to be so:—

(a) Our avowed aim is to create a Civil Service that is truly professional —expert both in the subject-matter and in the methods of public administration. Long experience and accumulated knowledge are essential parts of this concept. While it involves a constant inflow of new men and ideas from outside, it must also involve for the majority a professional career in the Service.

(b) Civil servants must be able to give forthright advice to their superiors and to Ministers without fearing that a clash of views might lead to dismissal from the Service.

(c) Really able young men are more likely to come into the Service if they know that the top jobs are open to them; if too many of the senior posts were filled from outside the Service, this would produce frustration among those already in the Service and discour-age recruitment.

(d) At a time when there is greater intermingling between the public and private sectors, and when the decisions of civil servants are of immediate concern to firms and other organisations, we want to see a substantial increase in the flow of staff, both long-term and short-term, between the Service and commerce and industry. But

46

this should take place in a professional atmosphere fostered by the fact that the majority of civil servants expect to remain in the Service for a life-time's career. It is important that civil servants should not come to think of those who do business with their departments as their prospective employers, and that firms, which are increasingly required to reveal their technical and financial affairs to government, should be able to do so with confidence.

TERMS OF SERVICE AND PENSION ARRANGEMENTS

135. We thus propose greater mobility into and out of a Service that still continues in the main to be a career service. As a consequence, important changes need to be made in the Service's pension arrangements and the terms on which civil servants are employed.

136. At present the rules of the pension scheme greatly restrict the sort of movement we wish to see. While there is a well-developed system for transferring pension rights in moves between employments in the public sector, this does not extend to moves between the Civil Service and private employment. A person who enters the Service from private employment cannot transfer his pension rights into the Civil Service pension scheme and thus continue to build up a continuous pension entitlement (though he may be able to preserve his rights in his old scheme); and a civil servant under 50 and below the rank of Assistant Secretary who by his own choice leaves to go to a private employment loses his pension rights altogether. Clearly this is a serious impediment to movement both into and out of the Service. We recommend therefore that the Service should, wherever practicable, make transfer arrangements with private employers to facilitate late entry, and that all civil servants who have served for an appropriate qualifying period should be able to transfer or preserve their pension rights on voluntarily leaving the Service.

137. Most temporary staff are now unpensionable, though a small number are members of the Federated Superannuation System for Universities. We think that every person—subject to having served for a specified qualifying period—should be entitled to a pension related to the length of his service. We therefore recommend that the pension scheme should be extended to cover temporary staff.

138. We also believe that the Service needs wider and more flexible powers than those provided in the present Superannuation Act in two respects:—

(a) to provide reasonable severance arrangements for those who are obliged to retire in the interests of the Service before they reach the normal retiring age, as proposed in paragraph 133;

(b) to offer improved pension arrangements where these are needed to attract into the Service individual late entrants with special ability, qualifications or experience, who are unable because of the shortness of their prospective period of service to earn a good pension by the time they reach the retiring age.

139. The present pension scheme is non-contributory. It could be suitably adapted to give effect to the proposals in paragraph 136 and 137

c

above. We think, however, that it would be marginally easier to deal with short periods of service, and that other advantages would accrue, if the scheme were put on to a contributory basis. This proposal has been made more than once before, notably by the Tomlin Commission in 1931, but has never been proceeded with. We understand that the basis of the Civil Service pension scheme, as indeed of all public-service pension schemes, will need to be re-examined when the proposed system of National Insurance retirement pensions related to earnings is introduced; and that the question of contributions is bound to be reviewed in that context. We hope that this review will be speedily conducted and will take full account of the arguments in favour of a contributory scheme.

140. The recommendations in paragraphs 136 to 139 above are discussed in greater detail in Appendix H.

141. We now turn to the terms on which civil servants are employed, and in particular to the question of established status. The origin and meaning of establishment are set out in a note by the Treasury, which we publish at Volume 4, Section IV. Briefly, an established civil servant is (in most cases) one who has been admitted to the Civil Service with a certificate from the Civil Service Commission (certifying that he satisfies the conditions laid down for his appointment); and only those who have been so certificated are pensionable. Established civil servants have much greater security of tenure than unestablished. We have recommended above that the link between establishment and pensionability should be broken. The question is whether the concept of establishment should then remain.

142. In our view, it should be abolished. The term " establishment " has acquired overtones of comfort and complacency, and damages the reputation of the Service. More important, the concept of established status has engendered an atmosphere within the Service that in practice, though not in theory, offers too much protection. It is not true that a civil servant, once established, is completely secure in his job, however lazy or inefficient he may be. But establishment has come to imply a presumption of security until retirement, which goes beyond what is genuinely needed and, we believe, hampers the elimination of the small minority who do not earn their keep.

143. In our view, the new terms of employment required to produce greater mobility into and out of a largely career service are as follows:—

(a) For all appointments, except the temporary staff discussed in paragraphs 125 and 126 above, there should be a two-year period of probation.

(b) On successful completion of probation an individual should be informed of this by letter and offered indefinite employment, subject to a reasonably long period of notice: we suggest up to six months on each side. The Service should be able to end the employment only on one of the following grounds:—

(i) redundancy, in circumstances in which he cannot appropriately be found a comparable job in another branch or department;

(ii) ill health;

(iii) disciplinary reasons such as misconduct or unreasonable refusal to move to another job in the Service when mobility is one of his conditions of service;

(iv) culpable inefficiency;

(v) early retirement in the interests of the Service, as proposed in paragraph 133.

In each case there should be appropriate safeguards for the person concerned. We have not examined the procedures, formal and informal, that now govern (i) to (iv), and therefore have no changes to propose. We discuss the procedure appropriate to the new proposal at (v) in Appendix H.

(c) The temporaries at paragraphs 125 and 126 above should, wherever possible, be offered short-term appointments for a specified number of years.

144. We think that the process of confirming a civil servant in his appointment (paragraph 143 (b) above) should be handled in a way that reduces the administrative complications now involved in the process of establishment. First, it should be delayed until successful completion of the probationary period; this should help to speed up recruitment, delays in which are today partly attributable to the procedures for establishing successful candidates. Secondly, there should be considerable delegation of authority. At junior levels (i.e. below the level of the graduate entry), we think that the employing department should determine that a person has successfully passed his probation and confirm him in his appointment accordingly. It should however report each case to the Civil Service Department, which should watch over the general standards observed by individual departments, and should conduct spot checks to see that standards are being maintained. At the graduate entry and higher levels, the authority should be the Civil Service Department. At the end of the probationary period, a department recommending a recruit for confirmation should submit a report stating that he has the necessary qualifications and is showing satisfactory performance and adequate promise for his grade.

CHAPTER 5

THE STRUCTURE OF DEPARTMENTS AND THE PROMOTION OF EFFICIENCY

145. To function efficiently, large organisations, including government departments, need a structure in which units and individual members have authority that is clearly defined and responsibilities for which they can be held accountable. There should be recognised methods of assessing their success in achieving specified objectives.

146. The organisation of a government department today usually defines with great clarity the area of a civil servant's responsibility; his position within his hierarchy is also clearly established. But it is not easy in the Civil Service clearly and distinctly to allocate to individuals or units the authority to take decisions. There are two reasons for this. Decisions often have to be referred to a higher level than their intrinsic difficulty or apparent importance merits; this is because they involve the responsibility of the Minister to Parliament and may be questioned there. At the same time, many problems overlap departments; they often involve wide consultations at many different levels both between departments and with a variety of interests outside the Service. Decisions therefore are frequently collective decisions achieved through a sequence of committees—culminating, if need be, in the collective responsibility of the Cabinet.

147. For these reasons clear delegation of authority is particularly difficult in the Civil Service. This has led well-informed observers, including some who have given evidence to us, to conclude that large-scale executive operations cannot be effectively run by government departments, and that they should be "hived off" wherever possible to independent boards. We discussed this suggestion in the concluding section of this chapter. We believe, however, that the work of departments can be so organised as to enable responsibility and authority to be defined and allocated more clearly than they often are at present. Individuals and units could then be called to account for performance which is measured as objectively as possible. In our view, this is true in different ways of many sides of a department's work. We consider this principle of organisation to be a necessary condition for achieving maximum departmental efficiency and for enabling men and women to get the greatest satisfaction from their work.

148. There can be no standard pattern of departmental organisation to achieve these ends. The responsibilities of government departments are extremely diverse. Each department, therefore, has to organise its staff in the way most appropriate to its own tasks. Nevertheless, there are certain common elements in the work for which the top-level direction of each department has to provide. Our proposals concentrate on four of these: —

    (a) The management of the department's executive activities, many of them laid down by legislation. These constitute the work of most civil servants and vary widely. They include, for example, much research and development work, all kinds of procurement, the management of technological projects and programmes, inspection and monitoring work of many kinds and the management of social services, such as the running of employment exchanges and National Insurance offices.

    (b) Administrative activities, mostly of a non-executive character, concerned often with the operation and adaptation of existing policies. Examples of these are high-level case-work arising from the detailed application of policy, exercising the department's financial controls over its expenditure, and dealing with the wide variety of problems arising from the services administered by local authorities (education, housing, roads, town and country planning, etc.).

    (c) The day-to-day organisation of the department's staff and work and the provision of its internal services (i.e. the work of personnel and organisation divisions).

    (d) The formulation and review of policy under political direction.

149. The precise application of our recommendations to these broad aspects of departmental work will differ from department to department. They will, however, involve substantial changes in the present basic pattern. In particular, for each major department (and, where applicable, smaller ones) we recommend: —

    (a) the organisation of executive activities in such a way that the principles of accountable management can be applied;

    (b) the provision of high-level management services;

    (c) the creation of a long-term Planning Unit or Units;

    (d) a top departmental structure in which, while overall direction under the Minister must rest unequivocally with the Permanent Secretary, there should be closely associated with him a Senior Policy Adviser or Advisers and, where appropriate, a chief scientist, engineer or other senior specialist.

ACCOUNTABLE AND EFFICIENT MANAGEMENT

150. Accountable management means holding individuals and units responsible for performance measured as objectively as possible. Its achievement depends upon identifying or establishing accountable units within government departments—units where output can be measured against costs or other criteria, and where individuals can be held personally responsible for their performance.

151. The establishment of such units must involve an addition to the Service's traditional accounting methods. The present system of vote accounting does not automatically provide complete cost figures for the work and expenditure of individual divisions and branches or for particular activities; only recently have arrangements been introduced in some departments to supplement the formal parliamentary accounts with cost data of this kind. Accountable management requires the identification of those parts of the

51

organisation that form convenient groupings (or "centres"), to which costs can be precisely allocated as the responsibility of the man in charge. We regard this as essential to systematic management control.

152. There is a complementary need to establish for the same groups and units standards of achievement by which their performance can be judged. Clearly this is more easily done in some parts of the Service than in others.

153. Wherever measures of achievement can be established in quantitative or financial terms, and individuals held responsible for output and costs, accountable units should be set up. We believe this to be practicable over a very wide area of the executive work in paragraph 148(a). Much of this work is done in establishments outside headquarters; some is nation-wide. The most straightforward cases are where there is a physical output, e.g. in stores or supplies. But it is also possible to measure output against costs wherever a large number of similar and defined operations are performed. For example, in the registration of applications, the payment of benefits and the handling of individual employment problems, local offices could establish standards of achievement by using the statistical data they already collect relating to transactions handled. At present this information is largely used to determine the number and type of staff required; it could be used to measure the comparative efficiency of different units. These accountable units would correspond to the "budget centres" which have been widely developed as an instrument of managerial control in progressive industry.

154. Work of this kind should thus be organised into separate "commands". The manager of each command should be given clear-cut responsibilities and commensurate authority and should be held accountable for performance against budgets, standards of achievement and other tests. Within his unit he should set up sub-systems of responsibility and delegated authority on similar lines.

155. Different considerations apply to much of the administrative work mentioned in paragraph 148(b). Here measurable output cannot always be made the criterion for assessing performance. One cannot lay down in advance how long it should take to review effectively the investment programme of a nationalised industry, or to study and make a sound recommendation on the acceptability of a proposed company merger. The assessment of administrative work is also complicated by the unpredictable demands that arise from the Minister's responsibility to Parliament, and by the fact that much of it contains a major element of new policy-making, involving consultation, negotiation and the preparation of legislation.

156. It is still, however, important that those engaged on administrative work of this kind should know what their objectives are and that their performance should be judged by their results. The principle to be applied here is management by objective. Whether the branch is primarily concerned with administering existing policies (paragraph 148(b) above), with planning new policies or with research, its objectives and priorities need to be clearly established. To some extent, of course, many branches work in this way now. But the principle of management by objective is not applied as systematically or widely in the Service as it should be. It should be normal practice everywhere for heads of branches doing this kind of

work to agree with their superiors and subordinates the tasks assigned, relative priorities and dates for completion, and regularly to review progress. Individuals at all levels should know what they are responsible for and what authority they have. The effectiveness of the branch and the contribution of its individual members could then be more objectively assessed.

157. Further changes in the way in which many departments organise their work are also needed if the principles of accountable management are to be applied as fully and as widely as they ought to be. Three main obstacles at present stand in the way of the effective allocation of responsibility and authority.

158. The first of these arises when several departments, or several branches within a department, have a substantial interest in the same problem. With responsibility diffused, the need for wide consultation may mean that all can move forward only at the pace of the slowest. This limitation is inherent in much government work. Despite this, it should be possible, especially where the problem is reasonably self-contained, to devise methods of concentrating in one man or group the responsibility for organising the relevant material and putting forward a solution. Where problems involve several departments, it may often be the right course to set up a team. This is, in fact, often done now. There is however too much of a tendency at present for members of groups of this kind to try to carry their departments with them at each step of the way. We feel that more specific allocation of responsibility to individuals, both departmentally and inter-departmentally, is needed. The interests of many different Ministers are often, if not usually, involved. Nevertheless, the problem-solving approach, has great value, since it reduces the temptation to " pass the buck ", and it can do much to develop the competence and confidence of the individuals concerned. We recommend that departments should make opportunities for adopting it whenever they can.

159. Another general obstacle to the clear allocation of personal responsibility and authority frequently arises from the number of levels in the hierarchy of most Whitehall departments. Usually there are at least seven organisational levels in administrative work (from Executive Officer to Permanent Secretary), rather more than there would be in a typical industrial situation, and spans of control (i.e. the number of subordinates reporting directly to a superior) are very narrow, usually only two or three. Similar narrow spans of control are found in other hierarchies, e.g. in the organisation of much engineering work. Often, from Executive Officer upwards, each level " has a go " at a paper or a problem, adding comments or suggestions as it goes up the hierarchy until it reaches the point at which somebody takes a decision. This point is often higher than it would otherwise be because decisions may involve the Minister in having to answer for them in Parliament. In consequence, personal responsibility and authority are obscured; delay follows. We think that the number of working levels in the traditional organisation of the flow of business should be reduced. The level or levels omitted will obviously vary in different situations. Much more often than now, for example, an Executive Officer should work direct to a Senior Executive Officer, or a Principal direct to an Under Secretary. With " flatter " structures there can be a more precise allocation of responsibility and authority. We think the Service ought to make bold experiments in this direction.

53

160. The third obstacle arises in those areas of the Service where administrators and specialists (e.g. engineers, architects, quantity surveyors and planning officers) are jointly engaged on a common task like the design and preparation of military installations and the supervision of their construction by outside contractors. Where this happens, the two main systems of organisation at present are known as " parallel hierarchies " and " joint hierarchies ". In parallel hierarchies, the responsibility is bisected: financial and overall policy control is entrusted to administrators organised in one hierarchy, while advice on the technical merits of a case and the execution and development of technical policy is laid to specialists organised in a separate but parallel hierarchy. In joint hierarchies, an administrator and a specialist are designated joint heads of a block of work, but at lower levels the separation of functions still occurs, with financial control in the hands of the administrators. The way these arrangements work is described in more detail in the report of the Management Consultancy Group.

161. We are aware of the advantages claimed for these forms of organisation, but we are satisfied that they are outweighed by their very considerable disadvantages. They produce delay and inefficiency because of the need for constant reference to and fro between the hierarchies. They prevent the specialists from exercising the full range of responsibilities normally associated with their professions and exercised by their counterparts outside the Service. In particular, they obscure individual responsibility and accountability; no single person at any level has clear-cut managerial responsibility for the whole task.

162. These common tasks frequently include a large volume of non-technical work—some of it routine, some of it requiring considerable expertise, e.g. in preparing legislation and regulations and in the financial procedures of government. Nevertheless we consider that the best organisation for this kind of work is a single integrated structure under a single head. The head of the structure should be the man with the most appropriate qualifications for the job. Beneath the single head, administrators and specialists should be integrated in teams or unified hierarchies, where individual posts are filled by administrators or specialists according to the requirements of the task. Part of the Ministry of Technology already operates on the basis of a unified hierarchy incorporating all necessary technical, financial, administrative and other specialist staff. The speed with which this new pattern can replace joint and parallel hierarchies throughout the Service will depend on the availability of men and women with the right training and experience; it will take time to find and develop the skills required.

THE DEPARTMENTAL MANAGEMENT SERVICES UNIT

163. Implementing the proposals we have so far outlined would not by itself be enough to guarantee full efficiency and the maintenance of the highest standards of management. The Service will also need to devise the right machinery for ensuring that each department keeps its organisation up to date, conducts a regular audit of its efficiency, and constantly applies the best available methods and techniques to its tasks. The use of outside consultants could help and the central management services of the new Civil Service Department should be an effective spur. But the primary

responsibility must lie with the department itself. Thus departmental personnel and organisation divisions have a key role to play. These divisions are primarily concerned with personnel and efficiency and therefore have a powerful influence on the total operation of departments at all levels. We discuss their role in personnel management in Chapter 3. Here we concentrate on their task of promoting and maintaining efficient organisation and methods of work.

164. Although the Civil Service has played a major part in the development of organisation and methods (O and M) is this country, the work of departmental O and M divisions in promoting efficiency is at present often inadequate. The findings of our Management Consultancy Group indicate that the reasons for this are as follows:—

(a) O and M staff tend in practice to focus on methods to the exclusion of organisation, and too rarely question whether a particular task actually needs to be done at all. Normally, there is little, if any, investigation of work above the lower and middle levels of a department. There is, too, the serious weakness that the staff employed on this work (nearly always members of the Executive Class and not normally above Senior Executive Officer) have not the rank or authority to operate effectively at higher levels.

(b) O and M investigations begin for the most part only by invitation from the head of an operating division when he decides that he has a problem. Some departments conduct planned reviews of selected areas but the current emphasis is on *ad hoc* assignments. And when such assignments (or reviews) have been completed, O and M staff usually do not sufficiently participate in seeing their recommendations put into effect.

(c) The separation of staff inspection (assessing the numbers of staff required for the efficient performance of a given amount of work) and O and M (analysing the tasks and the methods by which they are performed as well as the organisation required for the purpose) divides what should be a unified operation. We are aware that these separate responsibilities usually converge at the Under Secretary level. It is the separateness of the two actual operations that we are criticising. We acknowledge that there are occasions when a limited rather than a full-scale operation is all that is required, for example to investigate a request for one or two additions to a division's staff; but this cannot justify the present separation.

(d) The staff engaged in O and M and staff inspection work are not sufficiently expert; they are frequently " generalists " who, because they spend too short a time on the job, lack the necessary qualifications and experience.

165. In our view, each major department should contain a management services unit with wider responsibilities and functions than are given to O and M divisions today. In particular, we should like to see the following changes:

(a) Efficiency audits should be introduced involving all aspects of the department's work at all levels. This should take place as part of a constant and phased review of the total operation of the department. In particular, special attention should be paid to studies designed to improve organisational efficiency.

(b) The management services unit should be fully and clearly responsible for promoting throughout the department the use of the best management techniques.

(c) O and M should be equipped to operate effectively at all levels in a department and not just at the middle and lower levels.

(d) The functions of O and M and staff inspection should be assimilated and combined in the same unit; this would mount operations of varying scope and depth according to the nature of the problem.

166. The management services unit must be properly staffed. It cannot carry these enlarged responsibilities if it consists of inexpert general administrators assigned to the unit as part of a regular three- to four-year rotation between widely differing jobs. The work demands specialisation from men and women with high qualifications. The staff should be drawn from the groups of administrators referred to in Chapter 2, from appropriate specialists, including accountants, and from those with experience of similar work outside the Service, including some with practical experience of management in industry. Many should spend long periods—in some cases the better part of their careers—in this type of work gaining additional qualifications and experience, moving between different departments, including the Civil Service Department, and between the Service and similar work in other employments outside.

167. The qualifications and training of the management services staff of the Civil Service must compare favourably with those doing similar work outside, e.g. in large management consultancy firms. Many should have a relevant degree or equivalent professional qualification and not less than five years' experience as manager or administrator in an operating division. This needs to be followed by more specialised training in management techniques and a great deal of refresher training subsequently. There is almost no-one now in departmental establishment work with qualifications and experience of this order.

168. Our proposals are not intended to discourage departments from bringing in outside consultants for special assignments. Departments have done this to an increasing extent over the last few years. It is in our view a necessary supplement to the work of their own management services units; it will help to keep the units themselves fully up to date and it can be of particular value when problems of organisation arise at the highest levels within departments.

169. It is important that the creation of stronger management services units should not detract from the responsibility of members of operating divisions for their own efficiency. The prime responsibility for the efficiency of their work must rest with them. The role of the management services unit should be to give any assistance that is needed and generally to act as a spur to the achievement of higher standards.

170. We are convinced that the creation of management services units

of this kind in departments is the only way to ensure that all unnecessary work is eliminated and that staffs are kept to the absolute minimum. We believe that there are substantial savings to be achieved by such units, staffed and operating in the way we have described. These units too should themselves be subjected to an external efficiency audit about every five years; it might be done by a team drawn partly from central management services and partly from outside management consultants.

171. We wish to draw special attention to one other factor which is a source of inefficiency at present. Office services (notably secretarial assistance) are frequently inadequate. Much more needs to be done to improve the physical surroundings in which civil servants work. Conditions vary widely; some are lamentable. Squalor is not conducive to pride in the job. We discuss this further in Appendix I.

POLICY PLANNING

172. We emphasised in Chapter 1 the growing need for long-term planning if the problems of modern government are to be foreseen, and the groundwork for decisions prepared in good time. We believe that this responsibility, like the complementary responsibility for the execution of policy, needs to be more clearly defined and allocated. At present policy-making, especially long-term policy thinking and planning, is the responsibility of officers over-burdened with more immediate demands arising from the parliamentary and public responsibilities of Ministers. The operation of existing policies, and the detailed preparation of legislation with the associated negotiations and discussions, frequently crowd out demands that appear less immediate. Civil servants, particularly members of the Administrative Class, have to spend a great deal of their time preparing explanatory briefs, answers to Parliamentary Questions, and Ministers' cases. Generally this work involves the assembly of information to explain to others (civil servants, outside bodies and so on) the policies of the department, how they are operating, and how they apply in particular cases. Almost invariably there are urgent deadlines to be met in this kind of work. In this press of daily business, long-term policy-planning and research tend to take second place.

173. We propose that a department's responsibility for major long-term policy-planning should be clearly allocated to a planning and research unit. In the rest of this chapter, we call these "Planning Units". Research is, however, the indispensable basis of proper planning, and the phrase should be understood as referring to a unit equipped to assemble and analyse the information required for its planning work. The unit should be relatively small. Its main task should be to identify and study the problems and needs of the future and the possible means to meet them; it should also be its function to see that day-to-day policy decisions are taken with as full a recognition as possible of their likely implications for the future. The Planning Unit should not carry any responsibility for the day-to-day operations of the department. It will, however, be important to ensure that it does not become too much detached from the main stream of the department's work. In some departments, e.g. the Home Office, with widely

separated fields of activity, it may well be that more than one Planning Unit should be set up.

174. The staff of Planning Units should develop close contacts with the appropriate experts both inside and outside the Service. They should be aware of, and contribute to, new thinking in their field. They should also be trained in, and have the capacity to use, the relevant techniques of quantitative analysis.

175. We think that Planning Units should be staffed by comparatively young men and women. Thus some of the most able, vigorous and suitably qualified young civil servants will be able to have an early and direct impact on top policy-making, as they do so impressively in France and Sweden. Planning Units also offer scope for the employment of men and women on short-term contracts or temporary secondment to the government service. By offering these opportunities both to young civil servants and to "outsiders", Planning Units will help to generate the thrust and drive that are needed; they should also provide an environment in which those who possess qualities of imagination and foresight can be identified and developed.

176. We think that people should not normally remain in these units beyond their mid-forties (except for the head of the Planning Unit—see paragraph 182). After a period of service in Planning Units they should then expect to move—some returning to work outside government, others into the operating sections of their departments.

177. Many of the problems handled by Planning Units will have implications extending beyond the boundaries of a single department. These units may therefore need a measure of central direction if the emerging problems of the country are to be tackled systematically and comprehensively and on the basis of common major hypotheses. The status and location of this central direction, whether by the Cabinet Office, the Treasury or the development of other machinery, is a question of machinery of government and therefore beyond our terms of reference.

THE OVERALL DIRECTION OF DEPARTMENTS

178. The proposals we have made so far in this chapter have important implications for the highest levels of responsibility in departments. Today, responsibility at the top is concentrated in the Permanent Secretary. He has four functions. He is the Minister's most immediate adviser on policy; he is the managing director of the day-to-day operations of the department; he has the ultimate responsibility for questions of staff and organisation; as the Accounting Officer (in nearly every department), he also has the ultimate responsibility for all departmental expenditure.

179. This is a heavy burden. In some departments (the Treasury, Ministry of Defence, Board of Trade and Ministry of Technology) the post of " Second Permanent Secretary " has been introduced. We have strong doubts about it. It attracts a salary of £8,100—£500 below the Permanent Secretary and £1,800 above the Deputy Secretary. The role and status of the Second Permanent Secretary have never been satisfactorily defined: he is below the Permanent Secretary, but not far enough below to occupy a clear position in the chain of command. If, as we propose in Chapter 6, a common grading structure

embracing all the present classes is introduced, special attention should, in our view, be paid to the grading of posts at this level.

180. We believe, however, that the present structure of departments needs reinforcing and diversifying at the highest levels. No Permanent Secretary would claim to be equally skilful at all aspects of his job. However much he delegates, the day-to-day service of his Minister (including helping to deal with the political squalls of the moment) must take priority, and this often prevents him from giving his full personal attention to the long-term objectives and planning of his department. We have already drawn attention to the lengthening time-span of government work and to the increasing emphasis on forward thinking that this demands. Top management outside government is everywhere increasingly concerned with anticipating the needs of the future; it is vital that such forward thinking in the Service should not be impeded by the constant pressure to deal with the needs of the moment.

181. Our proposals for accountable management and for enlarging the role of departmental personnel and organisation divisions will inevitably add still further to the burdens of the Permanent Secretary. He will have to devote more time to his managerial function—to be the spearhead of the constant drive to improve the efficiency of his department at all levels and among the various accountable units; and, with the greater emphasis on career management that we recommend, the Permanent Secretary's responsibility for the selection and movement of staff will become even more important and demanding.

182. We consider, therefore, that in most departments, if not all, there should be a Senior Policy Adviser to assist the Minister. This adviser should be head of the Planning Unit. His prime job, like that of the unit, would be to look to, and prepare for, the future and to ensure that day-to-day policy decisions are taken with as full a recognition as possible of likely future developments. He should be an authority in the department's field of activity. Where a department's responsibilities are so varied that no single adviser can be an authority on all of them, he would be a specialist in a major part of the department's work; the other specialisms required might be included in the Planning Unit*. It would be the job of the Senior Policy Adviser, like his staff, to know the other experts in the field, both inside and outside the Service, at home and abroad; he should be aware of all the important trends in new thinking and practice that are relevant. We hope that the adviser would often be a relatively young man. (We think that considerable advantages are gained in France and Sweden from the system by which the average age of the French *directeurs du cabinet* is 46 and of Swedish under-secretaries 45. The average age of Permanent Secretaries in Britain is 56.) On occasions he might be appointed by the Minister from outside the Service to give a new impetus to its forward thinking. More often, however, we should expect him to be a career civil servant with a long experience in, and expert knowledge of, the field covered by the department, though we think it would be advantageous if he had also had some experience outside.

*Alternatively, in some cases it might be necessary to have more than one such adviser. The precise pattern may differ from department to department but the basic concept is of a departmental Planning Unit or Units with one or more heads, but all detached from responsibility for day-to-day operations and charged with planning for the future.

183. For the proper discharge of his duties, we consider that the Senior Policy Adviser must have direct and unrestricted access to his Minister, both personally and in writing. He should also be free to determine, after consultation with the Permanent Secretary but subject only to the approval of the Minister, what problems his Planning Unit should tackle. While the adviser should have the chief responsibility for planning the longer-term departmental policy, he should not have responsibility for the day-to-day operations of the department; these should remain under the direct control of the Permanent Secretary.

184. We have considered what the status of the Senior Policy Adviser needs to be if he is to fulfil most effectively the role described. Much will depend on the way the Minister wishes to organise his top-level advice. The Permanent Secretary, as we have said, will have enlarged responsibilities for managing his staff and for the efficient organisation and running of the department. We do not wish to make specific recommendations about the Senior Policy Adviser's rank, provided that it is clearly understood that he should have the status commensurate with his being the Minister's main adviser on long-term policy questions and on their implications for the day-to-day policy decisions that have to be taken. This suggests to us that his rank should not normally be below that of Deputy Secretary. To find the right solution needs experiment; no doubt the long-term pattern should vary according to the needs of different departments at different times.

185. In some of the big technical departments there may well be a case for a further top post. For example, where a department is engaged on large-scale scientific research or on major building or engineering projects, it might be right to appoint a chief scientist or a chief engineer to be in charge of these operations. His job would be to take the chief responsibility for the direction of the department's technical work; he would have direct access to the Minister as his main adviser in these matters; he would also be the professional head of the specialist staff. In exceptional cases there might be a need for two such posts.

186. We do not propose that these senior officers, together with the Permanent Secretary, should constitute a formal board. The working arrangements should be informal and variable from department to department and from time to time; different Ministers' individual ways of working will do much to determine the pattern.

187. In any event, we consider that there should be one person who has the overall responsibility under the Minister (subject to the reservation about long-term policy in paragraph 183) for all the affairs of the department, and that this person should, as now, be the Permanent Secretary. He has the main responsibility for the day-to-day service of the Minister and for accounting to Parliament for expenditure. He cannot discharge these responsibilities unless he is ultimately in charge of the departmental machine. In carrying his responsibilities for current operations, he cannot lose his concern for their long-term policy implications, just as the Senior Policy Adviser must have some concern with current policy issues. The Permanent Secretary therefore should still be head of the office under the Minister. At the same time, our proposals about Senior Policy Advisers and chief specialists

60

should provide Ministers with a wider range of expert advice at the highest
level than at present.

THE DELEGATION OF RESPONSIBILITY TO AUTONOMOUS PUBLIC BOARDS

188. We return now to the question referred to in paragraph 145, whether there are areas of Civil Service work that should be " hived off " from the central government machine and entrusted to autonomous public boards or corporations. It has been put to us that accountable management is most effectively introduced when an activity is separately established outside any government department, and that this solution should be adopted for many executive activities, especially the provision of services to the community. These boards or corporations would be wholly responsible in their own fields within the powers delegated to them. Although they would be outside the day-to-day control of Ministers and the scrutiny of Parliament, Ministers would retain powers to give them directions when necessary. There are a number of commercial enterprises within the public sector that are already run on this principle, and it is also shortly to be applied to part of the Civil Service by " hiving off " the Post Office. There are also non-commercial activities in the public sector that are similarly organised, for example, the Atomic Energy Authority.

189. We have seen such a system operating in Sweden where the principle of " hiving off " is much more widely applied than has so far been attempted here. In Sweden central departments deal in the main with policy-making; they are quite small and are predominantly staffed by younger men. The task of managing and operating policies is hived off to autonomous agencies whose senior staff are mainly older men of mature experience. This system is used not only for activities of a commercial kind, but also for public services in social fields. We were much impressed by it. On the other hand, we are aware that in the United States the application of the " hiving-off " principle, as evidenced in the work of the independent regulatory commissions, has attracted a good deal of criticism.

190. Much new policy is a development of that which already exists and springs from practical experience in its operation. Any complete separation of policy-making from execution could therefore be harmful. However this does not appear to happen in Sweden, and we see no reason why the risk should not be provided against. There is indeed a wide variety of activities to which it might be possible to apply the principle of " hiving off ". They range from the work of the Royal Mint and air traffic control to parts of the social services. We have not been able to make the detailed study which would be needed to identify particular cases; but we see no reason to believe that the dividing line between activities for which Ministers are directly responsible, and those for which they are not, is necessarily drawn in the right place today. The creation of further autonomous bodies, and the drawing of the line between them and central government, would raise parliamentary and constitutional issues, especially if they affected the answerability for sensitive matters such as the social and education services. These issues and the related questions of machinery of government are beyond

our terms of reference. We think however that the possibility of a considerable extension of " hiving off " should be examined, and we therefore recommend an early and thorough review of the whole question.

191. Meanwhile, we believe that the other recommendations in this Chapter should make it possible to gain some of the benefits that could arise from " hiving off ", even where activities and services remain the direct responsibility of Ministers, by making it possible to allocate responsibility and authority more clearly. In this connection, we attach particular importance to our proposals: —

(a) to distinguish those within departments whose primary responsibility is planning for the future, from those whose main concern is the operation of existing policies or the provision of services;

(b) to establish in departments forms of organisation and principles of accountable management, by which individuals and branches can be held responsible for objectively measured performance.

CHAPTER 6

THE STRUCTURE OF THE CIVIL SERVICE

192. We have recommended a number of far-reaching changes in the way the Civil Service is run. We have reached the conclusion that for these changes to be fully effective, there must also be a fundamental change in the structure of the Service. Civil servants are at present organised in a large number of separate classes, almost all with their own different grading and career structures. This is a major obstacle to the application of the principle we have set out in Chapter 1. We recommend that classes as such should be abolished. In our view, all civil servants should be organised in a single grading structure in which there are an appropriate number of different pay-levels matching different levels of skill and responsibility, and the correct grading for each post is determined by an analysis of the job.

193. The change we are recommending will have massive repercussions on all aspects of Civil Service work and on the way it is organised. We believe it to be necessary, because the present structure of the Service stands in the way of what we consider to be the only efficient method of matching men to jobs—rigorously examining what each post demands before selecting the individual who is best fitted to fill it. The structure we recommend will improve the opportunities of civil servants fully to develop their talents and to get the experience they need for jobs of higher responsibility. It will provide a sound foundation for the application of the principles of accountable management, and hence for the efficient working of government departments. It will mean that the organisation of a block of work can be determined by the best way of doing the job rather than by the need to observe the traditional hierarchy of particular classes. Since it will enable success in achieving set objectives to become the determining factor in promotion, it will be a powerful stimulus to civil servants at all levels. Finally, the opening-up of opportunities, which it will offer to all civil servants, will, we believe, provide the constant competitive challenge needed for the achievement of maximum efficiency.

194. We develop all these points later in this chapter. We also give a fuller description of the new structure we recommend. First, however, we deal with the existing organisation and its defects; we survey it against the objectives which, in our view, the structure should seek to achieve.

THE OBJECTIVES

195. The Civil Service must have a clearly articulated and relatively formal structure; jobs must be graded in distinct bands which determine the pay of their occupants on a rational and fair basis; and relative positions of authority and subordination must be clearly established.

196. The problems of structure would in some ways be much simpler if

each department employed its own staff independently, and constructed its own grading system to fit the precise needs of its own work and staff. But the Civil Service cannot be run in this way. Departments have to work closely together in the achievement of common goals; the boundaries between them are subject to constant revision; the complex interlinking of departmental tasks requires a common approach and methods of work; it is necessary for the effective discharge of the tasks of the Service that staff should be able to move easily between departments—though, as we have stressed, mostly between related kinds of work. To meet these needs, the Service must be a flexible, integrated whole; it must continue to be a unified service. Its structure should be designed accordingly as a structure that is common throughout. Within such a structure two objectives are of overriding importance.

197. The first is that the structure should enable all civil servants, whatever their background, skill or discipline, to make their full contribution to the work of government; in particular, scientific and other specialist staff should be able to bring their professional training and outlook to bear effectively upon today's major problems of policy-making and management. This means an open road to the top of the Service for all kinds of talent. It also means that suitable specialists must be able to take part in policy-making and management at the lower and middle levels of the Service; quite apart from the valuable contributions they can make to management at these levels, it is unrealistic to expect specialists to reach top managerial positions without this earlier experience.

198. The second objective is that the structure should promote the effective management of the work, and especially the organisation of mixed teams in the growing areas of work in which solutions to problems need the partnership of different skills and disciplines. Effective management calls for clear allocation of responsibility and chains of command designed to meet the needs of the particular job in hand. It also requires a structure flexible enough to accommodate future changes in the work and in the combinations of skills needed from time to time.

THE PRESENT STRUCTURE

199. The present structure is still fundamentally the product of the Northcote-Trevelyan report. One of its basic principles was that a proper division of labour depended on the clear separation of intellectual from routine work, and on the separate recruitment and deployment of staff for each. Recruitment was directly linked to the output of the educational system; graduates were recruited for the intellectual work and non-graduates for the rest. This principle has been endorsed as regards initial recruitment by the recommendations of subsequent Royal Commissions and Committees of Inquiry, and supported in the past by the Treasury in its responsibilities for the overall management of the Service (though it has been tempered by a measure of class-to-class promotion after entry). Hence the division of the Service into upper and lower classes in the same broad areas of work. The Administrative, Executive and Clerical Classes are an example of these divisions; direct recruitment to each is in the main linked to the educational system—graduates at 22 or 23 going mainly into the Administrative, school-

leavers with "A levels" into the Executive and school-leavers with "O levels" into the Clerical Classes.

200. Over the years, as the government has taken on new tasks, it has been necessary to recruit large numbers of specialists—scientists, engineers, architects and others. They have been organised separately in their own occupational groups; in the terminology of the Service, the separate grading structures which resulted are also called classes. Within the largest of these occupational groups, further divisions have been drawn between higher and lower classes. For example, there are three scientific classes—the Scientific Officer Class, the Experimental Officer Class and the Scientific Assistant Class —which broadly correspond to the Administrative, Executive and Clerical Classes. Similarly the Works Group of Professional Classes is supported by separate and parallel classes comprising technical officers and draughtsmen.

201. The classes so far mentioned, together with others such as the Legal, Medical and Accountant Classes, are "general service" classes. That is to say, their members are employed in all or in a substantial number of departments, each class with its own separate grading structure and scale of pay. They have been created over a long period of time as a means of unifying the Service. A hundred years ago, each department was largely independent in recruiting and managing its staff. The object of general service classes was to promote common standards and a sense of unity among all those who did similar work in different departments; it was also to enable staff to be moved between similar jobs in different departments. The Administrative, Executive and Clerical Classes were the first of these general service classes; the scientific classes were set up in the 1930's; the Works Group of Professional Classes after the second World War. The most recent addition was the general service Economist Class in 1965.

202. In addition to the general service classes there is a great number of departmental classes, ranging in size from the very large (e.g. the 20,000 or more in the Tax Inspector and Tax Officer Classes in the Inland Revenue) to those comprising only handfuls of staff, whose members are employed in one department only. Departmental classes account for 124,000, or some 27 per cent of all non-industrial civil servants.

203. As a result there are today 47 general service and similar classes whose members are distributed across the Service as a whole and over 1,400 departmental classes whose members work in one department only. Each civil servant is recruited on entry to a particular class, depending on the kind of work he applies for and his educational qualifications for it. His membership of his class determines his prospects, since most classes have their own different grading structures, reflecting responsibility and pay. It largely determines, too, the range of jobs on which he may be employed; there are conventions governing the allocation of types of work to each class, some of which are buttressed by agreements with staff associations. Although there is provision for individuals subsequently to move from one class to another, the processes are formal and restrictive. Thus, in practice, whether they move between departments or, as is more usual, remain in one department, civil servants do not normally think in terms of a career in the Service—they have a career in a class.

204. It is an important feature of the system that there are separate pay

scales for each class. These are determined for each class in accordance with the principles established by the Priestley Commission of 1955. The primary principle is that of "fair comparison with the current remuneration of outside staff employed on broadly comparable work". Internal relativities are used as a supplement to the principle of fair comparison in settling Civil Service rates in detail, and they become the primary consideration when outside comparisons cannot be made.

205. It is also an important feature of the system that the policy-making and general managerial jobs in the Service are generally reserved for members of the Administrative and Executive Classes. Specialists who seek broader managerial responsibilities normally have to transfer to one or other of these classes.

DEFECTS OF THE PRESENT STRUCTURE

206. The basis of the divisions between higher and lower classes is no longer valid. The work of the Service cannot now be broken down for the purposes of recruitment into two simple categories, the intellectual and the routine, the one appropriate for graduates and the other for the rest. The changing tasks of civil servants refuse to conform to this outmoded division, and the Service can discharge its modern responsibilities only by drawing on many different kinds of ability at every level. Higher-level posts still call for the ability to give advice to Ministers on complex policy issues. But many now also require the ability to run large projects and programmes, and to manage large numbers of staff. The practical, managerial qualities thus required at these levels are not necessarily identified by success in a written degree examination taken many years before or, indeed, by any selection method for testing young people in the late 'teens or early twenties.

207. In the middle ranges, too, there are already jobs for graduates—for example, in the Executive and Experimental Officer Classes. This will certainly continue and the number may grow. But it makes no sense to maintain a class distinction between two groups of people that has now to be based on the often narrow difference between one degree and another—between an upper second and a lower or between a second and a third. It is also difficult to maintain the present sub-division of clerical work into two separate classes, with four or five passes at "O level" required for the Clerical Officer Class and two or three for the Clerical Assistant Class. In addition, as the report of our Management Consultancy Group shows, there is often no discernible difference in content between work done at the lower levels of one class and the upper levels of the one beneath it. We have also to recognise the importance of the man whose promise is latent at the start of his career, but who then proves his worth by his performance. The present structure increases the risk that his talent will remain undiscovered.

208. The occupational divisions between separate disciplines and specialisms are also under strain. They are not at present constructed on any uniform principle. Thus physicists and biologists are grouped in one class, while doctors have a separate class of their own, as do psychologists. Secondly, not all members of the same discipline or occupation are classed together. For example, some electrical and mechanical engineers engaged on research are in the Scientific Officer Class, while others, engaged on construction, are in the Works Group of Professional Classes; but the Works Group also

contains some who are engaged on research. Similarly, there is no clear-cut occupational difference between the work done by members of different classes; for example, it is frequently difficult to distinguish between the tasks given to the following members of three classes—Technical Officer Grade II (Technical Works, Engineering and Allied Classes), Assistant Experimental Officer (Experimental Officer Class) and Senior Scientific Assistant (Scientific Assistant Class.)

209. This structure, as operated today, presents serious obstacles to the most flexible use of staff: —

(a) It prevents the best deployment and use of individual talent. The formal and relatively rigid procedures involved in moving from one class to another place unnecessary barriers in the way of the movement of individuals, both upwards to posts of higher responsibility and sideways between different kinds of related work. It also impedes the rapid development and promotion of young people with outstanding potential.

(b) It is a major obstacle to the ability of the Service to adapt itself to new tasks. Each class tends to regard the posts that its members usually fill as its own preserve, guaranteeing a career structure with a fixed number of posts at various levels. Men and women enter these classes in their youth and form expectations about their prospects, to which they cling with increasing tenacity as the years go by. Staff associations naturally tend to serve as the guardians of these territories, and to resist any proposal that seems likely to reduce the number of posts to which they feel their members have a right. This rigidity in the deployment of staff is particularly serious at a time when the tasks are changing rapidly and new techniques are being developed to meet them. For example, as we point out in Appendix D, accountants could make a useful contribution to financial forecasting and control, procurement and O and M work; they are not in a position to do so because these duties are the province of other classes.

(c) The career opportunities that are thus defined for the different classes vary greatly in their attractiveness and scope, even for people with similar educational qualifications. For example direct graduate entrants to both the Administrative and Scientific Officer Classes need a first or second-class degree. But 46 per cent of the posts in the Administrative Class carry salaries in excess of £3,500 a year, compared with 23.5 per cent of the posts in the Scientific Officer Class. The point of this criticism is not that these proportions should necessarily be equal; the work may not demand a higher proportion of purely scientific posts at middle and high levels. It is that separate classification at these levels encourages the idea that opportunity is not equal—an idea that is justified to the extent that scientists cannot move easily into appropriate middle and higher management posts except through the relatively rigid process involved in moving from one class to another.

(d) The word "class", and the structure it represents, produce feelings of inferiority as well as of restricted opportunities. This is most

67

marked in the attitude of other classes towards the Administrative Class, but it can be seen in greater or lesser degree between lower and higher classes generally.

210. The structure also leads to the inefficient organisation of work. It does so in three ways: —

(a) Each class has its prescribed functions. For example, financial and policy work are generally reserved for the Administrative Class with appropriate support from the Executive Class, while technical or scientific work belongs to the specialist classes. Where administrators and specialists are engaged in a common task, parallel or joint hierarchies are the usual devices to enable them to work together. But within these hierarchies the administrator is normally responsible to another administrator in the next higher grade, and the specialist similarly to another specialist; thus the separation of prescribed responsibilities is maintained. These forms of organisation, which are a major source of inefficiency and frustration, are discussed in Chapter 5; but their roots lie in the structure of the Service.

(b) The separation of functions has a particularly damaging effect in blurring responsibility and authority in command. There are many joint tasks, especially projects and programmes with a high technical content, in which good management depends upon putting a single person in charge and holding him responsible for the result; the rest of the team should be responsible to him. Often, however, the separation of functions results in twin heads being in charge, one a specialist, the other an administrator.

(c) A man's career is primarily thought of as a career within his class. There is therefore a natural pressure to maximise the opportunities of the class, in each area of work that it occupies, by making use of as many of its grades as possible. The presumption thus grows up that the organisation of any area of work should reflect in full the grading structure of the class concerned—e.g. that the Assistant Secretary is always needed between the Principal and the Under Secretary, and the Executive Officer between the Clerical Officer and the Higher Executive Officer. This is also true of the specialist classes. The convention can be, and is, broken from time to time, but not enough. The structure makes it more difficult to do so, and to introduce experiments in the organisation of the work.

211. Underlying many of these criticisms is the fundamental point to which we drew attention in paragraph 193: that the system of classes stands in the way of the most efficient method of matching men to jobs. This is because classes are too crude an instrument for the purpose. They involve two assumptions: that any job can be categorised as appropriate to one or other of the classes; and that it will then be most appropriately filled by selection from the members of that class, all of whom are in principle more likely to be good candidates for it than any member of another class. These assumptions seem to us no longer sound, particularly in view of the work the Civil Service now has to do.

212. There are many jobs that can be filled only by qualified doctors or

engineers; and many that will require the training and experience of the economic or social administrators discussed in Chapter 2. But a growing proportion of jobs in the Service require both technical and managerial knowledge and ability, and cannot now be properly classified as either technical (and therefore reserved for the appropriate specialist class), or managerial (and therefore normally reserved for the Administrative or Executive Class). These jobs are to be found not only in the highest reaches of the Service; they exist at much more modest levels from about £1,500 a year upwards, especially in the big technological departments. Taking the Service as a whole, they may be a relatively small proportion at present. But as the work of the Service continues to change, and as new specialisms emerge, they are certain to multiply. Thus, the categorisation of jobs by class becomes less appropriate year by year; and, when it comes to selection for posts, there is a steadily increasing area of work in which the implied assumption that the best man for the job will be found within a given class has clearly become invalid. In our judgment, therefore, a principle of organisation that rests upon this assumption and relies mainly upon formal procedures for inter-class transfers in order to provide for exceptions is no longer satisfactory and will, if it is not changed, become an increasingly serious obstacle to the proper deployment of talent.

213. Finally, the present system of classes is a major obstacle to the proper application of the principles of accountable management which we recommend in Chapter 5. This is because in analysing jobs the Service now concentrates its attention and thought on the duties and tasks appropriate to particular *classes* and the various levels within them. In contrast, accountable management requires that the main weight should be placed upon an analysis of the results required from each individual *job*, their relative importance to the work of the Service as a whole, and the consequent search for the man with the right qualities and qualifications to produce those results; in this context, the practice of assigning duties to individuals by reference to their membership of particular classes is at best an irrelevant distraction and at worst a serious obstacle to the kind of job evaluation that is needed.

THE NEW STRUCTURE WE PROPOSE

214. The structure the Service needs should in our view be based on the following principles:—

(a) Both the grading of a post and the selection of the man to fill it should be based first and foremost on an evaluation of the job.

(b) Management should appoint to each post the person it considers best fitted by his qualifications and experience to fill it.

(c) No posts should be the preserve of any group, except in so far as the individuals comprising the group may be uniquely qualified for them, e.g. doctors for medical posts.

(d) Since the qualifications and experience required for particular posts will vary from time to time, it should be the right and duty of management to determine the new qualifications and experience required for them.

(e) In filling individual posts, management should promote the right man even if he is not the next in the order of seniority, or bring him in from outside the Service if he cannot be found within it or if it believes that an appointment from outside would bring a valuable reinforcement of skill and experience.

(f) The pay for posts should continue to reflect the rate for the job on the basis of fair comparison with market rates for jobs of comparable responsibility and authority outside the Service.

(g) The structure should permit work to be organised in such a way that chains of command reflect the demands of the task and, where necessary, cut across any groupings by discipline or type of skill.

The application of these principles demands two fundamental and complementary changes in the structure of the Service. Together they produce the single, unified grading-system running across the whole Service that we referred to in paragraph 192. For the sake of clarity, however, we present them separately at this stage.

215. First, we recommend that the divisions between higher and lower classes should be abolished, and that a continuous grading-system from bottom to top should be substituted in each occupational group. Thus, for example, we propose the merger of the Administrative, Executive, and Clerical Classes, as recommended to us by the Treasury. But we also propose mergers of the Scientific Officer, Experimental Officer and Scientific Assistant Classes and of the Works Group of Professional Classes, the Technical Works, Engineering and Allied Classes and the Architectural and Engineering Draughtsman Classes. Movement upwards, e.g. from clerical to executive or from experimental to scientific work, should be by promotion from a lower to a higher grade; and this should lie within the direct authority of the management of each department, subject to appropriate central supervision of standards and numbers. We also consider that the supporting grades (e.g. messengers, typists, machine operators) should be brought into this structure. We discuss this further in Appendix J.

216. Although this reform will bring the Civil Service into line with other large organisations in this country, where divisions into higher and lower classes are rare, it will present a radical change for the Service itself. It is not simply a question of linking together classes that now operate at completely separate levels of pay and responsibility. There is a good deal of overlap at present between the levels at which these various classes operate and the types of work they do. Thus, to replace the present class structure by a continuous grading structure from bottom to top for each occupational group will involve a major programme of job evaluation: a fresh examination of what each job or kind of job is for, and of the qualifications and experience it requires.

217. Secondly, we believe that the principle of the best man for the job should apply between civil servants of different occupations no less than between those who enter the Service with different levels of educational qualification. No posts should be the preserve of any one group, except in so far as individuals in the group may be uniquely qualified for them. This calls for another radical structural change. It means bringing to an end the system in which an individual can normally move between jobs now reserved for different occupational groups only if he himself moves into a different class.

218. To give full effect to our proposals at paragraphs 215 and 217, we believe that it is necessary to replace the present multitude of classes and their separate career structures by the creation of a classless, uniformly graded structure of the type that is now being adopted in many large business firms and similar to the system used by the Civil Service in the United States. The basis of the system we are proposing is the establishment of a number of successive grading levels that together would embrace all the jobs in the Service. Each grade would carry a range of pay. The number of grades required can be determined only after a more detailed analysis of the existing structure than we have been able to make; but on the basis of the advice we have received, we think that some twenty grades could contain all the jobs from top to bottom in the non-industrial part of the Service.

219. An essential feature of the system is that the salary range (or scale) for each grade should be relatively broad, and that there should be over-lapping of salaries between grades (see as an example the salary grading structure of the United States civil service shown in Appendix C). This is to provide scope for advancement within grades. Thus, while the most able will be promoted well before they reach the maximum of their grade, others can continue to earn salary increases within the same grade.

220. All the jobs now performed by the many different classes should be fitted into the appropriate grade. This will require careful job evaluation. This should be based on such factors as the " end-results " required, the degree of personal responsibility involved, the importance attaching to the work and the qualifications and experience needed in the holder to achieve the prescribed results. At the same time, the process of job evaluation should take into account the market rate for jobs of similar responsibilities outside the Service. The system is equally applicable to all types of job. A scientific job in a research establishment, high-level case-work in an administrative division, an engineering job, and a line-management job in an executive-clerical establishment can all be analysed and ranked within the same grading-system.

221. This is essentially a pay structure; it is not designed to determine the actual organisation of work. The precise organisation of each block of work, and the number of working levels in it, should be determined solely by what is required for the most efficient achievement of its objectives. Thus, in any division, job evaluation would show that only a selection of the twenty or so grades should be used—the smallest number needed. There should be no set pattern.

222. Within this overall structure, there will, of course, continue to be a great variety of groups of staff. At the highest levels of the Service, we think it useful to distinguish the top management, comprising all posts in all grades from the Head of the Civil Service down to, and including, grades that are today equivalent to Under Secretary; we refer to this here and elsewhere in our report as the Senior Policy and Management Group. Although the work of these grades is not sharply different from those immediately below, never-theless the higher one goes in the Service, the more one's work is likely to consist of policy-making and higher management rather than the exclusive practice of a particular skill or discipline. As a civil servant approaches these levels, his responsibilities become steadily heavier and usually less

specialist. He begins to share in a real collegiate responsibility to the Minister for the policy and management of the department as a whole; increasingly, too, he has to take interdepartmental considerations into account. At these levels an individual's particular occupational group is thus often of less significance than his range of experience, and personal qualities and qualifications should be the main criteria for filling posts with these wider horizons. There comes a point, therefore, where promotions become matters affecting the interests of the Service as a whole, and the Civil Service Department should play a part in them. We distinguish the Senior Policy and Management Group in order to define the area to which this should apply.

223. Below this level, the occupational content of the work is often greater than the managerial content. Thus occupational groupings of staff have a greater significance. They vary greatly in kind. The majority of civil servants are employed in supporting grades (see Appendix J), where the work has little or no managerial content and its occupational content consists more of the practice of a skill (e.g. typing, filing or operating machines) than the application of a discipline. At higher levels, the development and application of a particular discipline, and the need for specialisation by subject-matter, becomes much more important, and in many parts of the work its managerial content steadily increases as a man rises towards the senior levels referred to above. At all levels however where the work requires civil servants to specialise (whether in administrative, specialist or the various kinds of supporting work), occupational groups will be needed, and civil servants should generally be recruited and trained as members of them. They should include the present specialist disciplines, the two groups of administrative staff identified in Chapter 2 and the supporting grades discussed in Appendix J.

224. At least during the earlier years of their career, most civil servants should work in the field of their specialism. Those whose main inclinations and aptitudes lie in this direction could spend their whole careers in their specialised field, and we recognise that many people will wish to do this. Others, however, should progress after appropriate training and experience to work that becomes steadily more managerial in character in areas adjacent to their specialism; and posts at all levels which offer the right kind of experience in management should be open to members of all occupational groups who are fitted for them. In a system of this kind civil servants could be given a clear indication of their career prospects if they remained in their specialised field—the extent and shape of the structure of higher posts open to them if they develop in this direction. We attach high importance to a structure in which people are able to take part in the development of their own career patterns.

225. It is likely that occupational groups will tend to develop their own career patterns. Men and women will enter the Service at different grades, depending upon the level of the work they have been recruited to do. Thereafter, it may become usual for members of particular occupational groups to skip certain grades. This should be kept flexible; but it should be established that it is normal to skip grades on promotion, and thus that the field of candidates for promotion is not limited to the grade immediately below.

226. Though we have not examined in any detail the pay of the Civil Service, we feel bound to make one comment on the implications for pay of the structure we propose. The proposal does not in our view imply a departure from the principle of " fair comparison with the current remuneration of outside staffs employed on broadly comparable work " which was established by the Royal Commission on the Civil Service 1953-1955. In our view this principle remains valid and will continue to be necessary to the efficiency as well as to the contentment of the Service. But if our recommendations for a unified grading structure are accepted, we should expect the outside comparison to be made as part of the process of job evaluation: assessing the importance of the job to the work of the Service and establishing the rate for jobs of similar responsibility outside the Service.

227. We recognise that the Civil Service attaches great value to negotiation and arbitration in the settling of pay claims. These should be preserved. It will be necessary to ensure that the system we propose does not result in the extension of formal negotiation and arbitration to cover those questions, such as the grading of individual jobs, that should remain a matter for management to determine. But the general pay-scales of the grades, and claims for higher pay on the basis of comparisons with pay outside the Service, should continue to be dealt with by negotiation and arbitration, adapted as necessary to fit the new structural pattern we propose.

228. We have said in paragraph 218 that each grade should carry a range of pay. This, in our view, should be true of all grades except the very top one—which should be a flat rate varied only in the case of the Head of the Civil Service (see Chapter 7, paragraph 258)—and possibly the grade immediately below*.

229. In all except the top grade, we think it important that there should be more flexible progression through the pay-scale of the grade. Fixed annual increments, in our view, do not give enough incentive to effort, and make possible too easy a progress for those who do not pull their full weight. We believe that it should be possible to reward merit by extra pay as well as by promotion. Thus, up to the level of the Senior Policy and Management Group, we recommend that, while annual increments should continue, there should be the following modifications:—

(a) Additional increments should be granted both for especially good work and for success in gaining relevant qualifications.

(b) Increments should be withheld when they have not been earned.

---

*Sir William Cook, Sir Norman Kipping and Sir John Wall make the following reservation on paragraph 228:—

    We see no reason why the principles of job evaluation and outside comparison should not extend to the most senior posts in the Civil Service. This applies both to the level and to the range of pay. Some Permanent Secretaries carry responsibilities comparable to those of the chairmen of the great nationalised undertakings, who command much higher salaries; others are in posts which, though demanding, are less onerous. We believe that these differences should be reflected in their pay. We do not think it wise to make a man who has perhaps been appointed to a top post at 48 or 50 feel that he has reached his ceiling at that age. Unless there is still something for him to look forward to, the temptation for him to leave must be great. We think that even the highest posts should therefore be paid on a salary band.

Above this level, regular annual increments seem to us unsuitable and the numbers are small enough to make a different system practicable. The range of pay for each grade should in effect become a " band " of pay, in which only the maximum and minimum points for each grade would be published, and the progress of each officer through the band would not be on a regular incremental basis but determined by an annual review of his performance. Individual salaries would not be published.

ADVANTAGES OF THE UNIFIED GRADING STRUCTURE

230. We think that the structure we propose would have five main advantages. First, we believe that the system will remove the obstacles to the flexible deployment of staff to which we referred in paragraph 209. It will thus offer wider opportunities to all civil servants.

231. In particular, the unified grading-system we propose will enable the Service to gain the full contribution which scientists, engineers and other specialist staff could, but do not now, make to policy, management and administration. At present all these people have careers in their own separate classes. To move into more general management, they have to transfer to the Administrative and Executive Classes. A few make the first move; practically none the second (although the Executive Class occupies managerial positions in the Service up to a salary level of £5,250). For specialists, the difficult problem arises of deciding whether they are likely to do better by transferring in mid-career to a new class which fills most of the top managerial and policy jobs; or by continuing to move up the ladder of their existing class, with its narrower range of posts, which does not generally take a man to the highest levels in the Service. The decision to seek a transfer also involves at least the appearance of a formal severance from a man's original discipline—a dividing-line which has to be crossed again if he wishes to return. With the abolition of classes, such problems and difficulties should be significantly lightened.

232. This does not apply only to the higher levels of the Service. It is equally, if not more, important lower down. The present system makes it particularly and unnecessarily difficult for specialists to be tested and given experience in general management sufficiently early in their careers. There are many members of the specialist classes at present in grades carrying between £1,500 and £2,500 a year., e.g. accountants, engineers, scientists, Experimental Officers, Technical Grades A and B, who should be getting some experience of management in areas where their specialist knowledge would be valuable. This is not only because it would fit them for higher management later on; it would also enable them to make a useful contribution to middle and junior management here and now.

233. A unified grading structure will also provide a more flexible career pattern for administrative staff, by enabling the Service to deploy them to the best advantage without the need for transferring from the Executive Class to the Administrative Class or vice-versa. Here again difficult decisions now confront the most able members of the Executive Class. Their areas of work are often similar to those of the Administrative Class. The able Executive who stays in his class has good prospects of promotion to comparatively senior posts. The top posts in the Service, however, are open to him only if he seeks a transfer to

74

the Administrative Class; but if he gets a transfer he may in the end do less well than if he had remained a member of the Executive Class since his chances of reaching senior posts in the Administrative Class are relatively smaller. Some play safe and stay; some of those who gain class-to-class promotion regret it. At the same time there is at present almost no movement from Administrative to Executive Class jobs (which would look like demotion under the existing system). Thus, members of the Administrative Class are not normally considered for the major management jobs that are reserved for the Executive Class, although some may well have the aptitude for them. The structure we propose will allow completely flexible posting to suit the aptitudes of administrators as they develop in the course of their careers.

234. A unified grading structure will thus offer wider opportunities to all civil servants. This is not, of course, to say that it will offer better prospects to all members of all the present classes. The widening of opportunities should lead to keener competition, and favour the most able civil servants regardless of their occupational group. Our proposal is designed, among other things, to bring this about.

235. In addition to providing the framework for the more flexible deployment of staff, we believe the second main advantage of a unified grading structure is that it would promote more efficient and accountable management and the more economical use of manpower. In Chapter 5 we define accountable management as a system in which individuals and units are held responsible for performance and output measured as objectively as possible, and we make more detailed proposals there about the departmental organisation needed for this. We believe that a unified grading structure would of itself result in a far more effective method of grading and manning jobs in the Service and thus promote greater efficiency. This is because: —

(a) The detailed job-evaluation system needed to set it up and run it will define and measure the " end-result " required of each post. An individual's performance can then be judged against this specification and by his actual achievement. The present system of grading and evaluating jobs concentrates on assessing whether the duties are appropriate to a particular level of a particular class, and not on the end-result of the job.

(b) With the disappearance of classes, the present pressures to use all possible grades in the organisation of a block of work (to which we referred in paragraph 210) will also be reduced. This is because members of different groups will have more varied career opportunities than they have now. In a common grading structure of twenty or so grades, there can be no set pattern for their use; it will, therefore, be necessary to ensure, by analysis of the work itself, that only the right selection of grades and occupational groups is used for each block of work.

(c) Common grading will help to get rid of the separate and parallel hierarchies which we criticised as the wrong way of applying a variety of skills and disciplines to a common task. The practice of allocating defined kinds of work to different classes will disappear with the classes themselves. In consequence, it will become easier to construct integrated hierarchies and teams that embody different

75

skills at appropriate levels under the single command of the officer in charge.

(d) If grading is made to depend upon the rigorous analysis of individual jobs, it will become an effective mechanism, built into the structure of the Service itself, for guarding against the inefficient use of manpower and the perpetuation of unnecessary jobs. The process of job evaluation, properly applied, tests both the value of the job itself and the levels of qualification it requires. It should therefore become an effective safeguard against the misuse of qualified manpower and should help to ensure that unnecessary jobs are eliminated.

236. We believe too that job evaluation in the context of a common grading structure offers the only rational method of solving the problems which now beset the classification and grading of the work of the specialist classes, to which we have referred in paragraph 208. The evidence makes clear* that the present frontiers between the Scientific Officer and Works Group Classes in the engineering field, for example, are wholly unsatisfactory. We are convinced that such problems are inherent in class structures, and that, in this as in other fields, the selection of the right man for the job (neither over-qualified nor under-qualified to fill it) must depend, not on membership of a class, but on the continual re-evaluation of the post and of the varying skills and levels of qualification it may demand from time to time.

237. Thirdly, a structure on these lines will make easier much-needed improvements in the system of promotion which we have criticised in Chapter 3. At present a civil servant is normally promoted within his class to a higher post in the area of work reserved for it. Opportunities for promotion vary greatly between different classes and also within the same class between different departments; promotion is too much determined by a man's seniority in his present grade in his class in a particular department. Promotion boards cannot generally consider a man's fitness for promotion to a job *outside* the field of work allocated to his class, even though his qualifications and experience might bring a useful contribution to it. At the same time, promotions *within* a class are normally based on the criterion that, in order to qualify, a man must be fit to do any of the jobs assigned to his class at the higher level. In our view, these factors together result in a system of promotion that is insufficiently discriminating. Too little attention is given to finding for those who have achieved promotions, the precise jobs at the higher level for which they are best fitted; and some, who would be very adequate performers in a limited range of jobs at the higher level, fail to achieve the promotion they deserve.

238. The unified grading structure we propose would provide the necessary foundations for a new promotion system in which: —

(a) Promotion is based on the record of an individual's achievement in producing the " end-results " at which his job is aimed.

(b) The aptitudes and experience of the individual can be more directly and specifically linked to the requirement of a particular job at the higher level.

---

*See the paper submitted by the Treasury, the Ministry of Public Building and Works and the Ministry of Technology on Scientists, Engineers and the Works Group (Volume 5, No. 7).

(c) Promotion boards can consider candidates for higher posts, not only within the field of their specialisation, but also in management posts where their specialist knowledge may be useful.

(d) Because performance is taken properly into account, and selection based upon the aptitudes and experience of the individual rather than upon his membership of a particular class, there are more nearly equal promotion opportunities for all,

(e) Able individuals can skip grades.

(f) In so far as seniority denotes valuable experience, it can be given its proper weight; but that weight will not be excessive if the main emphasis in promotion questions is on the assessment of individuals by results achieved and by their aptitudes, skills and relevant experience for particular jobs at higher levels.

This reform of the grading structure should enable the system of promotion to be adapted to what we see as the main objective: that a man's experience and qualification to do a particular kind of job at a higher level should be the main factor in promotion decisions; and that, in assessing this, full weight should be given to his performance in the job that he has been doing. In order to give full effect to this change, methods of reporting on staff will need to be revised. In particular, we recommend that report forms should be re-cast in such a way as to oblige reporting officers to give a much fuller assessment of performance (i.e. of success in achieving definite objectives) than they normally give at present.

239. Fourthly, a common grading structure which extends across the whole Service offers, in our view, the only practicable means of dealing with the fragmentation of over 1,400 departmental classes, each with its own separate pay and career structure. There is general agreement that this situation ought not to be allowed to continue; the existence of this vast number of separate classes produces unnecessary complexity in the work of management, not least by multiplying the number of separate pay negotiations. But our examination of the departmental classes has convinced us that so long as the Service maintains separate general service classes, there is no rational or logical basis on which the number of departmental classes can be significantly reduced. The great bulk of them can plead for separate existence on the same grounds as those put forward by any of the main general service classes. Within a unified grading structure, however, the whole problem of the separate departmental classes can be dealt with; after the necessary job-evaluation procedure they can be absorbed at the appropriate levels into the new structure. Many of them should continue to form distinct occupational groups, with their own recruitment, training and career management. But their members, like those of the more general groups, would also be available for employment in jobs of middle and junior management adjacent to the areas of their specialism.

240. Fifthly, we believe that a radical change in the structure of the Service is needed to give real effect to many of the other proposals we have made. The operation of the present structure has bred over a long period of years attitudes and practices that are deeply ingrained. Therefore we do not believe that it is sufficient to leave the structure basically as it is; incorporate in it some modifications; and then expect the Service to operate it in a

fundamentally new way. This is in essence what the Treasury have proposed. They have recommended the merger of the Administrative, Executive and Clerical Classes and a form of open structure at the top of the Service only; the remainder would continue in their existing classes. In our view this partial reform is inadequate. We intend no criticism of the future managers of the Service when we say that, with the best intentions, they could not carry it through to success. As long as a structure based on classes persists, the attitudes and practices associated with it will hinder the efforts of management to open up careers to all the talents and to make fully effective all the changes in organisation and practice we recommend.

PRIORITIES IN THE ESTABLISHMENT OF THE UNIFIED GRADING STRUCTURE

241. The introduction of the new system and its implementation throughout the Service will be a major undertaking. It will call for close and detailed consultations with the Staff Side on such matters as the general shape of the new structure, methods of settling pay claims, methods of job evaluation and a review of the existing criteria on which the annual report on the performance of each civil servant is based.

242. There will also have to be a substantial training programme for those who will carry out the necessary job evaluation. The subsequent application of job-evaluation techniques on the scale required to cover the whole Service will inevitably be a detailed and lengthy process. In this connection, however, it is important to stress that the total task may not be as massive as it might appear. Over wide areas of the Service, jobs can be grouped into "families" for grading purposes so that the numbers that have to be analysed in detail are only a proportion of the whole. It will take a large-scale operation to move the Service completely over to the new structure we recommend; how large will depend upon the extent to which present gradings are right.

243. Given acceptance in principle of our proposal for a unified grading structure throughout the Service, we think that it may be helpful to indicate what we believe to be the first priority. We think that the Civil Service Department should mount a major study to work out the details (including the number of grades and the system of job evaluation appropriate to the Service) of a scheme for a unified grading structure, together with a time-scale for its implementation. Our consultations have led us to believe that it will take from three to five years to produce a detailed scheme and implement it throughout the Service. In our view, the Civil Service Department will need to draw heavily on outside management consultants at all stages in this process.

CHAPTER 7

THE CENTRAL MANAGEMENT OF THE CIVIL SERVICE
AND RELATIONS WITH STAFF ASSOCIATIONS

244. The responsibilities of the Treasury at present cover both financial and economic policy, including the control of public expenditure, and also the central management of the Civil Service. By "management" in this context we mean the task of directing or running the Service itself—controlling its staffing and remuneration, its structure and organisation, and promoting efficient methods of work. In this chapter we discuss the task of central management, its location and staffing, and its relations with other departments. We also deal with the relations between management, both central and departmental, and the organisations that represent the staff.

245. The Treasury is divided into two parts to carry out its dual task. Its central management functions are discharged by the "Pay and Management" group under a Joint Permanent Secretary who is designated Head of the Civil Service. This side of the Treasury also has important central functions in relation to the pay and pensions of other public services and bodies. The "Pay and Management" group, however, has never been, and is not today, a fully-developed directing body at the centre with complete overall authority to manage the Civil Service. We have discussed the divided responsibility for recruitment in Chapter 3. The Treasury has the final responsibility and authority on questions of Civil Service pay (within overall considerations of incomes policy); on pensions; on the number of staff employed and the grading of posts (i.e. determining the level of responsibility demanded by the job), though it delegates certain powers to departments from time to time—in some matters, such as grading, quite extensively. The authority of the Treasury is less in O and M work, management services (i.e. the promotion of the best management practices), training and personnel management; in these, its role is mainly guiding and advisory. In machinery of government questions where political considerations are often paramount, the Treasury advises the Prime Minister.

246. As would be expected, the Treasury has developed its functions most fully in those fields where it has full authority—like pay and numbers of staff. Elsewhere, although its central management role has recently been extended, it has been patchy rather than systematic, with too few staff and too little expertise.

THE TASK OF CENTRAL MANAGEMENT

247. The proposals we are making for the Civil Service as a whole—the abolition of the present system of classes, a system of central recruitment more directly related to the needs of departments, the greater professionalism of administrators and specialists, the better career management, training and

D

deployment of staff, and the promotion of greater departmental efficiency—will all make greater demands than in the past on the central management of the Service. To make these proposals fully effective, the role of central management needs to be changed and enlarged.

248. The primary role of central management should be to ensure that the Service is continuously governed by the principle outlined in Chapter 1: that the Service should constantly review its tasks and the possible ways in which it might perform them; then consider what new skills and kinds of men are needed and how these can be found, trained and deployed. As we have said, this requires that recruitment, training and personnel management and organisation should be regarded as integral parts of a unified process: supplying and developing the talent the Service needs and deploying it to the greatest possible advantage. Clearly this constant adaptation of men and methods to changing tasks must be a joint responsibility, shared between central management and individual departments, but central management must have the appropriate degree of ultimate authority in those questions that affect the interests of the public service as a whole. We consider that its main responsibilities, including those that are at present discharged by the " Pay and Management " group of the Treasury, should be: —

(a) to stimulate and assist departments in reviewing the kinds of skill and forms of organisation needed for their tasks as they change and develop;

(b) in the light of this review, to determine manpower requirements both in quantity and quality, agree with departments how these requirements should be met, provide the necessary common services for new recruitment and internal transfer and satisfy itself that departments are efficiently and economically staffed;

(c) to specify in consultation with departments the qualities, qualifications and experience required of new recruits to the Service;

(d) to determine (after such negotiations as are necessary in each case) pay, pensions and other conditions of service;

(e) to determine training policy in consultation with departments, conduct central training courses, arrange external training, and stimulate and guide training within departments;

(f) to promote career development throughout the Service, and in particular to co-operate with and guide departments in fostering the promotion, and planning the future development, of the most promising members of all disciplines;

(g) to promote mobility both between departments and between the Service and outside employments;

(h) to discuss with departments (which should be required to consult central management on this matter) all promotions to the Senior Policy and Management Group, and to take the initiative in proposing individual moves between departments both within the group and at lower levels;

(i) to advise the Prime Minister on: —
  (i) appointments at the salary-level of Deputy Secretary and above; and
  (ii) the most efficient division of responsibility between departments;

(j) to study new developments in methods of organising work, in management techniques and in office machinery, and promote their use throughout the Service.

THE NEW CIVIL SERVICE DEPARTMENT

249. For these tasks of central management to be discharged effectively in the Civil Service of the future, two major institutional changes are needed.

250. First, as we have recommended in Chapter 3, the responsibility for recruitment and selection at present carried by the Civil Service Commission should be brought together with the other functions of central management within a single organisation.

251. Secondly, the expanded and unified central management of the Service should be made the responsibility of a new department created specifically for that purpose. Our reasons for this are as follows.

252. The Treasury's concern for public expenditure led to its development as the central managerial authority for the Service as a whole. But the British Civil Service is now almost alone in continuing to combine these functions in a single department. In our view, the central management of the Service is not, under modern conditions, an appropriate function for the central finance department, for three reasons:—

(a) The role of the central management of the Service needs to be enlarged. In particular, if it is to discharge its full responsibilities for senior appointments (which means ensuring that men and women from all disciplines are considered for these appointments on their basis of their individual qualifications and experience), it must follow that central management will need to have much greater knowledge than in the past of the most able civil servants of all disciplines, particularly those who are likely candidates for top posts, and influence over their appointments. If this enlarged responsibility for career development were added to the Treasury's responsibilities for financial and economic policy and for the control of public expenditure, there would be reason to fear too great a concentration of power in one department. The overall direction of the Service and the key to individual success within it should not both lie with the department that also uses the powerful weapon of central financial control.

(b) Each of the two sides of the Treasury needs to use an expertise separate and different from that required by the other; our proposals for increasing the professionalism of the Service will cause them to grow still further apart. We do not, therefore, think that central management should be predominantly staffed, as it is today at Assistant Secretary and Principal level, by those whose main training and experience have been in techniques of government finance and the control of expenditure. The present practice of manning both sides of the Treasury at this level by a constant interchange between them impedes the development of a full professionalism in each. A proportion of the staff of central management should come from other departments on loan, but the Treasury should not be the predominant source of this flow. It should come from all departments.

(c) Central management should be positively and creatively concerned with maintaining and improving the standards of the Civil Service. It should therefore be a separate institution with a single-minded devotion to its own professional purpose; and should be in a position to fight, and to be seen fighting, the Treasury on behalf of the Service.

253. In addition to these questions of principle, there is an important practical question of confidence. There is today among civil servants a lack of confidence in the Treasury as the centre of Civil Service management. In our judgment, the Treasury has contributed to this by employing too few staff on this work. A change is necessary for other sufficient reasons but also to demonstrate that a fresh start is being made. If our proposals are to have a fair chance of success, there must be no doubt about the effectiveness of the central direction. There will be no confidence that they will be implemented in the radical spirit we believe to be necessary, if central management is left where it is.

254. Accordingly we recommend as the first main step in the reform of the Service the setting up of a new Civil Service Department. This should absorb the functions of the Civil Service Commission and carry the responsibilities for central management outlined in paragraph 248*.

255. The staffing of this new department will be of critical importance. The full development of the responsibilities we have described will call for men and women who have knowledge and experience of personnel management and organisation, both inside and outside the Service. This will require a mixture of long-term and short-term appointments. The new department should not in our view be predominantly staffed by officers who have spent most of their careers in the Treasury, and can thus have little experience of direct responsibility for management. Departments generally should be prepared to release some of their best men for a period of service in the Civil Service Department, especially from among those with departmental experience of personnel and organisation work. We believe that the work of the new department will include some of the most challenging and creative jobs that the Service has to offer. We also consider it important that a number of appointments at senior levels within the new department should be made from outside the Service of people with appropriate knowledge and experience of managing large organisations both at home and abroad.

256. The department should also include specialists (e.g. scientists and engineers) who will be able to bring an intimate knowledge and experience to bear on the recruitment, training and career management of members of their own disciplines. There should be an appropriate measure of central management for all the major occupational groups, and the members of each group should be able to feel that their interests are being looked after

---

*We envisage in paragraph 266 below that this change may involve the consequence that the new department should also discharge the central functions in relation to the pay etc. of other public services and bodies that at present belong to the Pay and Management group of the Treasury. If this solution is adopted, " Civil Service Department " may not be the right title. It is however the most convenient term for the purposes of this report.

at the centre. In some cases, e.g. the lawyers, it seems appropriate for a senior practitioner of the specialism in question (not necessarily from the Civil Service Department itself) to be designated head of the profession or group, and to share with the Civil Service Department the responsibility for guiding the main lines of its management policy. Another helpful practice, already in use for some groups, is a management committee on which senior practitioners of a particular specialism and representatives of the Civil Service Department sit together. We see no reason why the pattern should not vary. But the Civil Service Department should itself command all the necessary information about the specialist groups and be so staffed as to be able to handle them with direct knowledge and professional management expertise.

257. The new department should include a Planning Unit on the lines we have discussed in Chapter 5. Some members of the department should have the prime responsibility for considering new developments in personnel management, training and management techniques; through contacts with the world outside, both at home and aboard, they should keep the management of the Civil Service abreast of experience elsewhere; and through their own expertise make it a model of progress in its field for others to follow.

258. We also recommend that the official head of the Civil Service Department should be designated Head of the Home Civil Service. We think that he should receive a sufficient lead in pay over the other official heads of departments in the Home Civil Service to mark his status. At present the lead of the Joint Permanent Secretary of the Treasury (see paragraph 245) is £600 a year, and similar leads are held by three other top officials: the other Joint Permanent Secretary to the Treasury, the Secretary to the Cabinet and (outside the scope of our inquiry) the Head of the Diplomatic Service. As far as the Home Civil Service is concerned, the other leads are something of a historical accident: the three offices were at one time held by a single individual; he had a lead of £1,000 over other Permanent Secretaries; when the offices were separated, the lead was split. We doubt if these other leads should be perpetuated; in our view it is hard to substantiate that the posts concerned carry greater responsibility than those of many other Permanent Secretaries. At the same time, we are clear that the responsibilities we propose for the Head of the Civil Service are of a different kind. We propose therefore that the other leads should be abolished when the present incumbents leave their posts, and that all Permanent Secretaries should receive the same rate of pay, with the exception of the Head of the Home Civil Service whose lead should be of the order of £1,000*.

259. The creation of a new Civil Service Department raises the important question of the relationship between the Head of the Civil Service and the Prime Minister. Today the Prime Minister has direct responsibility for senior appointments and for the machinery of government as well as for security in the Civil Service. On these subjects the present arrangement is that the Head of the Civil Service reports direct to the Prime Minister and

---

*The reservation that Sir William Cook, Sir Norman Kipping and Sir John Wall have made on paragraph 228 (Chapter 6) also applies here.

not to the Chancellor of the Exchequer. It is our strong hope that similar arrangements will be maintained in the new department, with the Head of the Home Civil Service maintaining his present responsibility for these matters and reporting direct to the Prime Minister.

260. There should however be a change in the machinery for making top appointments. At present the Head of the Civil Service makes his recommendations to the Prime Minister after consultation with the Ministers and others directly concerned. We have no reason to doubt that all the relevant views are taken into account. We think however that this arrangement vests too much responsibility in a single individual and in a way that creates the impression that his recommendations to the Prime Minister are within his sole discretion. Many civil servants criticise this—we think rightly. In future, we consider that in putting forward names to the Prime Minister the Head of the Civil Service should be assisted by a committee. The committee should have a variable composition, depending on the appointments and candidates under consideration. It should be drawn from a panel. The panel should have a rotating membership, appointment to it being for a term of, say, two or three years. Normally the committee would consist of two or three Permanent Secretaries, an approximately equal number of scientists or other specialists and not more than two eminent people from outside the Service. The " outsiders " might have no personal knowledge of the candidates, but their wide experience of business or other outside activity could in our view help to avoid an inbred and purely Civil Service attitude to these appointments. The Head of the Civil Service, after consulting the Ministers concerned and this committee, should put forward recommendations to the Prime Minister. We recommend that this procedure should cover all appointments at the salary-level of Deputy Secretary and above.

261. Making the right arrangements for the ministerial control of the new department will be decisive for its success. We therefore feel bound to comment on this. We have already expressed the hope that the Prime Minister will continue to be directly responsible for senior appointments, as for the machinery of government and security. We are also, however, strongly of the opinion that it is in the interests of the Service for the Prime Minister to be seen to be ultimately responsible, not just for these specific quesions, but also for the total task of managing the Service. No other Minister can assert the needs of the government service as a whole over the sectional needs of powerful departmental Ministers. At the same time, the Prime Minister cannot himself be expected even at present to handle all the day-to-day Civil Service problems that require ministerial attention. Still less will he be able to do so in the future if the central management of the Service becomes, as we propose, a much larger job than it is today. The Prime Minister will therefore need ministerial support. We do not believe that this responsibility should be allocated to a Minister who is also in charge of, and thus likely to be preoccupied by, the affairs of one of the other departments. We hope that we are not exceeding our terms of reference too much if we recommend that, outside the area for which he is directly responsible already, the Prime Minister should delegate day-to-day responsibility to a non-departmental Minister of appropriate seniority who is also a member of the Cabinet. His part will be of vital importance, especially during the period of reorganisation.

262. The Civil Service Department, charged with the management of the Service but divorced from direct contact with its work, could too easily become remote. We therefore attach great importance to the regular interchange of staff between the new department and other departments proposed in paragraph 255. This interchange should be mainly with the personnel and organisation branches of departments, but the Civil Service Department will also need those with direct and recent experience of ordinary work in departments.

263. The expanded role we recommend for the Civil Service Department in paragraph 248 above should not be allowed to develop into a take-over by central management of responsibilities that properly belong to the other departments. Our recommendations involve an expansion of their responsibilities as well, particularly in recruitment, career development and the promotion of departmental efficiency. The principle to be followed in all staff and organisation matters should be to delegate to individual departments the maximum authority compatible with the requirements of the Service as a whole. We put forward the following considerations to illustrate what we believe to be the right kind of balance between them: —

(a) Departments should play a greater part than at present in recruitment, both in the direct recruitment of specialist staff and in stating their future requirements for the various kinds of staff who will continue to be recruited centrally (see Chapter 3).

(b) In manning and grading, there should be the maximum delegation of authority to departments that is practicable from time to time. We do not wish to propose any change at present. We think that the balance should be carefully watched, especially in relation to specialist posts, where less authority is at present delegated than for non-specialist posts.

(c) On questions of internal departmental efficiency and organisation, the role of central management naturally varies as between small departments, which now rely upon the Treasury, and the larger departments, which have their own O and M teams. We recommend in Chapter 5 that the branches of the larger departments responsible for management services should in future have an enlarged role with more expert staff. The main role of the Civil Service Department should be to encourage the use of the most modern techniques rather than itself to implement the changes that are needed within departments. We think however that it may have a special part to play in assisting reorganisation at the higher levels of departments; and in the last analysis it should be in a position both to call all departments to account for failure to use the recommended techniques, and to put in its own men to investigate any departmental organisation and to recommend improvements.

(d) In the management of staff, especially in the planning of careers, the main responsibility must remain with the employing departments; we have recommended in Chapter 3 a considerable expansion of the part they play. At the same time we have argued that the Civil

Service Department will have to play a larger part than the Treasury does today and must have more ultimate authority. Although we recommend that civil servants, especially administrators, should move much less frequently between jobs in the same department, the development of the specialisms to which we have referred may make it desirable that there should be more movement, of both administrators and specialists, between departments. This applies especially to those civil servants, of whatever discipline, who are identified as being capable of filling the highest posts. The Civil Service Department should be responsible for informing itself about them, should consult with the employing departments about their training and development and should take the initiative in proposing appropriate moves for individuals in the longer-term interests of the work of the Service as a whole. In this way the total manpower of the Service will be most effectively used and the fullest opportunities given to each individual for widening his experience and for timely promotion. We think too that the Civil Service Department must have a voice, especially during the early years of the new system, in deciding upon promotions to the Senior Policy and Management Group; it will be important to make clear that the whole of the field has been given proper consideration and that every individual has had a fair chance. We recommend therefore that the Civil Service Department should be represented on all the departmental boards (see Chapter 3) that consider promotions to posts within the Senior Policy and Management Group but below the level to be covered by the service-wide committee proposed in paragraph 260. We expect that these moves and promotions would normally be agreed between the Civil Service Department and the departments concerned. If differences of opinion arise that cannot be resolved otherwise, it would be for the Prime Minister to decide.

RELATIONS WITH THE TREASURY

264. A separate Civil Service Department involves the co-existence of two central departments, the new department and the Treasury, each of which in its own sphere will be a centre of co-ordination, provide central services and occupy a position of central control. It will be important to ensure that the functions of these two departments and the relationship between them are clear and distinct.

265. We believe that all the functions now exercised by the " Pay and Management " group of the Treasury should be transferred to the Civil Service Department. This will include: —

    (a) responsibility for advising the Prime Minister on the machinery of government;

    (b) general supervision of departmental organisation;

    (c) the development and dissemination of administrative and managerial techniques

—in addition to the broad responsibility for the management of the Civil Service.

266. So far as the Civil Service is concerned, the principle on which the

division should be based is that all the functions that now belong to the Treasury in its role as " employer " should be transferred to the Civil Service Department, leaving to the Treasury responsibility for advising the Chancellor of the Exchequer on the overall control and allocation of public expenditure, on financial and fiscal policy and on the general management of the economy. Although this is strictly beyond our terms of reference, we think that the application of this principle will also involve the transfer to the new department of the functions at present exercised by the " Pay and Management " group of the Treasury in relation to other public services, e.g. the Diplomatic Service, the Armed Forces and other public servants such as teachers and nurses.

267. Over part of the field, this principle of division raises no problems. The Civil Service Department will clearly carry the whole of the central responsibility for Civil Service staff matters, including recruitment, training, career management and retirement, and advice on top-level appointments. Over other parts, however, where the functions of central management have a direct effect upon public expenditure, it will be necessary to devise arrangements that give the new Department a real base of independent authority without impairing the ultimate responsibility of the Treasury and the Chancellor of the Exchequer for the control of public expenditure as a whole. This means that the Treasury should retain its present concern for the total cost of particular services—costs which will include, in varying proportions, the cost of employing civil servants and other public servants. The precise allocation of functions between the two departments will need to be worked out; it may be helpful to examine how this is done in other countries more fully than we have been able to do. But we think that it should broadly follow this pattern:—

(a) *Pay*

The Treasury should retain a continuing interest in incomes policy as part of its responsibility for financial and economic management, but not in the staff costs as such of particular services. The Civil Service Department should be solely responsible for applying the government's incomes policy to the public services. Within the normal rules of collective Cabinet responsibility, this department should therefore have the final authority on any given pay settlement. The Minister who is to assist the Prime Minister in the running of the new department will thus be in a key position, both in relation to his Cabinet colleagues and in relation to all members of the public services. This reinforces our recommendation in paragraph 261 that he should be a member of the Cabinet.

(b) *Numbers*

Similarly, the central responsibility for ensuring that departments are efficiently and economically staffed should rest solely with the Civil Service Department. Staff costs are a part, in some areas a predominant part, of public expenditure, and would thus fall inevitably within the overall purview of the Treasury. But it should be the task of the Civil Service Department, rather than of the Treasury, to determine the scale of the staffs necessary for the efficient discharge of the tasks of departments; and the Treasury should in all cases have to accept that a given task demands the staff that the new department, after examination, is satisfied are needed. In practice, this would mean that departments proposing new policies would have to satisfy the Civil Service Department about the implications of their proposals for the numbers of staff needed and the Treasury about their other costs. The Treasury would look at the total costs of the proposed new policies; but it should not question the staffing requirements once these have been approved by the new department. In forward surveys of public expenditure and in the annual estimates, each of the two central departments would conduct its own examination of the costs falling within its own field. If the Treasury took the view that the total expenditure should be reduced, it would be free to challenge the policies of the spending departments, but not the assessment of staff costs approved by the Civil Service Department.

More generally, given the need to make the most economical use of manpower, we think it most important that the forecasting of demands for manpower in the various sectors of the economy should be considerably developed and improved. It should be for the Civil Service Department to speak for the public services in this field.

(c) *Organisation and management techniques*

The Treasury should retain responsibility for developing and disseminating techniques of financial analysis and systems of financial control, and this will give it an interest in certain aspects of departmental organisation as well as in interdepartmental procedures. It should therefore discuss with the Civil Service Department such changes in departmental organisation as it may think are needed for the improvement of financial control; when these have been agreed, it should be for the Civil Service Department to supervise their implementation.

268. On the basis of these general principles, working procedures should be devised, between spending departments and the two central departments, and between the central departments themselves, so as to reduce administrative complications to the minimum. They should be flexible. In many cases it would no doubt be desirable to set up joint teams for particular operations, e.g. for the examination of a spending programme or for a reorganisation of a part of the work in the interests of better financial control. But such arrangements should be based upon, and not allowed to blur, the clearest possible distinction between the functions and responsibilities of each of the two central departments.

WHITLEY COUNCIL MACHINERY AND THE ROLE OF STAFF ASSOCIATIONS

269. Staff relations in the Civil Service are organised through the collective machinery of Whitley Councils. The great majority of civil servants belong to staff associations, which represent grades or classes and are recognised as having the right to negotiate on their behalf. The main associations are members of the Staff Side of the National Whitley Council, and the associations recognised in each department constitute the Staff Sides of Depart-

mental Whitley Councils. The Official Side of the National Whitley Council normally comprises a number of Permanent Secretaries and a few Treasury officers; that of Departmental Whitley Councils comprises officers of the department.

270. Whitleyism in the Civil Service is now approaching its 50th anniversary. It has made an invaluable contribution to good staff relations. The high morale of the staff, and the fact that industrial disputes are rare in the Civil Service, owe a great deal to the universal acceptance of the principle of joint consultation. Co-operative responses to the wide-ranging changes brought about, for example, by the introduction of computers; the acceptance of domestic disturbances involved in the policy of dispersal of office staffs from London; and the smoothness with which pay settlements are generally reached and accepted, are attributable in no small measure to the activity of the staff associations in reaching agreements with management and subsequently defending them to their members. It is very much in the public interest that this atmosphere of agreement and of co-operation should be preserved. We have been much impressed by the thoughtful and constructive evidence that staff associations have sent us, and by the interviews we have had with their representatives. They can assuredly play a vital part in promoting and smoothing the way for the major reforms we recommend. We feel confident that they are willing, and indeed eager, to do so.

271. In some respects we consider that management, constrained by the existing structure of the Service, has allowed the Whitley system to operate in ways that hamper effective management: —

(a) Management has entered into agreements that have produced rigid arrangements in the promotion system in which seniority plays an excessive part.

(b) Resistance to changes in organisation tends to become formal and institutional; this has inhibited management from experimenting in the use of grades and classes.

(c) Managers of " operating " divisions are reluctant to become involved in questions of organisation and staffing, which are often the subject of complex and delicately balanced agreements with staff associations. These agreements are the responsibility of the personnel and organisation division of the department, and questions of organisation and staffing come to be regarded as their exclusive province. As a result, the manager is apt to see himself as less than fully responsible for the effectiveness of his branch.

(d) Success in reaching agreement with the Staff Side comes to be treated as an end in itself, and failure to reach agreement as a failure by management; this means that negotiations are sometimes too long drawn out.

272. These defects arise in our view from two main causes. The first is the structural framework of the Service within which Whitleyism has had to operate and in which we have recommended a radical change. It is because staff associations represent groups whose careers are largely limited to a single class that they are so sensitive on such matters as promotion within it, late entry into it and the number of jobs allocated to it. The second is that

management is sometimes less active and determined than it should be; arguments are allowed to go on too long, and rigid procedures are accepted where flexibility should be insisted upon. These defects however are in no way inherent in the Whitley system itself. Its principles are fully compatible both with a different structure and with more flexible methods of consultation.

273. Our recommendations, if accepted, are bound to have a profound effect upon the pattern of joint consultation. The introduction of a common grading structure; manning the work by job evaluation rather than by reference to membership of a class; training arrangements that lead to fast promotion routes; career management that will open up new and wider prospects of promotion; an increase in late entry and short-term appointments —all of these will call for co-operation and goodwill between departments and the Staff Side centrally, departmentally and locally. These changes will surely also lead to structural changes among the associations themselves.

274. A remodelling of the Service on this scale is bound to impose strains on the Official and Staff Sides alike. There will be both a short-term and a long-term problem. The period immediately following the publication of our report will be a particularly testing time. It will call for a high degree of adaptability and readiness for speedy decision in a situation in which the long-term pattern of staff associations and joint consultation for the future cannot yet have become completely clear. For the longer term, we think that the staff associations and the Civil Service Department should jointly take part in a review to determine the new pattern of joint consultation that will be appropriate for the Civil Service in the light of the Government's decision on our report. It is clearly essential that the pattern of joint consultation should reflect, not determine, the results of the changes we propose. We are convinced that its principles are of immense value to the Service and will continue to be so.

CHAPTER 8

THE CIVIL SERVICE AND THE COMMUNITY

275. We said in Chapter 1 that the Civil Service "must continuously review the tasks it is called on to perform and the possible ways in which it may perform them; it should then consider what new skills and kinds of men and women are needed and how they can be found." This has led us to emphasise throughout our report that the Service should develop greater professionalism among both specialists and administrators. For the specialists, it means more training in management and greater responsibilities. For the administrators, it means that the old concept of the gifted amateur, the all-rounder who passed easily from one job to another, should give way to one of greater specialisation. Our proposals are, therefore, designed to create a fully professional and dynamic Service.

276. It would be naive to suppose that our emphasis on professionalism will not produce its own problems. All professionals look both inwards and outwards: inwards to their fellow-professionals, outwards to the community they exist to serve. The Civil Service must keep these two aspects of professionalism in a healthy balance and thus guard against the danger of isolation. It is particularly important for a professional Civil Service to keep in mind that, in carrying out the tasks of modern government, it should remain the servant of democracy and be responsive to the control of Ministers. It is, too, a major public interest that the manpower of the Service should be kept to the absolute minimum required for the efficient and humane discharge of its duties. We discuss these problems in the following paragraphs; we also comment on the need for other complementary reforms and put forward specific proposals about the implementation of our report.

CONSULTATION AND SECRECY

277. We think that the administrative process is surrounded by too much secrecy. The public interest would be better served if there were a greater amount of openness. The increasingly wide range of problems handled by government, and their far-reaching effects upon the community as a whole, demand the widest possible consultation with its different parts and interests. We believe that such consultation is not only necessary in itself but will also improve the quality of the ultimate decisions and increase the general understanding of their purpose.

278. We welcome the trend in recent years towards wider and more open consultation before decisions are taken; and we welcome, too, the increasing provision of the detailed information on which decisions are made. Both should be carried much further; it is healthy for a democracy increasingly to press to be consulted and informed. There are still too many occasions

91

where information is unnecessarily withheld and consultation merely perfunctory. Since government decisions affect all of us in so many aspects of our lives, consultation should be as wide as possible and should form part of the normal processes of decision-making. It is an abuse of consultation when it is turned into a belated attempt to prepare the ground for decisions that have in reality been taken already.

279. We recognise that there must always be an element of secrecy (not simply on grounds of national security) in administration and policy-making. At the formative stages of policy-making, civil servants no less than Ministers should be able to discuss and disagree among themselves about possible courses of action, without danger of their individual views becoming a matter of public knowledge; it is difficult to see how on any other basis there can be mutual trust between colleagues and proper critical discussion of different hypotheses. But the material, and some of the analyses, on which these policy discussions are going forward, fall into a different category; unless there are overriding considerations to the contrary (e.g. on grounds of national security, the confidential nature of information supplied by individual firms, or to prevent improper financial gain), there would be positive advantages all round if such information were made available to the public at the formative stage of policy-making.

280. Civil servants, and perhaps also Ministers, are apt to give great and sometimes excessive weight to the difficulties and problems which would undoubtedly arise from more open processes of administration and policy-making. In this connection, therefore, we wish to draw attention to practice in Sweden. At the formative stages of policy-making, there is wide and prolonged consultation, which normally takes the form of setting up a committee of inquiry; its report is generally published; the report and the public discussion that follows are then a major part of the basis on which the Minister has to come to a decision. In addition, all files of any administrative office (in Swedish terminology, ministries and agencies) are open to the press and the public if not declared secret on grounds of military security, good international relations or for the protection of individuals named in them (e.g. because they may contain criminal or medical records); when policy decisions are in preparation, however, working material is not made available for public use. This shows that open government is possible; we suggest that the Government should set up an inquiry to make recommendations for getting rid of unnecessary secrecy in this country. Clearly, the Official Secrets Acts would need to be included in such a review. Some restrictions on the objective of " open decisions openly arrived at " will doubtless remain necessary; but a mature democracy rightly demands that they should be kept to the absolute minimum. The fuller the information, the closer the links between government (both Ministers and civil servants) and the community; and the smaller the gap of frustration and misunderstanding between " them " and " us ".

THE CIVIL SERVICE AND PARLIAMENT

281. We should also like to see Members of Parliament more purposively associated with the work of government than they are now. The traditional methods of parliamentary scrutiny have often failed to enlarge Parliament's

knowledge of what goes on or to secure for it a proper influence; at the same time they frequently impede the efficiency of administration. Even the work of the Public Accounts Committee has not escaped criticism for inducing a play-safe and negative attitude among civil servants (it has been referred to as a " negative efficiency audit "). We have noted the potential significance of the development of the new specialised Parliamentary Committees on agriculture, science and technology and education. We hope that these will enable M.P.s to be more closely associated with the major business of government and administration, both national and local, in these fields; we hope too, that their consultations with departments will increasingly include civil servants below the level of Permanent Secretary. It would be deeply regrettable, however, if these committees became an additional brake on the administrative process. We hope, therefore, that in developing this closer association with departments, Parliament will concentrate on matters of real substance, and take fully into account the cumulative cost (not only in time but in the quality of administration) that the raising of minutiae imposes upon them. We wish to draw special attention here to our proposals in Chapter 5 for accountable management and our recommendation that departments should be organised on the basis of acountable units. As we pointed out there, these proposals entail clear delegation of responsibility and corresponding authority. In devising a new pattern for a more purposive association with government departments, Parliament and its committees will need to give full weight to these changes.

282. We have noted the appointment of the Parliamentary Commissioner for Administration (Ombudsman). He has not been at work long enough for us to assess the full implications for Ministers and the Civil Service of this new office. It is clear, however, that the office of Parliamentary Commissioner is to be regarded as a further means of ensuring the proper responsibility and accountability of civil servants to Parliament and to the public.

THE ANONYMITY OF CIVIL SERVANTS

283. The argument of the preceding paragraphs has important implications for the traditional anonymity of civil servants. It is already being eroded by Parliament and to a more limited extent by the pressures of the press, radio and television; the process will continue and we see no reason to seek to reverse it. Indeed we think that administration suffers from the convention, which is still alive in many fields, that only the Minister should explain issues in public and what his department is or is not doing about them. This convention has depended in the past on the assumption that the doctrine of ministerial responsibility means that a Minister has full detailed knowledge and control of all the activities of his department. This assumption is no longer tenable. The Minister and his junior Ministers cannot know all that is going on in his department, nor can they nowadays be present at every forum where legitimate questions are raised about its activities. The consequence is that some of these questions go unanswered. In our view, therefore the convention of anonymity should be modified and civil servants, as professional administrators, should be able to go further than now in explaining what their departments are doing, at any rate so far as concerns managing existing policies and implementing legislation.

284. We do not under-estimate the risks involved in such a change. It is often difficult to explain without also appearing to argue; however impartially one presents the facts, there will always be those who think that the presentation is biased. It would be unrealistic to suppose that a civil servant will not sometimes drop a brick and embarrass his Minister. We believe that this will have to be faced and that Ministers and M.P.s should take a tolerant view of the civil servant who inadvertently steps out of line. On balance we think it best not to offer any specific precepts for the progressive relaxation of the convention of anonymity. It should be left to develop gradually and pragmatically, though the inquiry we have recommended in paragraph 280 above may well result in specific recommendations on this closely related problem. The further it develops, the closer the links between the Service and the community.

MINISTERS AND CIVIL SERVANTS

285. We considered whether we should recommend that Ministers at the head of departments should be served by a personal *cabinet* on the French model, or alternatively that they should make a substantial number of largely personal and political appointments to positions at the top of their departments as in the United States. These are both devices that could be used to strengthen the Minister's control of the departmental policy-making process and to increase the sensitiveness with which the department responds to the needs of Parliament and the public. We have welcomed in Chapter 4 the introduction of the practice whereby Ministers make a small number of temporary appointments. We think it important that Ministers should be free to arrange for the holders of such appointments to be closely associated with the work of the many " official " committees (i.e. committees of civil servants without ministerial membership) which make an essential contribution to policy-making; the work of these committees places a heavy responsibility on civil servants to ensure that the choices subsequently presented to Ministers are not unduly circumscribed*. In Chapter 5 we also propose that the Minister should be assisted by a Senior Policy Adviser as well as by the Permanent Secretary and we suggested that the Minister's own methods of working would determine the pattern of relationships at the top and the precise division of responsibilities. These developments should increase the control of Ministers over the formulation of policy in their departments. In the light of them (taken in conjunction with our proposals in the next paragraph), we see no need for ministerial *cabinets* or for political appointments on a large scale.

286. A related issue is the extent to which a Minister should be free to change the staff immediately surrounding him. There is no problem about those who have been personally appointed on a temporary basis by his predecessor; when a new Minister comes in, they will go anyway. Thus the issue really arises only over the positions of the Permanent Secretary, the Senior Policy Adviser and the Private Secretary. Because of the nature of the

*One of us (Dr. Norman Hunt) considers that junior Ministers should also be members of the more important of these committees. At present junior Ministers are sometimes not in a position to make a full contribution to departmental work. Their inclusion in official committees could strengthen the political direction of departments.

Private Secretary's duties, he must be personally acceptable to his Minister; there should therefore, in our view, be no obstacle in the way of a Minister's selecting from within the department, or on occasion more widely within the Service, as his Private Secretary the individual best suited to his ways of working; no stigma should attach to a person who is moved out of this job. As far as Senior Policy Advisers are concerned (whether career civil servants or those appointed from outside the Service on a short-term basis), we would hope that, as they will be selected for this job as men of technical competence and vitality, Ministers will not normally wish to replace them. This must however be possible when a new Minister finds the current holder of this office too closely identified with, or wedded to, policies that he wishes to change; or when an adviser's capacity for producing and making use of new ideas declines. It should be more exceptional, however, for a Minister to change his Permanent Secretary. Ministers change often, whereas the running of a department requires continuity. Even so, Ministers should not be stuck with Permanent Secretaries who are too rigid or tired. Any changes of this kind affecting Senior Policy Advisers or Permanent Secretaries will require the most careful consideration by the Head of the Civil Service and the Prime Minister, whose joint task it is in this context to safeguard the political neutrality of the higher Civil Service.

SERVING THE COMMUNITY

287. It is manifestly in the interests both of the Service and of the community at large that they should not be remote from one another. In the past the Administrative Class of the Civil Service has been on easy and familiar terms with the learned professions and particularly with the older universities, less so with the world of industry and commerce; familiar with London, less so with the regions; and so on. We would wish, not that familiar relationships should be lost, but that they should be enlarged and made more comprehensive.

288. Where recruitment is concerned, we hope that the proposals we have made in Chapter 3 will increase the attractiveness of the Civil Service to the graduates of the great civic and the newer universities. We have noted with satisfaction the recent trend towards an enlarged entry to the Administrative Class from these universities. Those of us who propose that emphasis should be placed in selection on the relevance of subjects studied for degrees believe that this development will give further impetus to the trend. In addition, a graduate entry drawn from a wider range of universities should help to ensure that graduate recruits to the Civil Service become more representative, geographically, educationally and socially, of the nation at large than they have been in the past; we regard this as a desirable objective in itself.

289. We have also set out in Chapters 3 and 4 our proposals for the sharing of post-entry training with staff from nationalised and private industry, business and local government, and for a greater flow, both of " outsiders " coming in for varying periods to work in departments, and of civil servants going to take part in work outside. We regard these proposals as a means not only of increasing the effectiveness of Civil Service work but also of avoiding the risks of professional isolation.

290. We are aware that service to the community demands more than

greater professionalism and efficiency. In formulating our recommendations we have tried throughout to bear in mind the overriding importance of good relations between the Service and the public. As the responsibilities of government have widened, so has the influence for good or ill of the Service itself. Ordinary citizens confront the State at many points in their everyday life: it taxes them and determines their rights to social benefits; it provides for the education of their children and the protection of their families' health. As householders, many are dependent on the State's housing policies; as employers or employees, they are deeply affected by its success or failure in its management of the national economy. In practice, most people can discharge many of their obligations to their families only with the help of the services provided and controlled by the State. The Civil Service, as the agent of the State, is bound constantly to touch very sensitive nerves. In consequence, its qualities of integrity, understanding and efficiency are profoundly important to ordinary men and women.

291. We believe that the measures we have proposed can make a contribution to a closer relationship between the Civil Service and the community. But this problem has to be grasped in the wider context of other, complementary reforms, which go well beyond the reform on the Civil Service.

COMPLEMENTARY REFORMS

292. Our proposals for the reform of the Civil Service need to be seen as part of the more general reappraisal that is being made of our inherited forms of government and social and economic organisation. For example, since we began our work Royal Commissions have been asked to examine the structure of local government in England and Scotland; the Royal Commission on Trade Unions and Employers' Associations has already reported; Parliament is modernising its procedures. The ability of the government to promote the country's well-being requires more than the reform of the Civil Service; so we attach great importance to the outcome of these other wide-ranging inquiries and developments, particularly those that affect the relationships between central and local government, between central government and private and nationalised industry, and between government departments and Parliament.

293. In this connection we considered whether we should propose a major review of the whole machinery of government, which has not been systematically examined by an outside body since the Haldane Committee in 1918. A number of witnesses who gave evidence to us thought that such a review was needed. Certainly, the division of responsibility between departments, and the lines drawn between the responsibilities of central government and those of other public bodies, have a decisive influence upon the work of the Civil Service. The speed and effectiveness of decision-making are inevitably affected when, under the current organisation of the work of government, several departments have a legitimate interest in most major social and economic problems, and when these problems accordingly have to be handled through a large network of departmental and inter-departmental committees. Machinery of government, however, was outside our terms of reference, and we have not examined whether or not there was merit in the proposals put to us on this subject; but if the review of " hiving off ", which we have proposed in Chapter 5, recommended substantial changes, this would

also provide the opportunity for simultaneous consideration to be given to a general review of the machinery of government.

MANPOWER

294. Throughout our work we have been conscious of the widespread public concern over the growing size of the Civil Service. The size of the Service (excluding the Post Office) since 1950 is shown below:—

	Adminis- trative	Executive	Clerical (including Clerical Assistant)	Profes- sional, Scientific and Technical	Other	Inland Revenue Customs and Labour [1]	Thousands Total [2]
1950	3·1	63·9	198·6	89·2	80·1	93·9	434·9
1955	2·7	62·7	155·4	104·5	62·5	88·4	387·8
1960	2·3	62·7	157·1	107·5	52·9	92·8	382·5
1964	2·5	68·7	168·9	121·4	55·1	95·1	416·6
1965	2·5	70·2	166·9	112·9	67·0	94·5	419·5
1966	2·3	73·4	172·1	123·1	49·5	98·4	430·6
1967	2·5	71·7	179·7	126·3	68·3	104·4	454·5
1968	2·7	83·3	191·9	132·3	61·4	110·9	471·6

[1] These are totals for the three departments. The figures are included in the other columns.
[2] Includes the Diplomatic Service which numbered 13,000 on 1st January 1968.

295. Naturally, the size of the Service is related to the size of the tasks directly carried out by the government. Today, although the Service accounts overall for less than 2 per cent of the working population, the figures conceal a larger claim on the qualified manpower of the country. It is regrettable that Civil Service and national statistics are inadequate to tell whether this claim is a growing one relative to other employments. But it is clear for example that the proportion of school-leavers with two or more " A levels " and equivalent qualifications in 1965 who joined the Civil Service was substantial. It is, therefore, of great importance to ensure that the Service uses its qualified manpower as efficiently and economically as possible.

296. Looking to the future, the Treasury have supplied us with short-term forecasts of the numbers of recruits who are expected to be needed, and the Department of Education and Science with longer-term projections of the output of the educational system, both at the various levels of educational qualification. We publish these papers, with other statistical material, in Volume 4, Section II. On the supply side, there is likely to be a shift in the pattern. Two main points are of particular significance. First, the actual output from the educational system to the labour market will increase at each of the graduate, " A level " and " O level " output points. Secondly, however, within these all-round figures, the increase in the output of graduates will be proportionately greater than the increase in the " A level " output, and the increase in the " A level " output will be proportionately greater than at " O level ". On the demand side, the future is necessarily more obscure. We think however that the general trend, a continuing rise in the demand for qualified manpower, which seems to be common to all advanced countries, is likely to be reflected in the British Civil Service as the work demands increasingly advanced management techniques and higher technological sophistication. We would therefore expect a steady advance in the standards of skill and qualification of the Civil Service as a whole. We discuss the

effect of this trend on the recruitment of graduates to the Service in Appendix F.

297. We see no reason in principle why the Civil Service should not be able in future to recruit the numbers of staff it needs, though there are, and will no doubt continue to be, temporary shortages of people with specific kinds of skill. The Service will however need to be truly competitive in what it offers, if it is to attract its share of really able men and women at all levels; our proposals are intended to make it so.

298. We are conscious that some of our own proposals call for increases in qualified staff. The main proposals that do so are:—

(a) the establishment of Planning Units;

(b) the creation of a Civil Service College and the expansion of the training programme;

(c) greater attention by departments to personnel management and career development;

(d) the expansion of departmental management services in the cause of increased efficiency and economy;

(e) the new Civil Service Department, which with its increased responsibilities will need to be larger than the present " Pay and Management " group of the Treasury.

In addition, the new grading-system we have recommended in Chapter 6 will require a comprehensive job evaluation throughout the Service; we doubt if it can be done without a further, even if temporary, increase of staff.

299. These increases must be viewed both against the size of the Service as a whole and against the benefits they will bring. As to the former, they are likely to be relatively very small, though as a claim on qualified manpower, they will be more significant. The case for them however depends wholly upon the latter; we can justify them only by the results we expect them to achieve.

300. We believe that the reforms we propose are necessary to make the Civil Service equal to the tasks of modern Government. In spite of the increases in staff to which we have referred, we believe that they will also lead in the end to worthwhile economies and greater efficiency in the use of manpower. This is not because we have found civil servants to be underemployed today. But we are not convinced that every job they do is essential in order to meet the demands that are placed on the Service by the country; there is not in our view adequate machinery for ensuring that this is so. We therefore set great store by the potential gains from the large-scale programme of job evaluation we have called for in Chapter 6 and from the expansion of management services proposed in Chapter 5. Together, they should do much to ensure that the nation gets value for money, by providing a built-in safeguard against over-staffing, both in quantity and in quality.

301. We stress that Ministers and civil servants alike should keep the need for economy in administration constantly in mind in devising their policies. Increasing sophistication in the methods and techniques of government, for example in those that arise from the large-scale introduction of computers, offers constant temptations to go in for complexity. Even in a

computer age, complexity costs time and money—a cost which often falls upon the organisations and individuals who have to respond to new government initiatives as well as upon the government itself. Since most new legislation involves additional tasks for civil servants, we attach considerable importance to the developing practice of recent years whereby new policy proposals are accompanied by detailed estimates of manpower costs. We think that these, no less than other costs, should be the subject of parliamentary and public debate. Simplicity, and thus economy, in administration should be a constant goal. We would also add that where work can be done more economically by outside organisations, the Civil Service should always be ready to take advantage of this.

THE IMPLEMENTATION OF OUR PROPOSALS

302. We have not spared our criticisms of the way in which the Service is run and of its other defects. We have however been deeply impressed by its very considerable strengths: its integrity, humanity, willingness at every level to carry the load of detailed work which composes so large a part of the country's public business. Any Minister or Parliamentary Secretary who has ever had to carry a complicated Bill through Parliament or to bear the brunt of an unpopular policy, knows this well. We have seen too, in the evidence we have received from civil servants, many signs of a strong desire that the organisation within which they do their work should be remodelled to enable them to do it more effectively.

303. Fully to implement our recommendations will naturally take a number of years. It will call for much discussion, especially with the various staff associations. As a first priority, however, there is an immediate need to:—

(a) set up the new Civil Service Department, designed and staffed to carry out the basic principles of our recommendations;

(b) set up an extensive training programme, so that present civil servants who have not been given adequate opportunities for training in the past can acquire the knowledge and skills they need.

304. For the longer term we hope that the government will take steps to review the progress made in implementing our proposals. This could be by means of an annual report to Parliament during the next five years. Alternatively, the Government might consider whether there is a need at the end of that period to set up a small committee to review progress and report to Parliament*.

305. A modern Civil Service reconstructed on the basis of these proposals (some of which are elaborated in more detail in the various appendices to this volume) will, we believe, make possible the progressive and efficient conduct of our affairs.

306. We have made far-reaching proposals on many important matters. We know that they will not be easy to carry out. A great deal of prolonged, difficult and complicated work will be needed. We have seen that the Service

---

*Five of us (Sir Philip Allen, Mr. W. C. Anderson, Sir James Dunnett, Sir Norman Kipping and Lord Simey) hope that the Civil Service, which has been in a state of uncertainty during the two years we have been sitting, will not have to face the prospect of a review by another committee after five years. A committee on the lines suggested would hardly limit itself to considering the implementation of our proposals.

has men and women with the ability, vision and enthusiasm to carry the task through to success. The new Service they will be creating will be one that offers a stimulating and challenging career to the men and women who work in it.

FULTON (*Chairman*)

NORMAN KIPPING

P. ALLEN

W. C. ANDERSON

EDWARD C. G. BOYLE

WILLIAM R. COOK

L. J. DUNNETT

N. C. HUNT

R. R. NEILD

ROBERT SHELDON

SIMEY

J. E. WALL

R. W. L. WILDING (*Secretary*)
M. A. SIMONS (*Assistant Secretary*)

19th June, 1968

100

RESERVATION TO CHAPTER 1

1. I sign Chapter 1 of the Report subject to the following reservations.

2. I think that the chapter is unfair to the Civil Service. While I agree that far-reaching changes are now desirable, the chapter fails to recognise, in my opinion, the contemporary relevance of the great contribution the Service made to the successful conduct of the war and, subsequently, in the transition from war to peace. I believe that full recognition should be accorded to the British Civil Service for its many achievements and qualities, and that the chapter's emphasis on the Service's present shortcomings gives a misleading impression of its future potentials. The Committee were told in France that those who were responsible for remodelling the French Civil Service at the end of the war had much in mind the qualities of the British Administrative Class. There have been recommendations also from time to time in the USA, that something equivalent to the British Administrative Class might, with advantage, be established.

3. Whilst it is no doubt true to say that the foundations of the Civil Service were laid in the second half of the nineteenth century, it is surely also true that the main characteristics it displays today are mid-twentieth-century developments. Although its creation has been called " the one great political invention of nineteenth-century England ", it is also evident that its continued growth is an achievement of our own times. The Northcote-Trevelyan reforms led to the creation of the Civil Service Commission, the open competition and to a structure which was the forerunner of what we have today. But events alone have produced a very different and more positive-minded Administrative Class over the years, starting perhaps with Lloyd George's Insurance Act, followed by two World Wars and all the developments since. After each of the World Wars the Service in fact did a good deal to reorganise itself and, if it has not gone as far as is called for in fully integrating the professional classes of the Service, the place that they have been given since the Second World War is very different from the one that they held before.

4. What we have now to face is essentially a situation which has arisen in the post-war world; this requires a capacity to face the truth at all costs, however inconvenient it may be to do so. This capacity is, I believe, already available to us in the Civil Service as it exists at present, but a degree of reorganisation and further development is required if its fullest potentialities are to be made available to us. This is common ground. I am therefore disappointed that the proposals embodied in this report, and foreshadowed in the present chapter, assume that what is required is something approaching revolutionary changes. My own view is that necessary reforms could be obtained by encouraging the evolution of what is basically the present situation, given the necessary amendments in direction and emphasis. The Treasury proposals before us already suggest many ways in which this may be achieved.

5. In particular, I do not agree that "the Service is essentially based on the philosophy of the amateur (or 'generalist' or 'all-rounder')". It has recently been pointed out that specialisation without a broad basis of foundation knowledge has profound disadvantages. It is true that modern economic and political organisation needs high specialism, but it also needs more general qualities of judgement and decisiveness, and the ability to understand how the reshaping of values may be embodied in and implemented by public policy. In effect, both specialists and generalists are required, and the problem becomes one of relationships and responsibilities, rather than the exclusion of the one in favour of the other. Modern techniques, such as linear programming, cost benefit analysis and other methods of specialised analysis are clearly needed and should be used to the full in the Civil Service. They do not, however, supersede the importance of the fundamental qualities of judgement which are vital to the successful prosecution of government business.

6. So far as generalist knowledge and experience are concerned, I am sure that Macaulay's argument was right and that the Civil Service needs nothing more, and nothing less, than the best brains known to teachers in schools and universities. I have little sympathy with the argument that the Civil Service of today must be fundamentally changed because the Administrative Class which dominates it is typified by the 'gifted amateur'. In the Finance and Public Sector sides of the Treasury there is an immense amount of expert knowledge in the Administrative Class and, although professional economists have helped, administrators have been very much to the fore in such matters as the better long-term planning of public expenditure. The charge of amateurism can indeed be pressed to a point where it puts too much importance on knowledge acquired and formally recognised by the award of a degree or professional qualification before a man enters the Service, and recognises too little the knowledge gained after joining. There are signs that big employers in industry are not now very interested in subject a man has read for a degree, unless they want him for scientific research, and the Administrative Class has in any case to face a problem of communication with non-experts in the form of Ministers and Committees of the House of Commons, which is fundamentally different from anything that industry has experienced. I do not therefore accept that there is a "cult of the generalist" in the Service today or that the "generalist" is obsolete at all levels.

7. More has already been done to improve the efficiency of the Service than the report recognises. There is still a long way to go in devising more effective forms of organisation, but the experience of, for example, Canada casts doubt on the suggestion that a reorganisation of class structure will of itself help the Service to work more smoothly. Reform should be discriminating. The statement that nowhere has it run ahead too rapidly takes no account of the informed criticism that too many economists have been introduced into the Service in recent years, in too short a time to make it possible to deploy their services to best effect. Although there may be a need for more knowledge in the Service of economics this cannot be obtained only by recruiting more specialist economists. Diminishing returns, it has been pointed out, are to be expected as their number grows.

8. In my opinion, it is evident that there is substantial agreement concerning the chief requirements of Civil Service reform, necessary to enable the Service to meet the rapidly changing demands of the present day more effectively. I agree that it was in the 1950s that it became apparent that the Service was not abreast of change; but I consider that it was only then that this happened. I therefore believe that the correct interpretation of the evidence summarised in this Chapter must lead to the conclusion that the task before us is not one of the total reconstruction of an obsolete institution. On the contrary, I am convinced that we have in the existing Civil Service an asset which it would be utterly foolish to discard. Its potentialities provide a more than adequate basis for any reforms that may be necessary both in the immediate and long-term future.

I have not sought to associate my Civil Service colleagues with me in stating this dissenting opinion.

SIMEY.

103

SUMMARY OF MAIN FINDINGS

1. The Home Civil Service today is still fundamentally the product of the nineteenth-century philosophy of the Northcote-Trevelyan Report. The problems it faces are those of the second half of the twentieth century. In spite of its many strengths, it is inadequate in six main respects for the most efficient discharge of the present and prospective responsibilities of government: —

   (a) It is still too much based on the philosophy of the amateur (or "generalist" or "all-rounder"). This is most evident in the Administrative Class, which holds the dominant position in the Service.

   (b) The present system of classes in the Service (there are over 1400, each for the most part with its own separate pay and career structure) seriously impedes its work.

   (c) Scientists, engineers and members of other specialist classes are frequently given neither the full responsibilities and opportunities nor the corresponding authority they ought to have.

   (d) Too few civil servants are skilled managers.

   (e) There is not enough contact between the Service and the community it is there to serve.

   (f) Personnel management and career planning are inadequate.

For these and other defects the central management of the Service, the Treasury, must accept its share of responsibility.

2. We propose a simple guiding principle for the future. The Service must continuously review the tasks it is called on to perform; it should then think out what new skills and kinds of men are needed and how these men can be found, trained and deployed.

3. A new Civil Service Department should be set up with wider functions than those now performed by the "Pay and Management" group of the Treasury, which it should take over. The new department should also absorb the Civil Service Commission.

4. The new department should be under the control of the Prime Minister. We hope that he will retain direct responsibility for senior appointments, machinery of government and questions of security. Outside this area, we suggest that the Prime Minister should delegate day-to-day responsibility to a non-departmental Minister of appropriate seniority who is also a member of the Cabinet.

5. The Permanent Secretary of the Civil Service Department should be designated Head of the Home Civil Service.

6. All classes should be abolished and replaced by a single, unified grading structure covering all civil servants from top to bottom in the

non-industrial part of the Service. The correct grading of each post should be determined by job evaluation.

7. The Service should develop greater professionalism both among specialists (e.g. scientists and engineers) and administrators (i.e. the new counterparts of the present Administrative and Executive Classes). For the former this means more training in management, and opportunities for greater responsibility and wider careers. For the latter it means enabling them to specialise in particular areas of government. We identify two such areas and accordingly recommend the development of a group of economic and financial administrators, and a second group of social administrators.

8. Employing departments should have a larger role in recruitment and there should be a speeding up of procedures. A majority of us consider that in the recruitment of graduates for one or other of the groups of administrators more account should be taken of the relevance of their university courses to the job they are being recruited to do.

9. A Civil Service College should be set up. It should provide major training courses in administration and management and a wide range of shorter courses. It should also have important research functions. The courses provided by the College should not be restricted to civil servants; a proportion of places should be set aside for men and women from private industrial and commercial firms, local government and public corporations.

10. More resources should be devoted to the career management of all civil servants. All must have the opportunity to progress as far and as fast as their talents and appropriate training can take them. This involves major changes in promotion procedures.

11. While the Civil Service should remain predominantly a career Service, there should be greater mobility between it and other employments. We, therefore, recommend an expanded late entry, temporary appointments for fixed periods, short-term interchanges of staff and freer movement out of the Service. These proposals involve substantial changes in the pension scheme and the replacement of " established " status by new terms of employment.

12. In the interests of efficiency, the principles of accountable management should be applied to the organisation of the work of departments. This means the clear allocation of responsibility and authority to accountable units with defined objectives. It also means a corresponding addition to the system of government accounting.

13. Management services units with highly qualified and experienced staff should be set up in all major departments.

14. Departments should establish Planning Units.

15. In addition to the Permanent Secretary, there should also be in most departments a Senior Policy Adviser to assist the Minister. The Senior Policy Adviser would normally be head of the Planning Unit. His prime job would be to look to and prepare for the future and to ensure that present policy decisions are taken with as full a recognition as possible of likely future developments.

16. In some of the big technical departments, there may be a need for a further senior post: a chief scientist, engineer or other specialist.

17. We do not propose that the Senior Policy Adviser and chief specialist, together with the Permanent Secretary, should constitute a formal board. The working arrangements should be informal and variable from department to department and from time to time; different Ministers' individual ways of working will do much to determine the pattern.

18. There should be one man who has overall responsibility under the Minister for all the affairs of the Department and he should continue to be the Permanent Secretary.

19. A Minister at the head of a department should be able to employ on a temporary basis such small numbers of experts as he personally considers he needs to help him.

20. We have suggested a number of further inquiries. Their subjects among others, should be: —

(a) the desirability of " hiving off " activities to non-departmental organisations;

(b) ways and means of getting rid of unnecessary secrecy both in policy-making and in administration;

(c) the new pattern of joint consultation that will be appropriate for the Civil Service in the light of the Government's decisions on our report. This inquiry should be conducted jointly by the Civil Service Department and the staff associations;

(d) methods of making recruitment procedures as speedy and objective as possible.

21. If our proposals are accepted, we hope that the Government will take steps to see that the progress made in their implementation is reviewed. This could be by an annual report to Parliament during the next five years. A small committee might be set up at the end of that period if needed.

22. We have seen that the Service has men and women with the ability, vision and enthusiasm needed to carry our proposals through to success. A Civil Service reconstructed on the basis of these proposals will, we believe, make possible the progressive and efficient conduct of our affairs.

APPENDIX A

THE SCOPE OF OUR INQUIRY

We were appointed on 8th February, 1966 to " examine the structure, recruitment and management, including training, of the Home Civil Service, and to make recommendations".

2. The Prime Minister, in his statement in the House of Commons, said that the decision to set up a Committee was reached in view of the changes which had taken place in the demands placed upon the Civil Service and of the changes in the country's educational system: and that the time had come to ensure that the Service was properly equipped for its role in the modern State. He added that the Government's willingness to consider changes in the Civil Service "does not imply any intention on their part to alter the basic relationship between Ministers and civil servants. Civil servants, however eminent, remain the confidential advisers of Ministers, who alone are answerable to Parliament for policy; and we do not envisage any change in this fundamental feature of our parliamentary system of democracy".

3. Our terms of reference refer to the " Home Civil Service ", and thus exclude the Diplomatic Service. The Home Civil Service is not easy to define precisely, but we have found it convenient broadly to follow the last two Royal Commissions on the Civil Service* in adopting " Servants of the Crown, other than holders of political or judicial offices, who are employed in a civil capacity and whose remuneration is paid wholly and directly out of moneys voted by Parliament ". This includes both permanent and temporary staff in public departments but excludes the staff of such bodies as the Research Councils, whose organisation, pay and conditions are similar to those of the Civil Service.

4. This definition also excludes the staff of the Post Office, whose salaries are not voted by Parliament but are paid out of Post Office receipts. They have continued to be civil servants by virtue of the Post Office Act, 1961, but we decided to omit them from our inquiry following the Government's announcement that legislation will shortly be introduced to separate the Post Office from the Civil Service. We have also followed the precedent of previous inquiries in omitting all industrial staff. The National Board for Prices and Incomes recommended in their report No. 18 of June, 1966 that the Government should aim over a period to build on what is common to the industrial and non-industrial parts of the Service with the ultimate objective of according equality of status to all government servants. This objective has been accepted, but the structure, management etc. of industrial staff are specially and separately determined, and we decided that we could not examine their different problems. Unless otherwise stated, all figures quoted in our report exclude both Post Office and industrial staff.

5. The field of our inquiry is thus the non-industrial staff of the Civil Service, excluding the Diplomatic Service and the Post Office. On 1st January, 1968, they numbered 459,000.

6. Our terms of reference excluded the machinery of government. We found at many points of our inquiry that this imposed limits on our work; questions about the number and size of departments, and their relationships with each other and the Cabinet Office, bear closely upon the work and organisation of the Civil Service. We have recommended (in Chapter 5) that the Government should examine the possibility of " hiving off " a number of functions now discharged by departments and entrusting them to independent public bodies; and we express the view (in Chapter 8) that this examination may also provide an opportunity for a wider review of the machinery of government.

---

* Royal Commission on the Civil Service 1929-31 (CMD. 3909). Royal Commission on the Civil Service 1953-55 (CMD. 9613).

THE NORTHCOTE-TREVELYAN AND MACAULAY REPORTS

1. THE NORTHCOTE-TREVELYAN REPORT

REPORT ON THE ORGANISATION OF THE PERMANENT CIVIL SERVICE

Presented to both Houses of Parliament by Command of Her Majesty

We now proceed to comply with that part of our instructions which states that, in connection with the inquiries which we were directed to make into each particular office, it is highly necessary that the conditions which are common to all the public establishments, such as the preliminary testimonials of character and bodily health to be required from candidates for public employment, the examination into their intellectual attainments, and the regulation of the promotions, should be carefully considered, so as to obtain full security for the public that none but qualified persons will be appointed, and that they will afterwards have every practicable inducement to the active discharge of their duties.

It cannot be necessary to enter into any lengthened argument for the purpose of showing the high importance of the Permanent Civil Service of the country in the present day. The great and increasing accumulation of public business, and the consequent pressure upon the Government, need only be alluded to; and the inconveniences which are inseparable from the frequent changes which take place in the responsible administration are matter of sufficient notoriety. It may safely be asserted that, as matters now stand, the Government of the country could not be carried on without the aid of an efficient body of permanent officers, occupying a position duly subordinate to that of the Ministers who are directly responsible to the Crown and to Parliament, yet possessing sufficient independence, character, ability, and experience to be able to advise, assist, and to some extent, influence, those who are from time to time set over them.

That the Permanent Civil Service, with all its defects, essentially contributes to the proper discharge of the functions of Government, has been repeatedly admitted by those who have successively been responsible for the conduct of our affairs. All, however, who have had occasion to examine its constitution with care, have felt that its organisation is far from perfect, and that its amendment is deserving of the most careful attention.

It would be natural to expect that so important a profession would attract into its ranks the ablest and the most ambitious of the youth of the country; that the keenest emulation would prevail among those who had entered it; and that such as were endowed with superior qualifications would rapidly rise to distinction and public eminence. Such, however, is by no means the case. Admission into the Civil Service is indeed eagerly sought after, but it is for the unambitious, and the indolent or incapable, that it is chiefly desired. Those whose abilities do not warrant an expectation that they will succeed in the open professions, where they must encounter the competition of their contemporaries, and those whom indolence of temperament, or physical infirmities unfit for active exertions, are placed in the Civil Service, where they may obtain an honourable livelihood with little labour, and with no risk; where their success depends upon their simply avoiding any flagrant misconduct, and attending with moderate regularity to routine duties; and in which they are secured against the ordinary consequences of old age, or failing health, by an arrangement which provides them with the means of supporting themselves after they have become incapacitated.

It may be noticed in particular that the comparative lightness of the work, and the certainty of provision in case of retirement owing to bodily incapacity, furnish strong inducements to the parents and friends of sickly youths to endeavour to obtain for them employment in the service of the Government; and the extent to which the public are consequently burdened, first with the salaries of officers who are obliged to absent themselves from their duties on account of ill-health, and afterwards with their pensions when they retire on the same plea, would hardly be credited by those who have not had opportunities of observing the operation of the system.

It is not our intention to suggest that all public servants entered the employment of the Government with such views as these; but we apprehend that as regards a large proportion of them, these motives more or less influenced those who acted for them in the choice of a profession; while, on the other hand, there are probably very few who have chosen this line of life with a view to raising themselves to public eminence.

The result naturally is, that the public service suffers both in internal efficiency and in public estimation. The character of the individuals influences the mass, and it is thus that we often hear complaints of official delays, official evasions of difficulty, and official indisposition to improvement.

There are, however, numerous honourable exceptions to these observations, and the trustworthiness of the entire body is unimpeached. They are much better than we have any right to expect from the system under which they are appointed and promoted.

The peculiar difficulties under which the Permanent Civil Service labours, in obtaining a good supply of men, as compared with other professions, are partly natural and partly artificial.

Its natural difficulties are such as these:-

Those who enter it generally do so at an early age, when there has been no opportunity of trying their fitness for business, or forming a trustworthy estimate of their characters and abilities. This to a great extent is the case in other professions also, but those professions supply a corrective which is wanting in the Civil Service, for as a man's success in them depends upon his obtaining and retaining the confidence of the public, and as he is exposed to a sharp competition on the part of his contemporaries, those only can maintain a fair position who possess the requisite amount of ability and industry for the proper discharge of their duties. The able and energetic rise to the top; the dull and inefficient remain at the bottom. In the public establishments, on the contrary, the general rule is that all rise together. After a young man has been once appointed, the public have him for life; and if he is idle or inefficient, provided he does not grossly misconduct himself, we must either submit to have a portion of the public business inefficiently and discreditably performed, or must place the incompetent person on the retired list, with a pension for the rest of his life. The feeling of security which this state of things necessarily engenders tends to encourage indolence, and thereby to depress the character of the Service. Again, those who are admitted into it at an early age are thereby relieved from the necessity of those struggles which for the most part fall to the lot of such as enter upon the open professions; their course is one of quiet, and generally of secluded, performance of routine duties, and they consequently have but limited opportunities of acquiring that varied experience of life which is so important to the development of character.

To these natural difficulties may be added others arising from what may be called artificial causes.

The character of the young men admitted to the public service depends chiefly upon the discretion with which the heads of departments, and others who are entrusted with the distribution of patronage, exercise that privilege. In those cases in which the patronage of departments belongs to their chief for the time being, the appointments which it commonly falls to his lot to make are either those of junior clerks, to whom no very important duties are in the first instance to be assigned, or of persons who are to fill responsible and highly paid situations above the rank of the ordinary clerkships. In the first case, as the character and abilities of the new junior clerk will produce but little immediate effect upon the office, the chief of the department is naturally led to regard the selection as a matter of small moment, and will probably bestow the office upon the son or dependant of someone having personal or political claims upon him, or perhaps upon the son of some meritorious public servant, without

109

instituting any very minute inquiry into the merits of the young man himself. It is true that in many offices some kind of examination is prescribed, and that in almost all the person appointed is in the first instance nominated on probation; but, as will presently be pointed out, neither of these tests are at present very efficacious. The young man thus admitted is commonly employed upon duties of the merest routine. Many of the first years of his service are spent in copying papers, and other work of an almost mechanical character. In two or three years he is as good as he can be at such an employment. The remainder of his official life can only exercise a depressing influence on him, and renders the work of the office distasteful to him. Unlike the pupil in a conveyancer's or special pleader's office, he not only begins with mechanical labour as an introduction to labour of a higher kind, but often also ends with it. In the meantime his salary is gradually advancing till he reaches by seniority, the top of his class, and on the occurrence of a vacancy in the class above him he is promoted to fill it, as a matter of course, and without any regard to his previous services or his qualifications. Thus, while no pains have been taken in the first instance to secure a good man for the office, nothing has been done after the clerk's appointment to turn his abilities, whatever they may be, to the best account. The result naturally is that when the chief of the office has to make an appointment of visible and immediate importance to the efficiency of his department, he sometimes has difficulty in finding a clerk capable of filling it, and he is not infrequently obliged to go out of the office, and to appoint some one of high standing in an open profession, or someone distinguished in other walks of life, over the heads of men who have been for many years in the public service. This is necessarily discouraging to the Civil Servants, and tends to strengthen in them the injurious conviction, that their success does not depend upon their own exertions, and that if they work hard, it will not advance them—if they waste their time in idleness, it will not keep them back.

It is of course essential to the public service that men of the highest abilities should be selected for the highest posts and it cannot be denied that there are a few situations in which such varied talent and such an amount of experience are required, that it is probable that under any circumstances it will occasionally be found necessary to fill them with persons who have distinguished themselves elsewhere than in the Civil Service. But the system of appointing strangers to the higher offices has been carried far beyond this. In several departments the clerks are regarded as having no claim whatever to what are called the staff appointments; and numerous instances might be given in which personal or political considerations have led to the appointment of men of very slender ability, and perhaps of questionable character, to situations of considerable emolument, over the heads of public servants of long standing and undoubted merit. Few public servants would feel the appointment of a barrister of known eminence and ability to some important position, like that of Under Secretary of State, as a slight, or a discouragement to themselves; but the case is otherwise when someone who has failed in other professions, and who has no recommendation but that of family or political interest, is appointed to a Librarianship, or some other such office, the duties of which would have been far better discharged by one who had been long in the department, and to whom the increased salary attached to the appointment would have been a fair reward for years of faithful service.

One more peculiarity in the Civil Service remains to be noticed. It is what may be called its fragmentary character.

Unlike the Military and Naval, the Medical, and the commissariat services, and unlike even the Indian Civil Service, the public establishments of this country, though comprising a body of not less than 16,000 persons, are regulated upon the principle of merely departmental promotion. Each man's experience, interests, hopes and fears are limited to the special branch of service in which he is himself engaged. The effect naturally, is to cramp the energies of the whole body, to encourage the growth of narrow views and departmental prejudices, to limit the acquisition of experience, and to repress and almost extinguish the spirit of emulation and competition; besides which, considerable inconvenience results from the want of facilities for transferring strength from an office where the work is becoming slack to one in which it is increasing, and from the consequent necessity of sometimes keeping up particular departments on a scale beyond their actual requirements.

Having thus touched upon some of the difficulties with which the public service is beset, we come to the consideration of the problem. What is the best method of providing it with a supply of good men, and of making the most of them after they have been admitted.

The first question which here presents itself is, whether it is better to train young men for the discharge of the duties which they will afterwards have to perform, or to take men of mature age, who have already acquired experience in other walks of life?

Our opinion is, that, as a general rule, it is decidedly best to train young men. Without laying too much stress on the experience which a long official life necessarily brings with it, we cannot but regard it as an advantage of some importance. In many offices, moreover, it is found that the superior docility of young men renders it much easier to make valuable public servants of them, than of those more advanced in life. This may not be the case in the higher class of offices, but is unquestionably so in those where the work consists chiefly of account business. The maintenance of discipline is also easier under such circumstances, and regular habits may be enforced, which it would be difficult to impose for the first time upon older men. To these advantages must be added the important one of being able, by proper regulations, to secure the services of fit persons on much more economical terms. A young man who has not made trial of any other profession will be induced to enter that of the Civil Service by a much more moderate remuneration than would suffice to attract him a few years later from the pursuit of one in which he had overcome the first difficulties and begun to achieve success; while to attempt to fill the ranks of the Civil Service with those who had failed elsewhere, and were on that account willing to accept a moderate salary, would be simply to bring it into discredit. It cannot be doubted that, even in the absence of proper precautions for securing good appointments, it is more probable that a fair proportion of eligible men will be found among a number taken at their entrance into life, particularly if pains be bestowed upon them after their appointment, than among an equal number taken after some years of unsuccessful efforts to open another line for themselves. The temptation to jobbing, and the danger of decidedly improper appointments being made, is also considerably less in the case of the selection of young men than in that of persons more advanced in life.

The general principle, then, which we advocate, is that the public service should be carried on by the admission into its lower ranks of a carefully selected body of young men, who should be employed from the first upon work suited to their capacities and their education, and should be made constantly to feel that their promotion and future prospects depend entirely on the industry and ability with which they discharge their duties, that with average abilities and reasonable application they may look forward confidently to a certain provision for their lives, that with superior powers they may rationally hope to attain to the highest prizes in the Service, while if they prove decidedly incompetent, or incurably indolent, they must expect to be removed from it.

The first step towards carrying this principle into effect should be the establishment of a proper system of examination before appointment, which should be followed, as at present, by a short period of probation. The necessity of this has been so far admitted that some kind of examination does now take place before clerks are admitted into any of the following offices:—The Treasury, the Colonial Office, the Board of Trade, the Privy Council Office, the Poor Law Board, the War Office, the Ordnance Office, the Audit Office, the Paymaster General's Office, the Inland Revenue Office, the Emigration Office and some others. These examinations vary in their character; in some offices more is required than in others, and in some cases what is required will be more rigidly enforced by one set of Examiners than by another.

The preliminary examination of candidates for civil employment, however, cannot be conducted in an effective and consistent manner throughout the Service while it is left to each department to determine the nature of the examination and to examine the candidates. Some on whom the duty of examining devolves feel no interest in the subject; others, although disposed to do their best, are likely to entertain erroneous or imperfect conceptions of the standard of examination which ought to be fixed, and to be unable to apply it properly after it has been settled. The time and attention of the superior officers are fully occupied in disposing of the current business

111

E

of their respective departments. To do this in a creditable manner will always be their primary object; and as the bearing of the subject under consideration upon the efficiency of their departments, although very important, is not of a direct or immediate kind, and is not likely to have much effect during their own tenure of office, what has to be done in reference to it will either be done by themselves in a hurried and imperfect manner, or will be left by them to their subordinate officers to be dealt with at their discretion. In a large department, in which numerous candidates have to be examined, want of time will prevent the superior officers from giving the subject the attention it deserves; and other matters, although of infinitely less real consequence, will have the precedence, because they press, and must be disposed of at the moment. Moreover, a large proportion of the persons appointed to a public department usually consists of young men in whose success the heads of the office or the principal clerks take a lively personal interest, owing to relationship or some other motive connected with their public or private position; and an independent opinion is hardly to be expected from an examiner who is acting under the orders of the one, and is in habits of daily intercourse with the other. A public officer ought not to be placed in a situation in which duty might require him to make an unfavourable report under such circumstances. Lastly, even supposing every other circumstance to be favourable, it is impossible that each department, acting for itself, can come to such just conclusions in regard to the nature of the preliminary examination, or can conduct it in such a fair, and effective, and consistent manner, as would persons having the advantage of a general view of the subject as it affects every public department, and who should have been selected for the duty on account of their experience in matters of this description.

We accordingly recommend that a central Board should be constituted for conducting the examination of all candidates for the public service whom it may be thought right to subject to such a test. Such board should be composed of men holding an independent position, and capable of commanding general confidence; it should have at its head an officer of the rank of Privy Councillor; and should either include, or have the means of obtaining the assistance of, persons experienced in the education of the youth of the upper and middle classes, and persons who are familiar with the conduct of official business. It should be made imperative upon candidates for admission to any appointment (except in certain special cases which will presently be noticed) to pass a proper examination before the Board, and obtain from them a certificate of having done so.

We are of opinion that this examination should be in all cases a competing literary examination. This ought not to exclude careful previous inquiry into the age, health, and moral fitness of the candidates. Where character and bodily activity are chiefly required, more, comparatively, will depend upon the testimony of those to whom the candidate is well known; but the selection from among the candidates who have satisfied these preliminary inquiries should still be made by a competing examination. This may be so conducted as to test the intelligence, as well as the mere attainments, of the candidates. We see no other mode by which (in the case of inferior no less than of superior offices) the double object can be attained of selecting the fittest person, and of avoiding the evils of patronage.

For the superior situations endeavours should be made to secure the services of the most promising young men of the day, by a competing examination on a level with the highest description of education in this country. In this class of situations there is no limit to the demands which may ultimately be made upon the abilities of those who, entering them simply as junior clerks, gradually rise to the highest posts in them. To obtain first-rate men, it is obvious that recourse should be had to competition. It would be impossible to impose upon each candidate for a clerkship, as a positive test of his fitness for the appointment, the necessity of passing an examination equal to that of first-class men at the universities; but if, on the occurrence of a vacancy, it is found that a number of candidates present themselves, of whom some are capable of passing such an examination, there can be no reason why the public should not have the benefit of such men's services, in preference to those of persons of inferior merit. It may be repeated that no other means can be devised of avoiding the evils of patronage, which, if, in this case, less objectionable because of the comparatively small number of superior appointments, is much more objectionable in its effects on the public business of the country.

Our proposal is not inconsistent with the appropriation of special talents or attainments to special departments of the public service. In the case, for example, of the subordinate grades from which collectors, surveyors, secretaries, junior commissioners, and other superior officers of the Revenue departments are usually selected, the nature of the examination should be adapted to the object of securing the scientific and other attainments which are so important to the efficiency of these great national establishments. In the same way provision might be made for securing the peculiar attainments to be required of persons to be employed in the Foreign Office, and in the diplomatic and consular services; and in respect to offices of account, arithmetic and book-keeping will be principally insisted on.

It next becomes a question, whether the competition which we have proposed should take place on the occasion of each vacancy, or whether there should be periodical examinations. We are of opinion that it would be desirable to adopt the latter alternative. There are peculiar advantages in a system of periodical examinations. It economises the number, and also the time of the examiners, who, instead of being over-worked half the year, have their employment regularly distributed. It is also more convenient to the candidates themselves. We propose, therefore, that examinations should be held at stated times; that an average having been taken of the number of situations of the class contended for, which periodically fall vacant, it should be announced, before the commencement of each trial, how many gentlemen were to be elected for admission into the public service on that occasion. The election having taken place, those who have succeeded should be distributed among the offices to which appointments are to be made, on the footing of probationers. The precise mode in which the successful candidates should be allotted to the several departments will require some consideration, but there will be no difficulty in it which may not easily be overcome. One obvious course of proceeding would be to send to each department a list of those who are selected for appointments, leaving to the head of each office to choose from among them as vacancies occur. Or it might be thought desirable that the Board of Examiners should recommend particular men to particular departments, according to their capacities, the head of the department in each case exercising his discretion in accepting them or not; or the choice might be given to the candidates themselves, some restriction being imposed to prevent any from choosing offices for which their peculiar education had not fitted them. If more have been elected (in order to maintain the average) than there is immediate demand for, they should be sent as supernumerary clerks to the offices in which the work happens to be the heaviest, unless there is any special service upon which they can with advantage be temporarily employed, or they might wait to take their turn. As vacancies occur from time to time before the next general examination, the supernumeraries should be appointed to them, and, if the whole have not been placed before that time, it will only be necessary to make the next batch the smaller. It would be desirable to retain the probation as at present, rendering it more efficient by precise reports of the conduct of the probationers.

In the examinations which we have recommended, we consider that the right of competing should be open to all persons, of a given age, subject only, as before suggested, to the necessity of their giving satisfactory references to persons able to speak to their moral conduct and character, and of producing medical certificates to the effect that they have no bodily infirmity likely to incapacitate them for the public service. It is only by throwing the examinations entirely open that we can hope to attract the proper class of candidates.

The choice of the subjects to be comprehended in the examination, as well as the mode in which the examination should be conducted, so as to diminish the labour by eliminating such candidates as have obviously no chance of success, should, of course, be left to the Board of Examiners. We will therefore only indicate the advantage of making the subjects as numerous as may be found practicable, so as to secure the greatest and most varied amount of talent for the public service. Men whose services would be highly valuable to the country might easily be beaten by some who were their inferiors, if the examination were confined to a few subjects to which the latter had devoted their exclusive attention; but if an extensive range were given, the superiority of the best would become evident. Besides, an opportunity would be afforded for judging in what kind of situation each is likely to be most useful; and we need hardly allude to the important effect which would be produced upon the general education of the country, if proficiency in history, jurisprudence, political economy, modern languages, political and physical geography, and other matters, besides the staple of classics and mathematics, were made directly conducive to the success of young men desirous of entering into the public service. Such an inducement would probably do more to quicken the progress of our Universities, for instance, than any legislative measures that could be adopted.

It would probably be right to include in the examination some exercises directly bearing upon official business; to require a precis to be made of a set of papers, or a letter to be written under given circumstances; but the great advantage to be expected from the examinations would be, that they would elicit young men of general ability, which is a matter of more moment than their being possessed of any special requirements. Men capable of distinguishing themselves in any of the subjects we have named, and thereby affording a proof that their education has not been lost upon them, would probably make themselves useful wherever they might be placed. We have before us the testimony of an eminent public officer, who was for many years connected with one of the chief departments of the State. He writes thus:—

"During my long acquaintance with the ———— Office, I remember four, and only four, instances of young men being introduced into it on the ground of well-ascertained fitness. I do not venture to mention any names, but I confidently affirm that the superiority of those four gentlemen to all the rest was such as to extort the acknowledgment of it from their rivals, and to win the high applause of each successive Secretary of State."

We feel satisfied that by the measures which we have suggested for ascertaining the fitness of each person before his appointment, the most marked and important improvement may be introduced into the public service.

We must remark that there will be some cases in which examination will not be applicable. It would be absurd to impose this test upon persons selected to fill the appointments which have been previously spoken of under the name of staff appointments on account of their acknowledged eminence in one of the liberal professions, or in some other walk of life. We think, however, that the circumstances under which any person is appointed to such an office should always be placed on record by an official correspondence between the department to which he is assigned and the Board of Examiners; and we would also suggest for consideration the expediency of making an annual return to Parliament of the names of persons who may be so appointed.

In dealing with the lower class of appointments, it will be necessary to make provision against the difficulty that if the examinations were all held at one place, a large proportion of those who might reasonably become candidates would be deterred from presenting themselves by the expense of the journey. If the scheme of examinations were more favourable to one locality than another, there can be no doubt that it would soon be set aside as unjust. We propose, therefore, that an arrangement should be made for holding examinations in various parts of the United Kingdom. A staff of assistant examiners might be formed; or the services of competent men might be engaged from time to time, or recourse might be had to the machinery of the Education Department of the Privy Council, for the purpose of holding district examinations at stated periods. Due notice should be given of the times and places at which such examinations are to be held, and all persons intending to compete should be required to send in their names by a certain day. The examinations should all take place on the same day—the examination papers being sent to each locality by the same post, as is done in the examinations conducted by the Education Department; and the papers, with the work of the candidates, being returned to the Central Board, which would cause them to be examined in the manner adopted at the Privy Council Office*. The required number should then be selected as probationers for the various appointments to be filled. The precise arrangements will, however, require much consideration, and we are of opinion that they cannot properly be determined otherwise than by experience, such as the proposed Board of Examiners, acting in concert with the Chiefs of the several Departments, would speedily acquire. We have satisfied ourselves, by communications with persons whose official position enables them to form sound opinions on the subject, that there will be no formidable difficulty in making the necessary arrangements to meet the vast majority of cases. Mr. John Wood, the Chairman of the Board of Inland Revenue, has, as far as he was able, acted on these principles in the selection of Excisemen; and the experiment has succeeded in a manner which is highly encouraging to further attempts in the same direction.

A suggestion to bestow a proportion of the inferior appointments in the public service upon the Pupils in Schools connected with the Privy Council was made by the Government of Lord John Russell in 1846, and a Minute was passed by the Education Committee upon the subject. No effect having been given to this Minute, it was repealed by the E ¦cation Committee, under Lord Derby's Government, as being inoperative.

It is obvious that no mere Minute of a Committee of Privy Council could give effect to such a scheme unless taken up as a part of the general policy of the Government.

With regard to the age of admission, we are of opinion that in the case of candidates for superior situations the limits should, as a general rule, be 19 and 25; in the case of candidates for inferior offices, 17 and 21.

Having thus completed our suggestions as to the best mode of obtaining a proper supply of public servants in the first instance, we have next to offer some remarks on what appears to us to be the best mode of regulating their employment, and their promotion, so as to maintain the efficiency of the Office at the highest point.

As we have already spoken of the importance of establishing a proper distinction between intellectual and mechanical labour, we need offer no further observations on this most vital point. The proper maintenance of such distinction depends more upon the discretion and management of the chiefs of offices, and those immediately below them, than upon any general regulations that could be made by a central authority. We consider that a great step has been taken by the appointment in several offices of a class of supplementary clerks, receiving uniform salaries in each department, and capable therefore of being transferred, without inconvenience, from one to another, according as the demand for their services may be greater or less at any particular time; and we expect that the movable character of this class of officers, and the superior standard of examination which we have proposed for the higher class, will together have the effect of marking the distinction between them in a proper manner.

We are aware that a measure has sometimes been recommended which, if adopted, would have the effect of establishing to a certain extent the separation which we have spoken of; we mean the creation of a general copying office, common to the whole or most of the departments in the neighbourhood of Whitehall, at which all of them might get their copying work done at a certain rate of payment by the piece.

We are, however, not prepared to recommend the adoption of such a measure. Copying is not the only work of a mechanical, or nearly mechanical, character which is performed in the public offices. A great deal of work of various kinds, such as registering, posting accounts, keeping diaries, and so forth, may very well be done by

---

* As the process adopted by the Education Department of the Privy Council may not be generally known, it is well to state that the papers of the candidates in all parts of the country are sent to the Central Office, where they are sorted according to subjects, and sent to different Inspectors, e.g., all the papers in Arithmetic to one, all in History to another, and so forth. Each Inspector assigns a number of marks to each paper, according to its merit. The papers are then returned; those of each candidate are put together again; the total number of marks which he has obtained is ascertained; and the candidates are finally arranged according to the result of the comparison.

supplementary clerks of an inferior class under the direction of a small number of superiors. Such work, however, could not be sent out of the office; and even with regard to copying, it would be found that several offices, which would be included in the proposed arrangements, would object to sending out a large proportion of their letters for that purpose, and that a great deal of copying is done in books which could not conveniently be parted with. Hence, it would be necessary, even were the copying office established, to maintain a class of supplementary clerks in each office in addition to it, or else the clerks would be employed nearly in the same manner as at present, that is to say, without a proper distinction between intellectual and mechanical duties.

Another point to which the attention of the chiefs of offices should be called is the importance of transferring the clerks from one department of the office to another, so that each may have an opportunity of making himself master of the whole of the business before he is called upon, in due course of time, to take a leading position. A proper system of transfers according to fixed rules in each office, and insured by periodical reports to the chief, must exercise a beneficial influence both upon the clerks themselves and upon the general efficiency of the establishment. Periodical reports upon the manner in which each clerk has been employed should be made to the chief of the office.

The advance of salaries in the public service is regulated upon a twofold principle. Each man, on being appointed to a clerkship in a particular class, receives for the first year, and in some cases for the first two or three years, what is called the minimum salary of that class, after which his salary increases, by a certain annual increment, to what is called the maximum salary, that is to say, if the minimum be £100 a year, the maximum £300 and the annual increment £15, the clerk receives £100 in the first year, £115 in the second, £130 in the third and so on till his salary reaches £300 at which point it must remain stationary unless he is promoted to a higher class. He may, however, at any time, whether before or after attaining the maximum salary of one class, be promoted to a higher on the occurrence of a vacancy, if he is considered deserving of such promotion, and he will immediately thereupon begin to receive the minimum salary of the higher class, and to advance therefrom by annual increments, without reference to the amount he was previously receiving. The theory of the public service is that the annual increase of salary, from the minimum to the maximum of the class, is given as matter of course as the reward of service, and with no reference to the comparative merits of the individuals; but that promotion from class to class is the reward of merit, or rather that it is regulated by a consideration of the public interests, and that those only are to be transferred from one class to a higher who have shown themselves capable of rendering valuable services in it. This salutary principle is, however, in practice often overlooked, and promotion from class to class, as well as the annual rise within the class, is more commonly regulated by seniority than by merit. The evil consequences of this are too obvious to require lengthened comment; it is, perhaps, more important to point out some of the difficulties which lie in the way of amendment.

If the opinions of the gentlemen engaged in the Civil Service could be taken on the subject of promotion, it would probably be found that a very large majority of them would object strongly to what is called promotion by merit. The reason they would assign would be that promotion by (so called) merit would usually become promotion by favouritism. The effect of the system of departmental patronage has been to inspire the clerks in each office with a feeling of jealousy towards any one who is supposed to enjoy the especial favour of the chief of the department, or, still more, of the principal permanent officer in it. Constituted as our official system now is, men feel, and not unreasonably, that the recognition of their merits, even within their own departments, is extremely uncertain, and that there is no appeal to any public tribunal if injustice is done them there. Even in an open profession a consciousness of unrecognised merit will sometimes weigh a man down, though he has always the hope that the justice which is denied him in one quarter will be done to him in another. In an office, if a clerk fails to please his immediate superior, he is probably condemned to obscurity for his whole life. The Parliamentary chief who presides over the department for a few years, and who is overwhelmed with business, can, as a general rule, know nothing of the merits of individual clerks in the lower ranks of the office, except through the permanent officers at its head. Now, setting aside cases of actual favouritism, there must be many instances in which the chief permanent officers fail to perceive, and properly to bring into notice, the valuable qualities of those beneath them. A man may be timid and hesitating in manner, and on that account may be passed over as dull, in favour of someone by no means his superior in real worth, but having more address in recommending himself, or, on the other hand, the chief officer may have taken a particular fancy to some young man on his first entrance into the department, and may have thrown in his way special opportunities of advancing himself, which others have not had. All such cases are watched with jealousy even now, and if promotion by seniority were wholly set aside, without the introduction of proper safeguards, they would be the cause of still more discomfort.

It ought, therefore, to be a leading object with the Government so to regulate promotion by merit as to provide every possible security against its abuse; and for this purpose we are of opinion that the following system should be adopted: On the occurrence of a vacancy in any class, the Chief Clerk, or other immediately superior officer, should furnish the Secretary of the department with a return of the names of a certain number (in no case less than three) of the Clerks at the head of the class below, accompanied by a special report upon the services and qualifications of each. In case there should be in the lower ranks of the class any man of merit decidedly superior to those above him, his name, with a note of his qualifications should be added. The Secretary should make what remarks he thinks proper upon the list, and should then submit it to the Head of the Office, who should select the person to be promoted, and should make out and sign a warrant for his promotion, setting forth the grounds upon which it is made. A Book should be kept in every office, in which should be entered the name and age of each Clerk or other officer, at the time of his appointment, the dates of his examination, first appointment, and subsequent promotions, together with notes of all the reports made upon him from time to time, either on the occasions afforded by the occurrence of vacancies, or at other times, in consequence of some special instance either of good or ill behaviour. A reference to this book on the occasion of promoting to vacancies will enable the Head of the Department to form a tolerably correct estimate of the merits of each individual. It may be noticed that such a book is kept, with very good results in the Commissariat Department.

With regard to the annual increase of salary, we are of opinion that it would be right to require that each clerk, before becoming entitled to receive the addition, should produce a certificate from his immediate superior, that he has been punctual in his attendance, and has given satisfaction in the discharge of his duties, during the preceding year. Such certificates are required from the heads of rooms in the Ordnance Department, and from each Inspector in the Audit Office. They would ordinarily be given as a matter of course, but the knowledge that they might be withheld would be useful in maintaining discipline, and in enforcing regularity of attendance, which in some cases is a matter of difficulty, the only penalties which can at present be imposed for irregularity being those of suspension and dismissal, which are too severe to be applied unless in aggravated instances.

The subject of pensions and retired allowances is one intimately connected with the matters treated of in this paper. We are aware that it is receiving separate consideration from the Government, and we therefore abstain from entering upon it so fully as we should otherwise have done. We desire, however, to call attention to the importance of establishing a uniform and consistent system of regulating the amounts to be granted to superannuated public servants, with reference to the character of their service. Whatever decision may be taken as to the maintenance of the superannuation deductions, or of the present scale of retired allowances, we presume that the course now followed in the Treasury, of apportioning the pension of each individual with some reference to the character he has borne and the abilities he has displayed, will still be pursued. As, however, the Superannuation Committee in the Treasury changes with every change in the Administration, and as no systematic record of the merits of public servants is kept at the Offices to which they are attached, the application of the principle, which has been rightly laid down, is attended with much difficulty, and with an amount of uncertainty which deprives it of much of its value.

The want of encouragement in the form of good service pensions and honorary

117

distinctions, is also severely felt in the ordinary Civil branch of the public service, which is the only one in which these classes of reward are not dispensed.

It is obvious that the proposed Board of Examiners might be turned to good account in supplying these defects. Duplicates of the books which we have recommended to be kept in the separate Offices should be transmitted to the Department of Examination, which should also be furnished with all information relating to promotions and other matters bearing on the services of the officers in each department. No grant of superannuation allowance or good service pension should be made by the Treasury without a previous report from the Board of Examiners embodying this information.

By this system, not only would greater certainty be introduced into the superannuation business, but a degree of consistency would be given to the whole scheme of promotion by merit, which would, we think, ensure its success. It would also have this further advantage, that it would serve to direct the attention of the Government to the merits of individual clerks—now seldom known beyond the sphere of their own offices— and would thus enable it to select deserving persons from the ranks of the public service to fill important situations which might become vacant. It is to be hoped that in future, if any staff appointment falls vacant in an office in which there is a deserving clerk well qualified to fill it, his claims will not be passed over in favour of a stranger; but this principle might advantageously be carried further, by filling the appointment with a person from another office, if there is no one in the department itself qualified to take it; and there might often be occasions in which the advantages of encouraging public servants, and at the same time introducing fresh blood into an office, might be combined; as, for instance, by filling a staff appointment in office A by the transfer to it of a meritorious staff officer from office B, and then supplying the vacancy caused in office B by the appointment to it of one of the most deserving clerks in office A. The extent to which this principle could be carried into effect must, of course, depend upon circumstances, and upon a careful observation of its working; but we do not see why it should not be tried.

Upon a review of the recommendations contained in this paper it will be seen that the objects which we have principally in view are these:—

1. To provide, by a proper system of examination, for the supply of the public service with a thoroughly efficient class of men.

2. To encourage industry and foster merit, by teaching all public servants to look forward to promotion according to their deserts, and to expect the highest prizes in the service if they can qualify themselves for them.

3. To mitigate the evils which result from the fragmentary character of the Service, and to introduce into it some elements of unity, by placing the first appointments upon a uniform footing, opening the way to the promotion of public officers to staff appointments in other departments than their own, and introducing into the lower ranks a body of men (the supplementary clerks) whose services may be made available at any time in any office whatever.

It remains for us to express our conviction that if any change of the importance of those which we have recommended is to be carried into effect, it can only be successfully done through the medium of an Act of Parliament. The existing system is supported by long usage and powerful interests; and were any Government to introduce material alterations into it, in consequence of their own convictions, without taking the precaution to give those alterations the force of law, it is almost certain that they would be imperceptibly, or perhaps avowedly, abandoned by their successors, if they were not even allowed to fall into disuse by the very Government which had originated them. A few clauses would accomplish all that is proposed in this paper, and it is our firm belief that a candid statement of the grounds of the measure would insure its success and popularity in the country, and would remove many misconceptions which are now prejudicial to the public service.

STAFFORD H. NORTHCOTE
C. E. TREVELYAN

November 23rd, 1853.

2. THE MACAULAY REPORT

COPY of the Report, dated November 1854, from the Committee who were requested to take into Consideration the Subject of the EXAMINATION of CANDIDATES for the CIVIL SERVICE of the EAST INDIA COMPANY; and, Copy of the LETTER addressed on the 20th November 1854, by the President of the Board of Commissioners for the Affairs of India, to the Chairman and Deputy Chairman of the East India Company, as to the Company's COLLEGE at HAILEYBURY.

REPORT ON THE INDIAN CIVIL SERVICE.

TO THE RIGHT HONOURABLE SIR CHARLES WOOD, BART., M.P.,
&c. &c. &c.

Sir,

WE have attentively considered the subject about which you have done us the honour to consult us; and we now venture to submit to you the result of our deliberations.

We do not think that we can more conveniently arrange the suggestions which we wish to offer than by following the order which is observed in the 39th and 40th clauses of the India Act of 1853.

The first matter concerning which the Board of Control is empowered by the 39th clause to make regulations is, the age of the persons who are to be admitted into the college at Haileybury.

The present rule is, that no person can be admitted under 17, and that no person can go out to India after 23. Every student must pass four terms, that is to say, two years at the college. Consequently, none can be admitted after 21.

It seems to us that it would be a great improvement to allow students to be admitted to the college up to the age of 23, and to fix 25 as the latest age at which they can go out to India in the civil service. It is undoubtedly desirable that the civil servant of the Company should enter on his duties while still young; but it is also desirable that he should have received the best, the most liberal, the most finished education that his native country affords. Such an education has been proved by experience to be the best preparation for every calling which requires the exercise of the higher powers of the mind; nor will it be easy to show that such preparation is less desirable in the case of a civil servant of the East India Company than in the case of a professional man who remains in England. Indeed, in the case of the civil servant of the Company a good general education is even more desirable than in the case of the English professional man; for the duties even of a very young servant of the Company are more important than those which ordinarily fall to the lot of a professional man in England. In England, too, a professional man may, while engaged in active business, continue to improve his mind by means of reading and of conversation. But the servant of the Company is often stationed, during a large part of his life, at a great distance from libraries and from European society, and will therefore find it peculiarly difficult to supply by study in his mature years the deficiencies of his early training.

The change which we propose will have one practical effect, to which we attach much importance. We think it desirable that a considerable number of the civil servants of the Company should be men who have taken the first degree in arts at Oxford or Cambridge. At present the line is drawn as if it had been expressly meant to exclude bachelors of those universities. It will, we believe, be found that the great majority of our academic youth graduate too late by a few months, and only by a few months, for admission into Haileybury.

We propose to fix 18 as the lowest age at which a candidate can be admitted into the college. We are indeed of opinion that, except in very rare and extraordinary cases, it is not desirable that a lad should be admitted so early as 18. But we are convinced that, except in very rare and extraordinary cases, no lad of 18 will have any chance of being admitted. Hitherto the admissions have been given by favour. They are henceforward to be gained by superiority in an intellectual competition. While they were given by favour, they were frequently, indeed generally, given to persons whose age was not much above the minimum. A director would naturally wish his son or his nephew to be handsomely provided for at 19 rather than at 23, and to be able to return to England with a competence at 44 rather than at 48. A majority of the students have, therefore, been admitted before they were 19, and have gone out before they were 21. But it is plain that, in any intellectual competition, boys of 18 must be borne down by men of 21 and 22. We may therefore, we believe, safely predict that nine-tenths of those who are admitted to the college under the new system will be older than nine-tenths of those who quit it under the present system. We hope and believe that among the successful competitors will frequently be young men who have obtained the highest honours of Oxford and Cambridge. To many such young men a fellowship, or a tutorship, which must be held on condition of celibacy, will appear less attractive than a situation which enables the person who holds it to marry at an early age.

The India Act next empowers the Board of Control to determine the qualifications of the candidates for admission to Haileybury. It seems to us to be proper that every person who intends to be a candidate should, at least six weeks before the examination, notify his intention to the Board of Control, and should at the same time transmit a list of the subjects in which he proposes to be examined, in order that there may be time to provide a sufficient number of examiners in each department. He should, at the same time, lay before the Board testimonials certifying that his moral character is good. Whether the testimonials be or be not satisfactory is a point which we conceive may safely be left to the determination of the Board.

The Board is then authorised by the Act to make regulations prescribing the branches of knowledge in which the candidates for admission to Haileybury shall be examined. Here arises at once a question of the gravest importance. Ought the examination to be confined to those branches of knowledge to which it is desirable that English gentlemen who mean to remain at home should pay some attention?—or ought it to extend to branches of knowledge which are useful to a servant of the East India Company, but useless, or almost useless, to a person whose life is to be passed in Europe?

Our opinion is, that the examination ought to be confined to those branches of knowledge to which it is desirable that English gentlemen who mean to remain at home should pay some attention.

It is with much diffidence that we venture to predict the effect of the new system; but we think that we can hardly be mistaken in believing that the introduction of that system will be an event scarcely less important to this country than to India. The educated youth of the United Kingdom are henceforth to be invited to engage in a competition in which about 40 prizes will, on an average, be gained every year. Every one of these prizes is nothing less than an honourable social position, and a comfortable independence for life. It is difficult to estimate the effect which the prospect of prizes so numerous and so attractive will produce. We are, however, familiar with some facts which may assist our conjectures. At Trinity College, the largest and wealthiest of the colleges of Cambridge, about four fellowships are given annually by competition. These fellowships can be held only on condition of celibacy, and the income derived from them is a very moderate one for a single man. It is notorious that the examinations for Trinity fellowships have, directly and indirectly, done much to give a direction to the studies of Cambridge and of all the numerous schools which are the feeders of Cambridge. What, then, is likely to be the effect of a competition for prizes which will be ten times as numerous as the Trinity fellowships, and of which each will be more valuable than a Trinity fellowship? We are inclined to think that the examinations for situations in the civil service of the East India Company will produce an effect which will be felt in every seat of learning throughout the realm, at Oxford and Cambridge, at the University of London and the University of Durham, at Edinburgh and Glasgow, at Dublin, at Cork, and at Belfast. The number of candidates will doubtless be much greater than the number of vacancies. It will not surprise us if the ordinary number examined should be three or four hundred. The great majority, and among them many young men of excellent abilities and laudable industry, must be unsuccessful. If, therefore, branches of knowledge specially Oriental should be among the subjects of examination, it is probable that a considerable number of the most hopeful youths in the country will be induced to waste much time, at that period of life at which time is most precious, in studies which will never, in any conceivable case, be of the smallest use to them. We think it most desirable that the examination should be of such a nature that no candidate who may fail shall, to whatever calling he may betake himself, have any reason to regret the time and labour which he spent in preparing himself to be examined.

Nor do we think that we should render any service to India by inducing her future rulers to neglect, in their earlier years, European literature and science, for studies specially Indian. We believe that men who have been engaged, up to one or two and twenty, in studies which have no immediate connexion with the business of any profession, and of which the effect is merely to open, to invigorate, and to enrich the mind, will generally be found, in the business of every profession, superior to men who have, at 18 or 19, devoted themselves to the special studies of their calling. The most illustrious English jurists have been men who have never opened a law book till after the close of a distinguished academical career; nor is there any reason to believe that they would have been greater lawyers if they had passed in drawing pleas and conveyances the time which they gave to Thucydides, to Cicero, and to Newton. The duties of a civil servant of the East India Company are of so high a nature that in his case it is peculiarly desirable that an excellent general education, such as may enlarge and strengthen his understanding, should precede the special education which must qualify him to despatch the business of his cutcherry.

It therefore seems to us quite clear that those vernacular Indian languages which are of no value except for the purpose of communicating with natives of India, ought not to be subjects of examination. But we are inclined, though with much distrust of our own judgment, to think that a distinction may properly be made between the vernacular languages, and two languages which may be called the classical languages of India, the Sanscrit and the Arabic. These classical languages are by no means without intrinsic value in the eyes both of philologists and of men of taste. The Sanscrit is the great parent stock from which most of the vernacular languages of India are derived, and stands to them in a relation similar to that in which the Latin stands to the French, the Italian, the Spanish, and the Portuguese. The Arabic has contributed, though not in the same degree with the Sanscrit, to the formation of the vocabularies of India; and it is the source from which all the Mahometan nations draw their religion, their jurisprudence, and their science. These two languages are already studied by a few young men at the great English seats of learning. They can be learned as well here as in the East; and they are not likely to be studied in the East unless some attention has been paid to them here. It will, we apprehend, very seldom happen that a candidate will offer himself for examination in Sanscrit or in Arabic; but, as such instances may occur, we think it expedient to include those languages in the list of subjects.

As to the other subjects we speak with more confidence. Foremost among those subjects we place our own language and literature. One or more themes for English composition ought to be proposed. Two papers of questions ought to be set. One of those papers should be so framed as to enable the candidates to show their knowledge of the history and constitution of our country: the other ought to be so framed as to enable them to show the extent of their knowledge of our poets, wits, and philosophers.

In the two great ancient languages there ought to be an examination not less severe than those examinations by which the highest classical distinctions are awarded at Oxford and Cambridge. At least three passages from Latin writers ought to be set, to be translated into English. Subjects should be proposed for original composition, both in Latin verse and in Latin prose; and passages of English verse and prose should be set, to be turned into Latin. At least six passages from Greek writers should be set, to be translated into English. Of these passages, one should be taken from the Homeric poems, one from some historian of the best age, one from some philosopher of the best age, one from some Attic orator, and at least one from the Attic drama. The candidates ought to have a full opportunity of exhibiting their skill in translating both English prose and English verse into Greek; and there should be a paper of questions which would enable them to show their knowledge of ancient history, both political and literary.

We think that three of the modern languages of the Continent, the French, the Italian, and the German, ought to be among the subjects of examination. Several passages in every one of those languages should be set, to be turned into English; passages taken from English writers should be set, to be turned into French, Italian, and German; and papers of questions should be framed which would enable a candidate to show his knowledge of the civil and literary history of France, Italy, and Germany.

The examination in pure and mixed mathematics ought to be of such a nature as to enable the judges to place in proper order all the candidates, from those who have never gone beyond Euclid's Elements and the first part of algebra up to those who possess the highest acquirements. We think it important, however, that not only the acquirements, but also the mental powers and resources of the competitors should be brought to the test. With this view the examination papers should contain a due proportion of original problems, and of questions calculated to ascertain whether the principles of mathematical science are thoroughly understood. The details will probably be best arranged by some of those eminent men who have lately been moderators in the University of Cambridge, and who know by experience how to conduct the examinations of large numbers of persons simultaneously. It must, however, be borne in mind that the extent and direction of mathematical reading, especially in the higher branches, differ greatly at the different universities of the United Kingdom. The mathematical examination for the Indian service must, therefore, in order to do justice to all candidates, embrace a wider range of questions than is usual at Cambridge, Oxford, or Dublin.

Of late years some natural sciences which do not fall under the head of mixed mathematics, and especially chemistry, geology, mineralogy, botany, and zoology, have been introduced as a part of general education into several of our universities and colleges. There may be some practical difficulty in arranging the details of an examination in these sciences; but it is a difficulty which has, we believe, been at some seats of learning already overcome. We have no hesitation in recommending that there should be at least one paper of questions relating to these branches of knowledge.

We propose to include the moral sciences in the scheme of examination. Those sciences are, it is well known, much studied both at Oxford and at the Scottish universities. Whether this study shall have to do with mere words or with things, whether it shall degenerate into a formal and scholastic pedantry, or shall train the mind for the highest purposes of active life, will depend, to great extent, on the way in which the examination is conducted. We are of opinion that the examination should be conducted in the freest manner, that mere technicalities should be avoided, and that the candidate should not be confined to any particular system. The subjects which fall under this head are the elements of moral and political philosophy, the history of the ancient and modern schools of moral and political philosophy, the science of logic, and the inductive method, of which the Novum Organum is the great text-book. The object of the examiners should be rather to put to the test the candidate's powers of mind than to ascertain the extent of his metaphysical reading.

The whole examination ought, we think, to be carried on by means of written papers. The candidates ought not to be allowed the help of any book; nor ought they, after once a subject for composition has been proposed to them, or a paper of questions placed before them, to leave the place of examination till they have finished their work.

It is, of course, not to be expected, that any man of 22 will have made considerable proficiency in all the subjects of examination. An excellent mathematician will often have little Greek, and an excellent Greek scholar will be entirely ignorant of French and Italian. Nothing can be further from our wish than to hold out premiums for knowledge of wide surface and of small depth. We are of opinion that a candidate ought to be allowed no credit at all for taking up a subject in which he is a mere smatterer. Profound and accurate acquaintance with a single language ought to tell more than bad translations and themes in six languages. A single paper which shows that the writer thoroughly understands the principles of the differential calculus ought to tell more than 20 superficial and incorrect answers to questions about chemistry, botany, mineralogy, metaphysics, logic and English history.

It will be necessary that a certain number of marks should be assigned to each subject, and that the place of a candidate should be determined by the sum total of the marks which he has gained. The marks ought, we conceive, to be distributed among the subjects of examination, in such a manner that no part of the kingdom, and no class of schools, shall exclusively furnish servants to the East India Company. It would be grossly unjust, for example, to the great academical institutions of England, not to allow skill in Greek and Latin versification to have a considerable share in determining the issue of the competition. Skill in Greek and Latin versification has indeed no direct tendency to form a judge, a financier, or a diplomatist. But the youth who does best what all the ablest and most ambitious youths about him are trying to do well will generally prove a superior man; nor can we doubt that an accomplishment by which Fox and Canning, Grenville and Wellesley, Mansfield and Tenterden, first distinguished themselves above their fellows, indicates powers of mind, which, properly trained and directed, may do great service to the State. On the other hand, we must remember that, in the north of this island the art of metrical composition in the ancient languages is very little cultivated, and that men so eminent as Dugald Stewart, Horner, Jeffrey, and Mackintosh, would probably have been quite unable to write a good copy of Latin alcaics, or to translate 10 lines of Shakespeare into Greek iambics. We wish to see such a system of examination established as shall not exclude from the service of the East India Company either a Mackintosh or a Tenterden, either a Canning or a Horner. We have, with an anxious desire to deal fairly by all parts of the United Kingdom, and by all places of liberal education, framed the following scale, which we venture to submit for your consideration:

English language and literature:

Composition	500
History	500
General literature	500
	1,500

Greek	750
Latin	750
French	375
German	375
Italian	375
Mathematics, pure and mixed	1,000
Natural sciences	500
Moral sciences	500
Sanscrit	375
Arabic	375
	6,875

It seems to us probable, that of the 6,875 marks, which are the maximum, no candidate will ever obtain half. A candidate who is at once a distinguished classical scholar and a distinguished mathematician will be, as he ought to be, certain of success. A classical scholar who is no mathematician, or a mathematician who is no classical scholar, will be certain of success, if he is well read in the history and literature of his own country. A young man who has scarcely any knowledge of mathematics, little Latin and no Greek, may pass such an examination in English, French, Italian, German, geology, and chemistry, that he may stand at the head of the list.

It can scarcely be necessary for us to add, that no expense ought to be grudged which may be necessary to secure the services of the ablest examiners in every branch of learning. Experience justifies us in pronouncing with entire confidence that, if the examiners be well chosen, it is utterly impossible that the delusive show of knowledge which is the effect of the process popularly called cramming can ever be successful against real learning and ability.

Whether the examinations ought to be held half-yearly or annually is a question which cannot, we think, be satisfactorily determined till after the first experiment has been made.

When the result of the examination has been declared, the successful candidates will not yet be civil servants of the East India Company, but only civil servants elect. It appears from the 40th clause of the Act to be the intention of the Legislature that, before they proceed to the East, there should be a period of probation and a second examination.

In what studies, then, ought the period of probation to be passed? And what ought to be the nature of the second examination?

It seems to us that, from the moment at which the successful candidates, whom we will now call probationers, have been set apart as persons who will, in all probability, have to bear a part in the government of India, they should give their whole minds to the duties of their new position. They must now be considered as having finished their general education, and as having finished it with honour. Their serious studies must henceforth be such as have a special tendency to fit them for their calling.

Of the special knowledge which a civil servant of the Company ought to possess, much can be acquired only in India, and much may be acquired far more easily in India than in England. It would evidently be a mere waste of time to employ a month here in learning what may be better learned in a week at Calcutta or Madras. But there are some kinds of knowledge which are not considered as essential parts of the liberal education of our youth, but which it is most important that a civil servant of the Company should possess, and which he may acquire in England not less easily, indeed more easily, than in India. We conceive that every probationer ought during the interval between his first and his second examination to apply himself vigorously to the acquiring of these kinds of knowledge.

The subjects of his new studies will, we apprehend, be found to range themselves under four heads.

He should, in the first place, make himself well acquainted with the history of India, in the largest sense of the word history. He should study that history, not merely in the works of Orme, of Wilks, and of Mill, but also in the travels of Bernier, in the odes of Sir William Jones, and in the journals of Heber. He should be well informed about the geography of the country, about its natural productions, about its manufactures, about the physical and moral qualities of the different races which inhabit it, and about the doctrines and rites of those religions which have so powerful an influence on the population. He should trace with peculiar care the progress of the British power. He should understand the constitution of our Government, and the nature of the relations between that Government and its vassals, Mussulman, Mahratta, and Rajpoot. He should consult the most important Parliamentary reports and debates on Indian affairs. All this may be done with very much greater facility in England than in any part of India, except at the three seats of Government, if indeed the three seats of Government ought to be excepted.

Secondly, it seems to us to be desirable that every probationer should bestow some attention on the general principles of jurisprudence. The great majority of the civil servants of the East India Company are employed in the administration of justice. A large proportion of them are judges; and some of the most important functions of the collectors are strictly judicial. That the general principles of jurisprudence may be studied here with more advantage than in India will be universally acknowledged.

Thirdly, we think that every probationer ought to prepare himself for the discharge of his duties by paying some attention to financial and commercial science. He should understand the mode of keeping and checking accounts, the principles of banking, the laws which regulate the exchanges, the nature of public debts, funded and unfunded, and the effect produced by different systems of taxation on the prosperity of nations.

124

We would by no means require him to subscribe any article of faith touching any controverted point in the science of political economy; but it is not too much to expect that he will make himself acquainted with those treatises on political economy which have become standard works. These studies can undoubtedly be prosecuted with more advantage in England than in India.

Fourthly, we think that the study of the vernacular languages of India may with great advantage be begun in England. It is, indeed, only by intercourse with the native population that an Englishman can acquire the power of talking Bengalee or Telugu with fluency. But familiarity with the Bengalee or Telugu alphabet, skill in tracing the Bengalee or Telugu character, and knowledge of the Bengalee or Telugu grammar, may be acquired as quickly in this country as in the East. Nay, we are inclined to believe that an English student will, at his first introduction to an Indian language, make more rapid progress under good English teachers than under pundits, to whom he is often unable to explain his difficulties. We are therefore of opinion that every probationer should acquire in this country an elementary knowledge of at least one Indian language.

If this recommendation be adopted, it will be desirable that the probationers should, immediately after the first examination, be distributed among the Presidencies. It will indeed be desirable that the division of the Bengal civil service into two parts, one destined for the upper and the other for the lower provinces, should be made here at the earliest possible moment, instead of being made, as it now is, at Calcutta.

In what manner the distribution of civil servants among the Presidencies ought henceforth to be made is a question which, though it has not been referred to us, is yet so closely connected with the questions which have been referred to us, that we have been forced to take it into consideration. We are disposed to think that it might be advisable to allow the probationers, according to the order in which they stand at the first examination, to choose their Presidencies. The only objection to this arrangement is, that, as the Presidency of Bengal is generally supposed to be the theatre on which the abilities of a civil servant may be most advantageously displayed, all the most distinguished young men would choose Bengal, and would leave Madras and Bombay to those who stood at the bottom of the list. We admit that this would be an evil; but it would be an evil which must, we conceive, speedily cure itself; for as soon as it becomes notorious that the ablest men in the civil service are all collected in one part of India, and are there stopping each other's way, a probationer who is free to make his choice will prefer some other part of India, where, though the prizes may be a little less attractive, the competition will be much less formidable. If, however, it should be thought inexpedient to allow the probationers to choose their own Presidencies in the manner which we have suggested, it seems to us that the best course would be to make the distribution by lot. We are satisfied that, if the distribution be made arbitrarily, either by the Directors or by Her Majesty's Minister for Indian Affairs, it will be viewed with much suspicion, and will excite much murmuring. At present nobody complains of the distribution. A gentleman who has obtained a Bombay writership for his son is delighted and thankful. It may not be quite so acceptable as a Bengal writership would have been: but it is a free gift; it is a most valuable favour; and it would be the most odious ingratitude to repine because it is not more valuable still. Henceforth an appointment to the civil service of the Company will be not matter of favour, but matter of right. He who obtains such an appointment will owe it solely to his own abilities and industry. If, therefore, the Court of Directors or the Board of Control should send him to Bombay when he wishes to be sent to Bengal, and should send to Bengal young men who in the examination stood far below him, he will naturally think himself injured. His family and friends will espouse his quarrel. A cry will be raised, that one man is favoured because he is related to the Chairman, and another because he is befriended by a Member of Parliament who votes with the Government. It seems to us, therefore, advisable that the distribution of the civil servants among the Presidencies, if it cannot be made the means of rewarding merit, should be left to chance. After the allotment, of course, any two probationers should be at liberty to make an exchange by consent.

But, in whatever manner the distribution may be made, it ought to be made as soon as the issue of the first examination is decided; for, till the distribution is made, it will be impossible for any probationer to know what vernacular language of India it would be most expedient for him to study. The Hindostanee, indeed, will be valuable to him, wherever he may be stationed; but no other living language is spoken over one-third of India. Tamul would be as useless in Bengal, and Bengalee would be as useless at Agra, as Welsh in Portugal.

We should recommend that every probationer, for whatever Presidency he may be destined, should be permitted to choose Hindostanee as the language in which he will pass. A probationer who is to reside in the lower provinces of the Bengal Presidency should be allowed to choose either Hindostanee or Bengalee. A probationer who is to go to the upper provinces should be allowed to choose among Hindostanee, Hindee, and Persian. A probationer who is to go to Madras should be allowed to choose among Hindostanee, Telugu, and Tamul. A probationer who is to go to Bombay should be allowed to choose among Hindostanee, Mahrattee, and Guzeratee.

It is probable that some probationers who have a peculiar talent for learning languages will study more than one of the dialects among which they are allowed to make their choice. Indeed it is not improbable that some who take an interest in philology will apply themselves voluntarily to the Sanscrit and the Arabic. It will hereafter be seen that, though we require as the indispensable condition of passing only an elementary knowledge of one of the vernacular tongues of India, we propose to give encouragement to those students who aspire to be eminent Orientalists.

The four studies, then, to which, in our opinion, the probationers ought to devote themselves during the period of probation, are, first, Indian history; secondly, the science of jurisprudence; thirdly, commercial and financial science; and fourthly, the Oriental tongues.

The time of probation ought not, we think, to be less than one year, nor more than two years.

There should be periodical examinations, at which a probationer of a year's standing must pass, on pain of forfeiting his appointment. This examination should, of course, be in the four branches of knowledge already mentioned as those to which the attention of the probationers ought to be specially directed. Marks should be assigned to the different subjects, as at the first examination; and it seems to us reasonable that an equal number of marks should be assigned to all the four subjects, on the supposition that each probationer is examined in only one of the vernacular languages of India. Sometimes, however, as we have said, a probationer may study more than one of these vernacular languages of India among which he is at liberty to make his choice, or may, in addition to one or more of the vernacular languages of India, learn Sanscrit or Arabic. We think it reasonable that to every language in which he offers himself for examination an equal number of marks should be assigned.

When the marks have been cast up, the probationers who have been examined should be arranged in order of merit. All those who have been two years probationers, and who have, in the opinion of the examiners, used their time well, and made a respectable proficiency, should be declared civil servants of the Company. Every probationer who, having been a probationer only one year, has obtained a higher place than some of the two-year men who have passed, should also be declared a civil servant of the Company. All the civil servants who pass in one year should take rank in the service according to their places in the final examination. Thus a salutary emulation will be kept up to the last moment. It ought to be observed, that the precedency which we propose to give to merit will not be merely honorary, but will be attended by very solid advantages. It is in order of seniority that the members of the civil service succeed to those annuities to which they are all looking forward, and it may depend on the manner in which a young man acquits himself at his final examination, whether he shall remain in India till he is past 50, or shall be able to return to England at 47 or 48.

The instances in which persons who have been successful in the first examination will fail in the final examination, will, we hope and believe, be very few. We hope

126

and believe, also, that it will very rarely be necessary to expel any probationer from the service on account of grossly profligate habits, or of any action unbecoming a man of honour. The probationers will be young men superior to their fellows in science and literature; and it is not among young men superior to their fellows in science and literature that scandalous immorality is generally found to prevail. It is notoriously not once in 20 years that a student who has attained high academical distinction is expelled from Oxford or Cambridge. Indeed early superiority in science and literature generally indicates the existence of some qualities which are securities against vice—industry, self-denial, a taste for pleasures not sensual, a laudable desire of honourable distinction, a still more laudable desire to obtain the approbation of friends and relations. We therefore believe that the intellectual test which is about to be established will be found in practice to be also the best moral test that can be devised.

One important question still remains to be considered. Where are the probationers to study? Are they all to study at Haileybury? Is it to be left to themselves to decide whether they will study at Haileybury or elsewhere? Or will the Board of Control reserve to itself the power of determining which of them shall study at Haileybury, and which of them shall be at liberty to study elsewhere?

That the college at Haileybury is to be kept up is clearly implied in the terms of the 37th and 39th clauses of the India Act. That the Board of Control may make regulations which would admit into the civil service persons who have not studied at Haileybury is as clearly implied in the terms of the 40th and 41st clauses. Whether the law ought to be altered is a question on which we do not presume to give any opinion. On the supposition that the law is to remain unaltered, we venture to offer some suggestions which appear to us to be important.

There must be, we apprehend, a complete change in the discipline of the college. Almost all the present students are under 20; almost all the new students will be above 21. The present students have gone to Haileybury from schools where they have been treated as boys. The new students will generally go thither from Universities, where they have been accustomed to enjoy the liberty of men. It will therefore be absolutely necessary that the regulations of the college should be altered, and that the probationers should be subject to no more severe restraint than is imposed on a bachelor of arts at Cambridge or Oxford.

There must be an extensive change even in the buildings of the college. At present, each student has a single small chamber, which is at once his parlour and bedroom. It will be impossible to expect men of two or three and twenty, who have long been accustomed to be lodged in a very different manner, to be content with such accommodation.

There must be a great change in the system of study. At present, the students generally go to Haileybury before they have completed their general education. Their general education and their special education, therefore, go on together. Henceforth, the students must be considered as men whose general education has been finished, and finished with great success. Greek, Latin, and mathematics will no longer be parts of the course of study. The whole education will be special, and ought, in some departments, to be of a different kind from that which has hitherto been given.

We are far, indeed, from wishing to detract from the merit of those professors, all of them highly respectable and some of them most eminent, who have taught law and political economy at Haileybury. But it is evident that a course of lectures on law or political economy given to boys of 18, who have been selected merely by favour, must be a very different thing from a course of lectures on law or political economy given to men of 23, who have been selected on account of their superior abilities and attainments. As respects law, indeed, we doubt whether the most skilful instructor will be able at Haileybury to impart to his pupils that kind of knowledge which it is most desirable that they should acquire. Some at least of the probationers ought, we conceive, not merely to attend lectures, and to read well-chosen books on jurisprudence, but to see the actual working of the machinery by which justice is administered. They ought to hear legal questions, in which great principles are involved, argued by the ablest counsel, and decided by the highest courts in the realm. They ought to draw up reports of the arguments both of the advocates and of the judges. They ought to attend both civil and criminal trials, and to take notes of the evidence, and of the discussions and decisions respecting the evidence. It might be particularly desirable that they should attend the sittings of the Judicial Committee of the Privy Council when important appeals from India are under the consideration of that tribunal. A probationer, while thus employed, should regularly submit his notes of arguments and of evidence to his legal instructor for correction. Such a training as this would, we are inclined to think, be an excellent preparation for official life in India; and we must leave it to the Board of Control to consider whether any plan can be devised by which such a training can be made compatible with residence at Haileybury.

We have, &c.

(signed)   *T. B. Macaulay.*

Ashburton.

Henry Melvill.

Benjamin Jowett.

November, 1854   *John George Shaw Lefevre.*

Gentlemen,   India Board, 30 November 1854.

I HAVE the honour to enclose to you, for the information of the Court of Directors of the East India Company, a copy of the Report which has been drawn up by the gentlemen who at my request have been kind enough to give me their valuable assistance in the consideration of the best mode of carrying into effect that part of the Act of 1853 for the government of India which provides that the public admissions to the civil service of the East India Company shall be by competition.

I concur in the general tenor of their Report. I propose that 20 candidates shall be selected at an examination to be held in the course of the ensuing year; and as soon as the necessary regulations, which require very careful consideration, have been framed, notice will be given of the time when it will be held.

I have also had to consider what course should be adopted with regard to the successful candidates at such examination, and the best means of imparting to them such further instruction as may be thought necessary before their final appointment to India. In this question is involved the continued maintenance of the College of Haileybury.

Upon the best consideration which I have been able to give to the subject, this college, as it is now constituted for the education of youths from the age of 17, appears to me to be altogether unsuited to the instruction of gentlemen, many of whom may have passed through the full course of education at one or other of the universities, and some of whom may perhaps have even entered upon their studies for the bar.

Nor does it appear to me that any change in the constitution of Haileybury would render it possible that gentlemen residing there would have the opportunity of acquiring the knowledge which it is most desirable that all the civil servants of the East India Company should possess.

No qualification is so necessary to them, whether they be employed in the judicial branch of the service or in the combined duties of collectors and magistrates in India, as a thorough knowledge of the principles of law, combined with a practical acquaintance with the mode of conducting civil and criminal suits. Nothing, in my opinion, can conduce so much to the acquisition of this practical knowledge as attendance during the progress of trials in courts of justice; and the opportunity of doing this is so much greater in the metropolis than elsewhere, that this circumstance alone would render London by far the most convenient place for their residence. It seems to me also that arrangements may be made in London more easily than elsewhere for their instruction in the other branches of knowledge, of which they ought to have some acquaintance, in order to enable them to discharge with efficiency the multifarious duties which are so often thrown upon the civil service in India.

I have come to the conclusion, therefore, that it is inexpedient permanently to maintain Haileybury College. It will be necessary, however, that it should continue in a state of efficiency so long as is requisite, in order to educate those gentlemen who have been nominated to vacancies which occurred previous to the 30th of April last. I see by the number of appointments not yet taken up that if the college is kept full they will be exhausted by the admissions of January 1856.

After that period, therefore, no admissions ought to be permitted, and the college will be maintained only so long as to enable those gentlemen to complete their education there.

I propose to introduce a Bill into Parliament for the purpose of relieving the East India Company from the obligation under which they now are to maintain the College of Haileybury, and due provision will of course be made for those officers of the establishment who remain upon it at the time of the closing of the college as have a claim to such a provision.

I have, &c.

The Chairs,   (signed)   *Charles Wood,*
    &c. &c. &c.

129

Appendix B

REGULATIONS for the EXAMINATION of CANDIDATES for Appointments to the CIVIL SERVICE of the EAST INDIA COMPANY

Note.—An examination will take place in July 1855, by examiners to be appointed by the Board of Commissioners for the Affairs of India, of candidates for appointments to the civil service of the East India Company.

Public notice will hereafter be given of the precise day on which the examination will be held. Twenty appointments will be awarded, if so many candidates are declared by the examiners to be duly qualified.

REGULATIONS

1. Any natural-born subject of Her Majesty who shall be desirous of entering the civil service of the Company will be entitled to be examined at such examination, provided he shall, on or before the 1st of May 1855, have transmitted to the Board of Commissioners:

(*a*) A certificate of his age being above 18 years and under 23 years.

(*b*) A certificate, signed by a physician or surgeon, of his having no disease, constitutional affection, or bodily infirmity, unfitting him for the civil service of the Company.

(*c*) A certificate of good moral character, signed by the head of the school or college at which he has last received his education; or, if he has not received education at any school or college since the year 1852, then such proof of good moral character as may be satisfactory to the Board of Commissioners.

(*d*) A statement of those of the branches of knowledge hereinafter enumerated in which he desires to be examined.

2. The examination will take place only in the following branches of knowledge: English Language and Literature:—

Composition	500
English literature and history, including that of the laws and constitution	1,000
	1,500
Language, literature, and history of Greece	750
,, ,, ,, Rome	750
,, ,, ,, France	375
,, ,, ,, Germany	375
,, ,, ,, Italy	375
Mathematics, pure and mixed	1,000
Natural science, that is, chemistry, electricity and magnetism, natural history, geology, and mineralogy	500
Moral sciences, that is, logic, mental, moral, and political philosophy	500
Sanscrit language and literature	375
Arabic language and literature	375
	6,875

3. The merit of the persons examined will be estimated by marks, according to the ordinary system in use at several of the universities, and the numbers set opposite to each branch in the preceding paragraph denote the greatest number of marks that can be obtained in respect of it.

4. No candidate will be allowed any marks in respect of any subject of examination unless he shall, in the opinion of the examiners, possess a competent knowledge of that subject.

5. The examination will be conducted by means of printed questions and written answers, and by *vivâ voce* examination, as the examiners may deem necessary.

6. After the examination shall have been completed, the examiners shall add up the marks obtained by each candidate in respect of each of the subjects in which he shall have been examined, and shall set forth, in order of merit, the names of the 20 candidates who shall have obtained a greater aggregate number of marks than any of the remaining candidates; and such 20 candidates shall be deemed to be selected candidates for the civil service of the East India Company. Their choice of the Presidency in India to which they shall be appointed shall be determined by the order in which they stand on such list.

7. In August 1856, and August 1857, further examinations of the selected candidates will take place by examiners appointed by the Board of Commissioners for the Affairs of India in the following subjects:

Law, including the ordinary rules of taking evidence and the mode of conducting civil and criminal trials	1,000
The history of India	400
Political economy	400
Any language of India in which the selected candidate shall have given notice of his desire to be examined	200

and such further examinations will be conducted in the same manner as that above described. (The numbers set opposite to each subject denote the greatest number of marks which can be obtained in respect of such subjects.)

8. Each selected candidate, desirous of being examined at either of the further examinations of 1856 and 1857, shall, two months previously to such examination, transmit to the Board of Commissioners for the Affairs of India a statement mentioning the language or languages of India in which he is desirous of being examined.

9. Any selected candidate, who, having been examined at the further examination of 1856, shall not have passed, may, nevertheless, be again examined at the further examination of 1857.

10. Any selected candidate who shall not have passed at one or the other of the further examinations of 1856 and 1857, shall be struck off the list of selected candidates.

11. The selected candidates who, at either of such further examinations, shall be deemed by the examiners to have a competent knowledge of law, the history of India, political economy, and at least one language of India, shall be adjudged to have passed and to be entitled to be appointed to the civil service of the East India Company; and the names of the selected candidates who shall have so passed shall be placed in a list in the order of their merit in such examinations, estimated as above by the total number of marks which they shall have obtained in respect of all the subjects in which they shall have been examined at such examination.

12. The seniority in the civil service of the East India Company of the selected candidates shall be determined by the date of the further examination at which they shall be adjudged to have passed; and, as between those who passed at the same further examination, their seniority in such civil service shall be determined according to the order in which they stand on the list resulting from such examination.

13. No person will, even after such examination, be allowed to proceed to India unless he shall comply with the regulations in force at the time for the civil service of the East India Company, and shall be of sound bodily health and good moral character.

India Board, 26 January 1855.   *R. Lowe.*

APPENDIX C

IMPRESSIONS OF THE CIVIL SERVICES IN FRANCE, SWEDEN AND THE UNITED STATES

In the course of our work a number of us paid visits to France and Sweden, and two of us to the United States. We wish to record our deep appreciation of the kindness which our hosts showed to us and of the great trouble they took to make our visits fruitful. We append below accounts of the impressions we carried away from each of these visits. But three main ideas particularly struck us.

2. First, in both France and Sweden we were struck by the youth of civil servants in the key positions nearest to Ministers. The size and complexity of the US Civil Service made it impossible to attempt a comparison there. But the French and Swedish systems are constructed in their different ways to provide senior policy-making posts for young men. The *directeur du cabinet* in France is the Minister's principal collaborator in policy matters and also plays a part in the control of the Ministry. The Under Secretary in Sweden is also the Minister's chief adviser on policy and is the senior official in a small Ministry whose function is that of a policy-making secretariat largely free of executive responsibility. Men in their 40s and even 30s are commonly appointed to these posts. The average age of *directeurs du cabinet* is 46; of Under Secretaries, 45. Neither post has an exact equivalent in Britain, but the average age of Permanent Secretaries, whose functions include that of being top policy adviser, is 56.

3. Secondly, in all three countries, the extent to which Ministers choose their own immediate staff.

4. Thirdly, the professionalism of high civil servants. It is achieved in different ways: in France by selecting and training elites, in Sweden and the USA by each department recruiting its own men for specific kinds of jobs. However achieved, the result was impressive in each of the three countries.

THE FRENCH CIVIL SERVICE

The Chairman, Sir James Dunnett, Dr. Hunt, Sir Norman Kipping, Mr. Neild and the Assistant Secretary visited France from 7th to 10th November, 1966. This note sums up their main impressions.

PROFESSIONALISM

2. We were much impressed by the quality of the men in the important, central jobs. They were lucid, expert and possessed of that confidence which comes from the achievement of high responsibility combined with a certainty that one knows one's subject as well or better than anyone else.

3. It is a remarkable achievement to have created two complementary elites on the technical and administrative sides—the *polytechniciens* and the products of the *Ecole Nationale d'Administration* (ENA). Each is a highly selected and highly trained breed. Yet because the *polytechnicien's* training is widened so as to include economics and managerial disciplines, the two elites have common ground on which they can meet. Both seem well equipped to assume responsibility for policy-making, the assessment of projects and the other tasks of the higher civil servant.

4. These qualities owe much to the systems of selection and training; and something also to the fact that the higher civil service is an attractive route to the top of French life both in the public and private sectors.

5. We were struck too by the fact that the men in positions of very high responsibility are often remarkably young compared to their British counterparts. Clearly, there are good arrangements for picking out promising young men; the system of ministerial *cabinets* plays a large part in it. It appears to be well accepted that a young man should be put into a central post close to Ministers and should later move away from the centre to take charge of a job of a more managerial character within a Ministry or great organ of state like the *Conseil d'Etat* or outside the Civil Service. The existence of these outlets to reward the older men makes possible the turnover in the central positions that affords opportunities to bring forward the younger men.

ELITES

6. The French Civil Service is extremely elitist, and there is an elaborate hierarchy of elites; there is a recognised order of precedence in esteem and standing for the different *corps* and Ministries.

7. On the administrative side, the highest status belongs to the *grands corps—Conseil d'Etat, Inspection-General des Finances, Cours des Comptes*. Apart from their own primary functions, they are an elite deployed throughout the Civil Service and elsewhere. At any time about a third to a half of their members may be employed in posts outside the *corps*, and there is also a substantial amount of part-time duties outside the *corps*. The jobs on which they are employed may be inside the Civil Service, in central posts like the Secretary-General of the Government (analogous to the Secretary of the Cabinet), in ministerial *cabinets*, in special directorates and commissions, etc., or outside the Civil Service in the public, semi-public and private sectors of industry and commerce, in international organisations, etc.

8. A second elite group is the top technical *corps*. As an elite, they resemble, mutatis mutandis, the administrative elite. There is a similar well-established order of precedence with the *Corps des Mines* first, the *Corps des Ponts et Chaussees* second, the *Corps des Telecommunications* third, and so on down the scale. The higher *corps* are general-purpose technical elites, not confined to their traditional functions as a *corps*, but deployed throughout the Service.

9. Certain Ministries are dominated by the great technical *corps* and have not been popular as allocations for administrators because their role has largely been in giving auxiliary administrative services to technical directors. It is, however, now an official policy to get more civil administrators from the ENA into the technical Ministries and to give them more equality of status within those Ministries. The Ministry of Equipment and Housing is perhaps an indication of the way the French are moving since it

is a recent creation, amalgamating the Ministries of Construction and Public Works. It includes both administrators and members of the top technical *corps*, mixed together with no fixed proportions or relations between them; at the senior policy-making and managerial levels a man's job does not depend on whether his background is on the technical or the administrative side.

10. The predominance of the elites is self-renewing: the *grands corps* get the best jobs because they are manned by the best men, and they attract the best men because they lead to the best jobs—outside the Service as well as inside. The danger in this system appears to be that to the man who gets an initial advantage more and more advantage is added; the gap between one man and another, perhaps only a matter of a few marks at the time of graduation from the ENA, gets continually wider. The structure of the Service, based on the *corps*, but not described at length in this note, is both fragmented and rigid. There is little class-to-class promotion in the British sense; the normal route of advancement is by limited competition, demanding an exceptional effort that is scarcely feasible for the older man in particular.

TRAINING
Ecole Nationale d'Administration

11. The ENA, founded in 1945, is one of the most famous features of the modern French Civil Service—in our view justly so. It carries out both recruitment and training for the higher Civil Service. One hundred places a year are filled from two competitions, an open competition for two-thirds of the places, and one limited to existing civil servants for the remaining third. The competition includes written, oral and physical tests. The subjects are political, economic and social history from the middle of the 18th century, political economy, political institutions, French administration, modern languages and physical training; the optional subjects include mathematics, statistics and science. Although part of the examination is oral, it does not include a general interview in the British style designed for the assessment of the character and personality, as distinct from the abilities, of candidates, and no attempt to evaluate such qualities is made in marking and selection. This is of course in striking contrast to British practice in the Civil Service and other employment, but this practice is regarded as alien to French ideas. One senior Frenchman told us that he thought that the British type of interview was an unfair and dishonest method of selection.

12. In order to stand a chance of success, candidates must have undertaken some special preparation beyond an ordinary degree. In effect, it is necessary to undergo thorough training, tantamount to a second degree course, in the modern subjects set in the competition. The limited competition covers much the same ground, but in principle more emphasis is given to practical experience and the benefits derived from it, and in practice it is admitted to be rather easier. But some special training is also necessary, and candidates are often given special leave from the Civil Service for the purpose. It appears that many candidates for the limited competition are of the same type and background as those for the open competition, who enter the Civil Service with the object of finding an easier way into the ENA and resign if they fail to do so.

13. Once admitted to the ENA, the students are salaried civil servants under service discipline. The course begins with a year's *stage*, usually in a prefecture. The student is attached to the prefect's office as an assistant, seeing the work of the office, handling files, attending meetings, etc. He spends some time in sub-prefectures and in the local offices of the various Ministries. He is given a report to do on some subject that is not only valuable to him as a training exercise but in itself useful to the prefect; copies are sent to the ENA with the prefect's comments for assessment and markings. At the end of the *stage* the prefect completes a report on the student. The *stage* is regarded by administration and the students alike as a particularly profitable part of the course.

14. The remaining 18 months of the course are mainly spent at the ENA in Paris. There is no full-time teaching staff. The instructors are mainly themselves civil servants, with some university teachers and others. There are few formal lectures

and classes. Most of the teaching is in discussion groups. Considerable use is made of group projects; a study group is required to produce a report on some current topic, and has to collect the material by visiting Ministries and other organisations. The main fields of study are judicial and administrative matters, economic studies, international relations and social questions. Statistics, public accountancy, business management, and organisation and methods are also included in the syllabus, and the students are expected to improve their practical grasp of their first foreign language and to acquire the elements of a second. The content of the course is under constant review to keep it up to date. Everyone does the same subjects, including those going into the Diplomatic Service (and indeed it is not known for certain who they are until the end of the course). Members of the Diplomatic Service therefore get a grounding in economics and other subjects, while members of the Home Civil Service get a grounding in international questions. Each has a means of communication with the other. Thus the course at the ENA is not broken down according to the specialisms that students will pursue as civil servants. Until 1958 it was divided into four sections specialising in administration, economics, social affairs and international questions, but since the practice of determining allocations to *corps* and to Ministries by the final order of merit was already followed, there was no necessary relation between the specialism a man pursued and his allocation.

15. Towards the end of a course there is a second *stage* of about two months, the *stage d'entreprise*, spent in a private firm, some of them quite small. The firms are asked to give the students real work and responsibility, but one may have doubts as to the extent to which that is practicable in two months. Our impression is that at present the *stage d'entreprise* is not regarded as one of the more important parts of the course.

16. Marks are awarded throughout the course, and determine a final order of merit which is announced at the end of the course. At the same time a list is published of the vacancies available in the Civil Service, equal in number to the students graduating. The student with top marks has first choice of all the available vacancies and so on down to the student with bottom marks who has no choice and takes the last vacancy left. The high degree of predictability of the students' choices has already been mentioned. Those at the top nearly always opt for the *Conseil d'Etat* and the *Inspection-Generale des Finances*, followed by the *Cours des Comptes* and so on through the various Ministries in order of standing. This system is justified in official French quarters on two grounds, first, as ensuring objectivity of allocation, and, secondly, as a necessary means of getting continued effort from the students, in view of the fact that once admitted to the ENA they are in the Civil Service and virtually certain of getting at least a decent job. It is admitted that as a consequence there is a degree of competitive tension that is sometimes unhealthy.

17. In European countries, where administration has a formal and juridical character, Civil Services traditionally have been manned by people educated in subjects proper to administration as a formal art; frequently by lawyers. (In contrast, British administration has been informal and pragmatic, and a formal education in administration was not required.) The achievement of the French Civil Service with the ENA, imitated in varying degrees by some other European countries, is to have broken away from the traditional mould and created a vocational education for a modern Civil Service. Administration remains an important subject at the ENA because French administration still has a formal and juridical framework but it is combined with the outward-looking disciplines relevant to the work of a Civil Service with a positive role in a modern society.

Ecole Polytechnique

18. The *Ecole Polytechnique* carries out training for the higher technical *corps* of the Civil Service, and also for the armed forces, research and the private sector. There are about 300 places a year, preparation for which is done in special classes in higher mathematics and special mathematics at about thirteen *lycees*. The competition consists of written, oral and phsyical tests, in mathematics, physics, chemistry, French composition, general education, a foreign language and physical training.

19. In the two-year course a larger element of formal lectures survives than at the ENA, probably because of the subjects taught, but nevertheless they only amount to a small proportion of the course. The rest of the time is taken up with seminars, individual and group projects based on real problems, and free study. The syllabus is the same for all students, consisting of courses in mathematics, mechanics, physics and chemistry and some instruction in the humanities, economics and a modern language. Again, marks are given throughout which go to make up the final order of merit at the end of the two years.

20. The graduates of the *Ecole Polytechnique* do not all become civil servants. Some become army officers or military engineers. A number go into research. About 100 resign from the public service and go into the private sector; the option may be left open until the allocation of places following the final classification, and many resign from the public service if they are not well enough placed to get into the top *corps* of their choice. A former student of the *Polytechnique* who leaves the public service within ten years of graduation must pay a *forfait*, a substantial sum; however, industrial firms are very willing to bear the charge in order to get a *polytechnicien*. There remain about 80 who go into one of the civilian engineering *corps*, of which there is a great variety from mines to meteorology, weights and measures to telecommunications. As already described, there is, especially at the higher level, a hierarchy of precedence between these corps. As at the ENA, allocation is made by the graduates themselves according to their final classification.

21. The *polytechnicien* who goes into a state engineering *corps* must go through the appropriate *ecole d'application*—an applied training school. Each technical Ministry runs its own schools to provide specialised training for its own staff and the associated industry. These schools take in direct entrants from *lycees* by competitive examination, as well as graduates of the *Polytechnique*, but for the most part it is the latter who go into the higher echelons while the direct entrants man the lower technical *corps* or go into private industry. The *Ecole des Mines* ranks highest among these schools. Ten or twelve of the best graduates from the *Polytechnique* enter annually, together with 50-70 direct entrants, but the direct entrants are not members of the *Corps des Mines* and have little chance of getting into it. The school has gone a long way from its original role of giving a specialised training in mining engineering. The three-year syllabus not only includes scientific, engineering and technical subjects, but also a year in industry as an engineer with production responsibilities, the study and solution on a team basis of a real business problem using a computer, and the development of economic, administrative and financial understanding, including study in depth of an actual technico-economic problem from one of the Ministries. At the end of the course, the former *polytechnicien* is a member of the *corps* and he may go into the state service in one of the Ministries or be detached to work in a nationalised industry or other public corporation. He may also go into private industry for a spell without necessarily severing his connection with the Civil Service, the test being his readiness to return if recalled; in effect there is a steady erosion of members of the technical *corps* to the private sector. This occurs in spite of the fact that the most successful are among the most highly paid French civil servants, and indicates that they are a much sought-after elite.

MINISTERS AND DEPARTMENTS

22. French Ministries do not have a Permanent Secretary. In a few Ministries, notably the Ministry of Foreign Affairs, there is the post of Secretary-General but in practice it is not a real equivalent. Ministries are divided into *directions*, headed by directors, in principle equal but in practice sometimes not all of the same importance and standing. There is also the Minister's *cabinet* headed by the *directeur du cabinet*. The role of the *directeur du cabinet* within the Ministry in relation to the directors varies considerably at different times from one Ministry to another. While the directors are responsible for administration and management within their spheres, the *directeur du cabinet* is specially concerned on the Minister's behalf with the political direction of the Ministry and the political implications of its policies and activities. It is through him and the rest of the *cabinet* that the Minister exercises control over the Ministry. The *directeur du cabinet* is therefore the official in a French Ministry who exercises

some of the functions of a Permanent Secretary; that his appointment is made by the Minister is a very important difference.

23. The *directeur du cabinet* is typically (but not always) a permanent civil servant, and frequently a young man of relatively junior rank (sub-director). He is carefully selected; the appointment is made by the Minister and must be approved by the Prime Minister. In the Ministry of Finance, for example, he has a staff of 25-30, including six or seven promising young men under him each with a specific concern with one or more *directions*. The young men are usually civil servants of about the equivalent rank of Principal. At the end of their spell in the *cabinet* they can usually expect promotion. In the case of the *directeur du cabinet* this would usually be to the rank of director, that is, to a more managerial job, or alternatively he (*directeurs du cabinet* are often members of the *grands corps*) might go back into his *corps* or on to some other important, special job.

24. Ministers appear to exercise more control over the appointment and dismissal of senior staff to and from posts than in this country. There is a network through which Ministers get recommendations and advice on the appointment of men to their *cabinets* and to other jobs. It certainly seems to work as a way of bringing promising young men forward. The staff of a *cabinet* are normally changed when a new Minister comes in, and a Minister may also change them at other times. The directors of the operational divisions in a Ministry may also be changed by a Minister, but in practice this happens less frequently. In each Ministry there is a director of personnel but he is commonly the weakest director in the Ministry, concerned in practice only with the personnel management of the junior grades.

CENTRAL MANAGEMENT OF THE CIVIL SERVICE

25. The central management of the French Civil Service is divided between two bodies. The *direction du budget* of the Ministry of Finance is responsible for financial control. The *direction de l'administration et de la fonction publique* is responsible for management control. The Prime Minister is the Minister responsible for the civil service, but his powers in relation to the civil service have usually been delegated to another Minister, at present the Minister of State for Administrative Reform to whom the *direction de la fonction publique* works. The *direction* deals with general policy on pay, pensions, conditions of service, manpower, recruitment, promotions, education and training, retirement, mobility, career management, management services, etc. It directly supervises the career management of individuals in certain classes. As regards the relationship between the two *directions*, the *direction de la fonction publique* concerns itself with pay and pensions through their effect on management, while the *direction du budget* concerns itself with anything that can be construed to have financial implications, and therefore has an interest in efficiency. It appears that the duality of responsibility works well. The existence of an independent department for the Civil Service has the effect in France that there is a positive force thinking of reforms and the interests of the service, and doing battle where necessary with the Ministry of Finance.

CONCLUSION

26. The French system produces highly professional elites on both the administrative and technical sides; their professionalism is maintained and constantly renewed by the flow of recruits who have undergone a high-powered, modern training. The elites are exclusive. It is difficult to enter them from within the Service except at the start of a career; and to do so requires intense preparation and a particular kind of higher education. We did not investigate the middle and lower levels of the Service, and cannot form a judgement on the extent to which a price has to be paid in the quality of the Service at these levels for the methods by which the elites are produced. But as to the quality of the elites themselves there is no doubt. They offer a highly attractive career, so eagerly sought after that the Service can pick from the cream of the educational output. It is an important feature of this system that elites export much talent to the upper reaches of other employments and that the methods by which they are selected and trained thus effectively serve a wider purpose than the manning of the higher Civil Service itself.

THE SWEDISH CIVIL SERVICE

The Chairman, Mr. Anderson, Sir James Dunnett, Dr. Hunt, Sir Norman Kipping, Mr. Neild, Mr. Sheldon and the Secretary visited Sweden from 6th to 9th February, 1967. This note sums up their main impressions.

THE MAIN FEATURE—THE SEPARATION OF MINISTRIES AND AGENCIES

2. The central government machine is very small. There are eleven Ministers with a total staff of not much more than 1,500 between them; the Ministry of Education, for example, has a staff of about 120. This is made possible by the fact that large blocks of work that would be done by government departments in Britain are entrusted to autonomous agencies in Sweden. The agencies include both commercial bodies (e.g. the Telecommunications Board) whose functions are similar to those of nationalised industries in Britain, and non-commercial bodies such as the National Schools Board and the National Labour Market Board.

3. The main function of the Ministry is to act as the Minister's secretariat; the staff advise the Minister on policy and draft briefs, speeches, parliamentary bills, etc. The execution of policy lies with the agencies. This separation enables the Minister and his closest advisers to concentrate on policy; and allocates executive responsibility to separate public bodies, each with its own accountable head. It also makes possible an enviable pattern of career management. The best young entrants to Ministries are employed straight away on secretarial work of high responsibility, rise quickly to the chief posts in the Ministry by the time they are about forty, and then commonly go out between the ages of forty-five and fifty to become the heads of agencies or to occupy senior positions in them. Ministers thus have as their chief advisers relatively young men and women who have energy and ideas and are capable of standing up resiliently to a high pressure of work. We noted that Ministries in Sweden do not have a single official head but (usually) three chief officers who are more or less co-equal —the Under Secretary who deals with policy, the Permanent Secretary who deals with administration and the Chief Legal Officer. The Under Secretary in particular is very close to the Minister and is generally a semi-political appointment.

4. The attractions of this system are great and clear. We considered its working under two broad heads:—
   (a) how the Swedish separation of functions works;
   (b) the pattern of staffing which it produces for the Swedish Civil Service.

HOW THE SEPARATION OF FUNCTIONS WORKS

5. The most striking feature of the system is that the Swedes do not rely upon a single, monolithic organisation, like a government department in the United Kingdom, both to make policy and to execute it. The responsibility is divided between two bodies, one close to the Minister, which is small, lively and staffed for the most part with younger men, the other with independent executive authority, which is larger and headed by older men with more managerial responsibilities. The distinction is not a clear one between policy-making and execution. Ideas come from many quarters, notably from the agencies themselves, which are regarded by Parliament and the public as responsible for their own field and are expected to be active in making policy proposals to their Ministries. The Ministries for their part are not absolved from all administrative work; in particular they deal with quite a lote of case-work and appeals. They may, within limits provided by parliamentary legislation, give agencies direct instructions about the way in which they execute policy, but they may not interfere with directives pertaining to a particular case; the handling of individual cases is the responsibility of the agencies, subject to appeal to the Ministry or to administrative courts where these are provided. The primary functions of each are thus distinct: the Ministry's to serve the Minister in his policy-making and legislative duties; the agency's to run and take public responsibility for executive operations.

6. The working of this system is regulated by law and conducted in the full light of publicity. The duties and responsibilities of the agencies are embodied in statutes or royal instructions. So is their structure and organisation; as an integral part of the

civil service, agencies, including the nationalised industries, have less freedom in this respect than British nationalised industries. The responsibilities of civil servants at all levels of the agencies are thus legally defined, and the agency civil servant is answerable to the courts for discharging them. As regards publicity, all official documents with limited exceptions are open to public inspection. An agency thus normally publishes the proposals it makes to a Ministry for a new policy, and always publishes its budget proposals. The responsibility then lies with the Ministry, which has not been consulted in advance, to accept or reject them, and give its reasons for doing so. Agencies thus have considerable power and influence; and their heads, who have great security of tenure, are major public figures in their own right.

7. This pattern of power and responsibility derives much from the political history and social characteristics of Sweden. It is a relatively small (less than eight millions) and very homogeneous society. There are big controversies, but the basis of the general consensus is remarkably wide. Political stability (the Social Democrats have been in power since 1932) means that the permanent heads of agencies have been matched by almost equally permanent Ministers, who know the business of their small departments inside out. The system of conducting government in public and on the basis of statute law produces a much narrower difference between Ministers and civil servants than in Britain; a Swedish civil servant may be a member of Parliament, and it is not thought surprising if, within certain limits, he speaks his mind on government policy in public.

THE STAFFING OF THE CIVIL SERVICE

8. The pattern of staffing that the structure produces nevertheless provides interesting comparisons with Britain. One of the most striking features is the young, expert and influential secretariat in each Ministry. Until recently these civil servants have been predominantly lawyers by training. Given the legal basis of Swedish administration, this was natural, and lawyers will continue to be needed in relatively large numbers (Ministries do a great deal of legal drafting). But there is now a considerable expansion in the recruitment of those with an education in political science and economics. In contrast to this country, arts graduates in Sweden rarely look for a career in Government service, and the Ministries for their part generally look for recruits with qualifications broadly relevant to their future work. It is however interesting to note that scientists and other specialists are not usually found in the Ministries; the Ministry of Health, for example, employs no doctors. The National Board of Health on the other hand employs many doctors in senior administrative positions; the present Director-General is a former university professor of medicine. Most Swedes thought this pattern was right; but a minority expressed an uneasy feeling that an important science-based approach was being missed in the Ministries and would be needed in future.

9. The able young men who rise quickly to top posts in the Ministries then go out to become heads or senior officers of important agencies in middle age. Others may also be exported to become provincial governors or directors of minor agencies. There is thus a constant flow through the Ministry secretariat; and the civil servant who is ceasing to make his full contribution to the policy-making process moves out to posts of high executive responsibility elsewhere. We noted that these civil servants do not receive professional management training before they move to this new kind of managerial work. We also thought it likely that the agencies would be at some disadvantage in their efforts to recruit and retain a fair share of the best talent if their top jobs were regularly reserved for imports from the Ministries. We found however that most people, in agencies as well as in Ministries, were well content with the system.

10. Otherwise, there is little movement, between Ministry and agency, between Ministries, between agencies or between the Civil Service and private employment. Relations between the private and public sectors, which are close, thus depend not upon movement but upon personal acquaintance and co-operation. The open system of government facilitates this; notably the practice of enlisting members of parliament from opposition parties, businessmen and trade unionists to serve on committees and the boards of agencies, and the tradition of exposing all questions for public comment before policy decisions are made.

11. The absence of internal movement reflects the fact that there is no central management of the Swedish Civil Service. A central Ministry is in charge of pay and the Ministry of Finance contains an Organisation and Methods Office. But no central body deals with recruitment, postings or promotions. Since a few years back, some limited training is under way; a small agency with limited resources was created in 1966 for training civil servants. The benefits of this system are that Ministries and agencies can recruit the men they need with a specific eye to the jobs to be filled, and that continuity produces a high expertise. Ministers and staff are both in their small departments for long enough to get to know each other intimately; a Minister can thus pick his closest advisers in full knowledge of the field. On the other hand, the absence of central recruitment produces competition in which some Ministries, e.g. the Ministry of Finance, regularly secure the best talent and some agencies do not get enough; we thought that the absence of central arrangements for subsequent movement would be apt to perpetuate this unevenness. Finally, dismissal is virtually unknown: a civil servant, once appointed, has a job for life.

CONCLUSION

12. The system of Ministries and agencies, the commanding feature of the Swedish structure, sets a high-powered and youthful secretariat for the Minister side by side with independent executive agencies within a political framework in which government is carried on in the open, the responsibility for innovation is widely diffused and policy-making is a matter of public debate. The staffing of the Civil Service is naturally designed to serve this system. Its main features are separate recruitment and staff management by each Ministry and agency, and the flow of able men from the secretariats to the executive agencies in middle age.

THE UNITED STATES CIVIL SERVICE

The Chairman and Sir Philip Allen spent five days in Washington in September 1966. In this note they record their main impressions of the United States Civil Service and give a brief summary of its structure.

STRUCTURE OF THE US CIVIL SERVICE

2. The structure of the Service is primarily governed by the Classification Act of 1949 and subsequent amendments. (The Classification Act, along with other personnel statutes, has been codified into Title V, United States Code.) The general purpose of the Act is to provide a plan for (i) pay rates and (ii) the classification of positions.

3. As regards (i), variations in rates of pay paid to different officers are, under the Act, to be in proportion to substantial differences in the difficulty and responsibility of, and the qualification required by, the work performed and to the contributions of officers to efficiency and economy in the Service. In determining the rate of pay the principle of equal pay for substantially equal work is followed (i.e. within the Service—the question of comparability with outside employment is touched on in paragraphs 10–13).

4. As regards (ii), the Act requires that individual positions, in accordance with their duties, responsibilities and qualification requirements, be so grouped and identified by classes and grades, and the various classes so described in published standards, that the resulting position-classification system can be used in all spheres of personnel administration. The term " position " is used to mean the work assignable to a particular officer. The term " class " includes all positions that are sufficiently similar, as to kind or subject-matter of work, level of difficulty and responsibility, and qualification requirements of the work, to warrant similar treatment in personnel and pay administration. The term " grade " includes all classes of positions that, although different in the kind or subject-matter of work, are sufficiently equivalent, in difficulty, responsibility and the level of qualification required, to warrant the inclusion of such

classes of positions within one range of rates of basic pay. In addition there are occupational groups embracing, generally, several series of classes or positions in associated or related occupations, professions or activities. A single grade will include persons from many occupational groups and they will often be at very different points in their own occupational hierarchy.

5. There are 18 grades in the Classification Act General Schedule, and posts are also classified by occupational groups. Thus the general administrative clerical and office services group is known as GS300 while the engineering and architecture group is GS800. These groups are broken down into series, so that GS305 is the mail and file series within the general administrative clerical and office services group. GS305-1 is the lowest level of file clerk while file supervisors may range up to GS305-9 or higher. GS810 is the civil engineering series within the engineering and architecture group. GS810-5 is the lowest grade of civil engineer. Civil engineers are also graded as 7 and 9 and in all the grades from 11 to 18.

6. The General Schedule includes the executive departments, the independent establishments and agencies in the executive branch, and such bodies as the Administrative Office of the United States Courts, and the Government Printing Office. It does not apply to the Field Service of the Post Office Department, the Foreign Service or industrial staff or to many of the dentists, doctors and nurses, college and school teachers, employed by the Federal Government. Also excluded from the General Schedule are posts above the level of GS18. These are known as Federal Executive posts and are listed in the Federal Executive Salary Act of 1964. This Act divides such posts into five salary levels. With some exceptions (especially at level V) these posts are outside the career service and tend to be filled by the administration in power, although they include many posts which in the United Kingdom would be civil service posts. Most of these appointments are subject to Presidential and Senate approval. Level I of the Federal Executive Salary Schedule includes Cabinet Ministers. Level II includes a number of heads of agencies and officers such as the Director of the Bureau of the Budget, the Chairman of the Atomic Energy Commission and some junior Ministers, but most Under Secretaries are in Level III together with a number of Chairmen of Boards and Commissions. Level IV includes the 11 Assistant Secretaries of State and a number of Assistant Secretaries in the other major departments. Level V includes a number of Heads of the more independent sections of the main departments and the less important independent departments. Below these senior posts covered by the Federal Executive Salary Act are the 18 grades in the General Schedule. Details of the salaries of officers covered by the Federal Executive Salary Act and of officers included in the General Schedule are in Note 1 at the end of this annex, which also shows the numbers of officers in the various grades.

7. In addition to positions under the General Schedule and the arrangements described in the last paragraph, there are about 800,000 Federal blue-collar workers who are paid at rates determined administratively in the light of local rates.

8. Apart from GS18, which has a fixed salary, all other grades in the General Schedule are paid on a scale which from GS1 to GS15 has 10 points. Progression within a grade by means of " within grade increase " is described in paragraph 15 below. The Civil Service Commission has issued elaborate classification standards indicating the kinds of positions which may be placed in the various classes and grades on the basis of duties, responsibilities and qualifications required. It is the concern of the agency or department, using the published standards, to determine the class and grade of individual jobs. If no published standards directly apply, agencies classify the positions consistently with published standards for related occupations. By periodic reviews and inspections the Commission determines if the agencies are correctly applying the accepted standards. The Commission has authority to revoke or suspend an agency's classification authority if necessary. With minor exceptions, the Commission classifies all positions in GS16, 17 and 18 for which grades no written standards have been published.

9. Two-fifths of the 1·1 million persons in GS positions are in GS3, 4 and 5 which contain the vast majority of clerical posts. Seventy per cent are in GS1 to 9. A very few supervisory clerical posts are found above this level. Only 10 per cent of the 1·1 million are in GS13 to 18. According to the law describing grades generally, GS1 to 3

are for different kinds of routine work of varying degrees of responsibility and difficulty, but not normally involving supervision. GS4 is the first grade for which minor supervisory experience is required and GS5 is the lowest grade which works under general supervision. GS5, 7 and 9 are the levels at which recent college graduates enter. A person with a Bachelor's Degree would normally enter GS5 or 7 and persons with a year's graduate study would enter GS7 or 9. Possession of a doctorate normally qualifies a person for entry to GS11, or in research posts GS12 if the person concerned holds special qualifications. Although the levels may range from GS7 to GS13, GS11 and 12 may be regarded as the most common journeyman levels for almost all professional and administrative positions. As described by law, GS13 includes assistant heads of major organisations within a department or doing comparable work under administrative direction, with wide latitude for the exercise of independent judgement, work of unusual difficulty and responsibility along special technical, supervisory or administrative lines, requiring extended specialised, supervisory, or administrative training and experience which has demonstrated leadership and marked attainments. GS14 includes heads of major organisations within a Bureau. In practice, both GS13 and GS 14 include many kinds of positions, both supervisory and non-supervisory.

10. The Federal Salary Reform Acts of 1962 and 1964 made major changes both in the levels of salaries and the means of fixing them. For the first time the Federal Government adopted a policy of comparability with private enterprise rates for the same level of work. Moreover the 1962 Act reaffirmed the principle of internal alignment, i.e. equal pay for substantially equal work and pay distinctions in keeping with work and performance distinction. This is fundamental to the Classification Act, but since World War II there had been many piecemeal pay adjustments which had gradually eroded much of this concept.

11. Comparability of pay with private enterprise was established by the 1962 Act. It is based on " national average rates " for about eighty occupational classes, made up of salaries in about eighty areas. This information is collected and analysed by the Bureau of Labour Statistics. Each of these classes can be matched with a particular Classification Act grade. From a number of such national average rates fitting a particular grade, a " grade average " is determined. This is then related to other grade averages and if necessary the resulting pay line covering all grades is smoothed out to give regular progressions. The resulting figure for each grade is then used, as the fourth point or rate on the scale. The survey is thus not, like our Pay Research Unit Survey, based on a study of particular posts the results of which are applied to particular classes, but on statistical averages which are then applied to service-wide grades.

12. The President has to report annually to Congress a comparison of Federal and private enterprise pay rates as revealed by the analysis of the Bureau of Labour Statistics survey results. He is also required to include in his reports any recommendations on Federal pay or pay policy he considers advisable. He must secure the views of employee organisations on these proposals.

13. Under the 1962 Act, GS1 to 7 were given fully comparable salary rates in two stages and GS8 to 15 partially comparable rates. The latter were increased so as to come nearer still to comparability under the 1964 Act. Although the 1962 Act gave an increase of salary to GS16, 17 and 18, it did not apply the principle of comparability at this level. The Senate Committee instead recommended that these salaries should be reviewed in conjunction with Federal Executive salaries outside the General Schedule, particularly as otherwise top civil servants would be paid more than their chiefs in the Cabinet. This was done under the 1964 Act, but the rates for GS16 to 18 were based not on the Bureau of Labour Statistics survey as this does not cover staff at this level, but on projections of the salaries of lower grades, i.e. on the principle of internal alignment rather than comparability. It is recognised that because of the high rates of pay at this level outside the government service full comparability cannot apply.

14. The 1962 Act also established clear relationships between the General Schedule and other Federal salary systems such as the Postal Field Service Schedule, the Foreign Service Schedule and those applying to medical staff. Although the Bureau of Labour Statistics survey does not cover occupations comparable with posts in these schedules

the fact that they are closely linked with the General Schedule means that changes in private enterprise rates affect them indirectly.

15. Increments, known as "within-grade increases", are not paid on an annual basis, but are granted at varying intervals depending on the time spent in the grade and on performance on the job. Under the 1962 Act the rule is that all grades move from rate 1 to 2 after a year, and to rate 3 after another year. They spend two years on rates 4, 5 and 6 and three years on rates 7, 8 and 9. This system was evolved because it is recognised that the greatest increase in work proficiency occurs during the earliest period of service at any grade level. But in addition agencies can grant within-grade increases based on "high-quality performance" above that ordinarily found in the position concerned. Such increases cannot be given more than once a year.

16. Recruitment is normally to the minimum salary of the grade concerned, but the 1964 Act permits a rate above the minimum rate of the grade to be offered to unusually well-qualified candidates for appointments to positions in grade GS11 or above. As the scales of GS grades overlap, promotees do not necessarily start at the minimum. They are guaranteed a pay increase at least as large as two "within-grade increases" in the grade from which they are promoted and if necessary can be paid the top rate of their new grade.

17. The Civil Service Commission directs the recruitment and examination of candidates for Federal posts, most of whom enter the civil service on a permanent basis. Agencies however decide how particular posts will be filled, e.g. by promotion, transfer or recruitment. When an agency decides to make an original appointment, a list is passed to the agency of names of qualified persons (in order of merit) who have passed the examination (or competition—a written test is not necessarily part of the examination). The agency has to take one of the first three. The Commission also holds examinations to fill actual or expected vacancies. Much of this work of announcing examinations, rating candidates, and maintaining lists of eligibles is done throughout the country by inter-agency boards of Civil Service examiners, operated by the Civil Service Commission.

18. Most members of the Civil Service are recruited on a permanent basis, but the career-conditional appointment system was introduced in 1955 to give staffing flexibility during expansions and contractions of work resulting from limited emergencies and to assure stability of the career service. Career-conditional appointees have to pass the open competitive "examinations" and are selected for posts in regular order from lists of eligibles. After that they have fewer rights than the permanent staff if redundancy occurs. In addition appointments to strictly temporary jobs may be made for periods not exceeding a year. Also if there is no list of eligibles, conditional appointments can be made, pending the establishment of such a list. Under a recent law, these conditional appointments may ripen into appointments with full career standing in three years. Temporary appointments are also made for jobs of a project nature that will be completed within four years.

SOME IMPRESSIONS

19. Attention is drawn in this paragraph to some of the more striking differences, in this context, between the two countries.

(a) There is no sharp distinction, such as we have, between the political head of a department and the top officials—between the Minister who publicly speaks on policy issues and the officials who do not. The "Minister" is not a member of Congress, and may not even be a professional politician. In this country we occasionally bring in outsiders to head departments as Ministers but when we do they have to become politicians and be provided with a parliamentary seat.

(b) The separation of powers is a very real thing. The legislature has its own staff.

(c) A good deal is prescribed by law in a very detailed form—for example, the total number permitted in certain grade 16, 17 and 18 positions, and salaries. (Positions in the scientific and engineering categories are not restricted by law.) There are those who would see advantage in altering the law so as to produce something corresponding to the British Administrative Class but there would be no likelihood of doing so, since the legislature is firmly set against anything

143

F

which tends towards establishing an exclusive elite. This is putting an extreme example: but it is a matter of history that the recommendations of the second Hoover Commission for the setting up of a senior Civil Service were not accepted.

(*d*) " Agencies " proliferate on a considerable scale, and they may or may not eventually be brought together under one ministerial head—as was happening at the time of our visit in the proposals for a new Department of Transportation, which to a large extent was taking over a number of agencies that have so far had a more or less independent existence. Nor is there always a straightforward hierarchical set-up within a department. Sometimes separate units continue to have a pretty well self-contained existence (for example the FBI and the Federal Bureau of Prisons within the Department of Justice); and at the Treasury, which is a much more unified structure than some, the departmental chart shows that something like fourteen people report direct to the Secretary to the Treasury, although in practice arrangements are made to ensure that some of them trouble him very little.

20. This paragraph summarises some comments on the US Civil Service at the time of the 1966 visit.

(1) The US Civil Service was an open Civil Service in that entry could take place at many levels. Although statistically most of the higher civil servants entered at relatively low levels, nevertheless the intake to the Service direct to the higher levels, and at later ages, was on a significant scale.

(2) It was a striking feature of the Service that a number of the top posts (including some which in this country would be filled by permanent civil servants) were filled by " in-and-outers "—people who come into the Government for a period of perhaps three years and then go back to private life in some form or other, to be available however for some future political appointment. It was still a feature of the organisation (and this was an underlying reason for the creation of the posts in Schedule C—see Note 1) that the bureaucracy should be made politically responsive to political leadership. But it was very much an over-simplification to think of the US system as being simply a dual system, in which a rather thin layer of political appointees rested on a substantial body of civil servants. The position was much more complicated than this. A number of top posts were indeed filled by political appointees from outside; but there was an even greater number of " political appointees " from within the Civil Service ranks, and movement to and fro blurred the sharpness of the distinction between appointees from outside on the one hand and civil servants on the other.

(3) In the main, the highest civil servants were in the " super grades " (grades 16 to 18). There were some 4,430 of them—394 in grade 18; 893 in grade 17; and 3,147 in grade 16. But there were a few top civil servants to be found in Level V of the Federal Executive appointments. Most of the Level V appointments (totalling 475 in all) were political appointments subject to Presidential and Senate approval, but not all. The executive head of the Civil Service Commission—the top civil servant there—was Level V, whereas the Chairman, a political appointee, was Level III.

(4) Some 11 per cent of the " super grade " appointments, and a few appointments above grade 18, were " Schedule C " posts. Quite a number of these were professional civil servants who had gone into Schedule C at their peril. There were 1,600 " Schedule C " appointments in all. These were not straight political appointments. They were described as a buffer zone between the political appointee and the professional civil servant. Those in Schedule C were either personal and confidential assistants to the head of an agency; or advisers on policy; or holders of posts which called for public advocacy of controversial programmes. The Civil Service Commission always had to approve that a particular post should be placed in Schedule C and that a particular individual nominated for a grade 16-18 post could be appointed to it—but in doing so the only test they applied was whether he had the right qualifications. Most of the 1,600 posts were " confidential " ones (e.g.

personal secretaries) and only a minority were " policy-determining " posts, but most of this minority was to be found in grades 16-18 and above. (Schedule C was however about to be abolished for the super grades and replaced by " non-career executive assignments ".)

(5) Many persons coming into the Civil Service at the entry level had to take only an intelligence test (other than specialists, such as doctors). Others, such as stenographers and typists, had to take performance tests. These were organised by the Civil Service Commission. But the appointment was made by the agency. There was an important exception to the general rule that entrants had to take only an intelligence test: those who wanted to come in as " management interns " (formerly known as " junior management assistants ") had in addition to take a general knowledge test. Recruitment of these management interns had fallen off to not much more than 200 in a year, but it was hoped to get the total back to 500 or 600. No individual agency could hire one of these management interns unless it had a training plan for him which the Civil Service Commission had approved: and the limitation so far has been not the lack of funds but of suitable jobs in the agencies. There was a considerable wastage among management interns. A lot of them went off after a few years to jobs outside the government service.

(6) The Federal Civil Service did not get enough high-quality scientists and engineers. The Federal Goverment put out a tremendous amount of scientific and engineering work to the universities, without attempting to do this work within the Service. Where the Service did well for recruitment was in the areas where they were producing expensive hardware of a kind not met within the private sector; and where very large-scale equipment was needed as, for example, in cosmic research. They did well too in the recruitment of economists, because the government service itself provided interesting work and career prospects which compared well with outside, and, unlike the position in the physical sciences, the Government did not finance any big support programme in the social sciences in the universities.

(7) One interesting development was the White House Fellowship scheme. This involved taking a number of people, mainly from the universities, and allocating them to jobs of personal assistant, or something like this, to people near the top of the hierarchy, for a year. The hope was to take in about eighteen a year. This was not so much a recruitment device as a means of spreading greater knowledge about government among the intellectual community, although a number of those who had come in the early days of the scheme wanted to stay on in government when their year's fellowship was up. This scheme was not financed from Federal funds, but by private foundations.

(8) Training was a responsibility of the agencies, but the Civil Service Commission provided central courses to which members of the agencies could go—on payment by the agency. The Commission were running short elementary courses in management, and were also thinking of setting up some form of staff college for those in their forties. An Act had been passed in 1958 putting duties on the Civil Service Commission to promote and to co-ordinate training. Very little money had however been made available, so that progress had been slow. But things were on the move.

(9) There was a good deal of concern that there was not enough mobility between agencies on the part of civil servants, and it too often happened that a specialised agency was run by an expert who had never seen life outside his bureau. A specialised civil servant who reached top management within his agency could find life somewhat uncomfortable if he found that he had to justify something to a Congressional sub-committee and had to answer questions, not in terms which were comprehensible only to members of his profession but in language that made political sense to the questioner. To meet these difficulties, the Civil Service Commission were in course of producing a new " executive assignment system ". This involved preparing a fairly elaborate inventory of promising people inside and outside the public service, and

requiring the various agencies to examine names on this list when making top appointments, instead of simply promoting their own people. This represented the limit of what the Civil Service Commission could do without an alteration in the law.

(10) As regards job classification, the Civil Service Commission explained that they issued detailed guidance on this but that it was not for them to operate this guidance. This was for the agencies. But all the agencies were inspected from time to time by the Commission, and one of the prime purposes of this examination was to ascertain whether the agency had a proper organisation to apply these job-classification principles. The risk of " grade escalation " (that is, the tendency for jobs to be more highly graded than the classifier deems necessary on his criteria) had always to be watched for.

(11) A number of those consulted thought that there were probably too many grades in the hierarchy, although in practice there was a good deal of skipping of the grades. There was a good deal of criticism of the restrictions on total numbers put by the Bureau of the Budget on those in grade 15, and by law on those in grades 16 to 18. The point was frequently taken also that the rates of pay in the super grades were too low. Lower down, regard was had to what was paid in comparable employment outside, but the scales were kept down at the top.

(12) There was a good deal of disquiet that the rates of pay in the upper grades (which, as explained in the previous paragraph, are not based on direct comparability with outside employment) were too low to attract the brightest recruits.

(13) An employee was entitled to a within-grade increase only if it was determined that he was performing at an " acceptable level of competence ". Each department head had the authority, which he might delegate, to decide what constituted an acceptable level of competence and if the employee met it. An employee whose level of competence was determined to be unacceptable had certain appeal rights to the Civil Service Commission. On the basis of a sample number of employees in 1966, it was found that less than 1 per cent of employees eligible were denied within-grade increases.

(14) Generally, an employee might appeal at any time (through a representative, if he wished) in regard to the class or grade of his position. He could make his appeal either to his agency or to the Civil Service Commission or both.

(15) Employee organisation impact on personnel policies and practices was variable. Where salaries and other conditions of employment were fixed by the Congress these matters were not subject to negotiation. However, when the Civil Service Commission was developing classification and qualification standards or was preparing pay legislation for the President to submit to Congress, for example, the comments of employee organisations were solicited and taken into consideration along with those of other interested parties. (A Commission survey in November 1967 showed that 45 per cent or 1,238,748 of all Federal employees had exclusive representation by labour organisations.)

(16) The superannuation arrangements for the Civil Service were fairly generous, but did not appear to provide any new solution to the problem of transfer with outside employment, although it was to be noted that a civil servant who put in a certain number of years and then left had pretty well an absolute right to return if he wanted to do so later on. It was noticeable that there was little interchange between Federal and state employment.

NOTE 1

I. *Federal Employees Salary Rates*

1.

Level I	$35,000
Level II	$30,000
Level III	$29,500
Level IV	$28,750
Level V	$28,000

2. For convenience, the General Schedule salaries are set out, not as they were at the time of the visit, but as for July 1968. (See page 149.)

3. There are separate scales for postal field service employees, medical directors, physicians, dentists and nurses and for the Foreign Service.

II. *Distribution by grades of full-time employees in the General Schedule grades, 30th June, 1967*

	Number	Per cent
1	4,039	0·3
2	56,498	4·5
3	157,986	12·6
4	181,367	14·5
5	154,662	12·4
6	59,377	4·7
7	109,044	8·7
8	17,661	1·4
9	134,165	10·7
10	15,623	1·2
11	128,699	10·3
12	101,536	8·1
13	75,090	6·0
14	34,455	2·8
15	17,003	1·4
16	3,129	0·2
17	903	0·1
18	366	negligible
Total	1,251,603	100·0

III. *Federal civilian employment, by type of appointment, in the United States* 30th June, 1964 (including Postal Field Service and other posts not covered by the General Schedule)

1. *Competitive Appointments*

Career	Per cent	Career Conditional	Per cent	Temporary	Per cent	Total
1,744,892	82	285,024	13	96,654	5	2,126,570

2. *Excepted Appointments*

Permanent	Per cent	Other	Per cent	Total
109,673	50	108,036	50	217,709

A considerable proportion of the excepted appointments were to posts excepted by action of the Civil Service Commission. These fell into a number of categories listed in three Schedules. Relatively few were true patronage jobs.

Particulars of the Schedules are as follows:

A. Positions for which it is not practicable to hold any examinations: chaplains; professional and technical experts for temporary consultation purposes; narcotics agents for undercover work; certain part-time, seasonal and temporary positions particularly at isolated localities; and attorneys. There are 115,000 positions in this Schedule.

B. Positions for which it is practicable to hold only " non-competitive examinations ": e.g. positions in the intelligence services of the armed forces.

C. Includes positions whose occupants serve in a policy-determining or confidential capacity to the politically appointed heads of agencies, and which are normally filled by the administration in power. There are about 1,600 jobs in this Schedule. Departments may recommend to the Commission that a post be placed in this Schedule if they feel the duties assigned are either policy-determining or require the incumbent to serve in a confidential relationship to a key official. If the Commission regards these conditions as satisfied the position can be authorised.

Over one-half of the excepted posts are excepted by statute rather than by the action of the Civil Service Commission. They include posts with the Veterans Administration (some 40,000), the Tennessee Valley Authority, Atomic Energy Commission and the Federal Bureau of Investigation.

Also the positions of approximately 75,000 foreign nationals overseas have been excepted by the President.

General Schedule Salaries
Annual rates and within-grade steps
1968

	1	2	3	4	5	6	7	8	9	10
	$	$	$	$	$	$	$	$	$	$
GS-1	3,889	4,019	4,149	4,279	4,408	4,538	4,668	4,798	4,928	5,057
2	4,231	4,372	4,513	4,655	4,796	4,937	5,078	5,219	5,360	5,501
3	4,600	4,753	4,907	5,060	5,214	5,367	5,521	5,674	5,828	5,981
4	5,145	5,316	5,487	5,658	5,829	6,000	6,171	6,342	6,513	6,684
5	5,732	5,924	6,115	6,307	6,498	6,690	6,881	7,073	7,265	7,456
6	6,321	6,532	6,743	6,955	7,166	7,377	7,588	7,799	8,010	8,221
7	6,981	7,214	7,447	7,680	7,913	8,146	8,379	8,612	8,845	9,078
8	7,699	7,956	8,213	8,470	8,727	8,984	9,241	9,498	9,755	10,012
9	8,462	8,744	9,026	9,308	9,590	9,872	10,154	10,436	10,718	11,000
10	9,297	9,607	9,917	10,227	10,537	10,847	11,157	11,467	11,777	12,087
11	10,203	10,543	10,883	11,223	11,563	11,903	12,243	12,583	12,923	13,263
12	12,174	12,580	12,986	13,392	13,798	14,204	14,610	15,016	15,422	15,828
13	14,409	14,889	15,369	15,849	16,329	16,809	17,289	17,769	18,249	18,729
14	16,946	17,511	18,076	18,641	19,206	19,771	20,336	20,901	21,466	22,031
15	19,780	20,439	21,098	21,757	22,416	23,075	23,734	24,393	25,052	25,711
16	22,835	23,596	24,357	25,118	25,879	26,640	27,401	28,162*	28,923*	
17	26,264	27,139	28,014*	28,889*	29,764*					
18	30,239*									

*These rates show the increases half way to comparability with private enterprise levels as required by section 212 of the Federal Salary Act of 1967, but section 216 of that law provides that no rate shall be increased to an amount in excess of the salary rate for Level V of the Executive Salary Schedule. Consequently, the salary for employees at these rates is limited to the rate for Level V of the Executive Salary Schedule, now $28,000.

APPENDIX D

PROBLEMS OF THREE SPECIALIST GROUPS:
ACCOUNTANTS, LAWYERS AND RESEARCH OFFICERS

It will be clear from the main body of our report that the position of specialists in the Civil Service is in our view one of the main problems that the Service has to solve. We have made proposals for change under a wide variety of heads. In general, these proposals apply to all groups of specialists alike, and thus cover most of what we have to say about them.

2. On three groups, however, accountants, lawyers and Research Officers, we have further comments and proposals which are not adequately covered by the general terms of the report. We make them in this appendix.

I. ACCOUNTANTS

3. In Chapter 2 we refer to accounting as an example of a specialist skill where the Civil Service has not recruited sufficient qualified people nor deployed them in positions of proper responsibility. In this appendix we develop this point at rather greater length.

4. We have received much evidence. The report of the Management Consultancy Group discusses the present role and status of the accountant (Volume 2, paragraphs 125-135). We have received papers from the Treasury (Volume 5, No. 9) and the Institution of Professional Civil Servants (Volume 5, No. 45), and taken oral evidence from the former. We have also taken evidence (oral and written) from the Accountants Joint Parliamentary Committee (Volume 5, Nos. 51 and 52) and (written) from the Institute of Cost and Works Accountants (Volume 5, No. 89). The basic facts relating to the Accountant Class are set out in the Treasury's Introductory Factual Memorandum, Chapter 9 (Volume 4, No. 1).

5. There can be no doubt that the present position is unsatisfactory and calls for substantial and early improvement.

6. In general the Service has failed to take advantage of important developments in industry and commerce during recent years. There, it is generally accepted that accounting is no longer a matter of book-keeping but of financial management in its widest sense. Internal audit is no longer a matter of routine but is an important element in management services aimed at increasing the effectiveness and efficiency of an organisation; and it is recognised that training and experience in accountancy can fit the right man for the highest managerial posts. In the Service, on the other hand, the role of the accountant is narrowly conceived. Accounting is still mainly concerned with the procedures of cash accounting carried out by the Executive Class under the direction, where necessary, of the Administrative Class. Professional accountants are employed mainly in work involving commercial accounting within a department or concerned with the financial operations of commercial organisations; examples are given in the Treasury's paper and in the report of the Management Consultancy Group.

7. This point can be put still more forcefully. In spite of the vast increase in expenditure by the public sector—much of it under the control of the Civil Service—there are posts for only 309 qualified accountants in the entire Service out of the 25,000 qualified accountants who make up the accountancy profession in this country. Of these 309 posts, none carries a salary over £4,500; six carry salaries above £3,650. Salaries for staff of the right qualification and competence are seriously out of line with those in the outside world.

8. Thus, at a time when qualified accountants are in increasing demand throughout industry and commerce, the Service can offer neither work of a sufficiently high level nor career prospects of sufficient attraction to bring in good men and women with these important qualifications and to pay them competitive salaries.

9. This is partly the result of a deliberate decision on the part of the management of the Service. It is the practice to employ private accountancy firms for major jobs outside the normal routine. There is much sense in this. It would be wrong for the Service to try to be self-sufficient in this field, and there is positive advantage in bringing in accountants from outside from time to time, especially because methods and skills are constantly changing. We do not propose that this practice should be discontinued. But it ought not to be a substitute for a strong force of highly-qualified professional accountants within the Service.

10. Some of the areas in which more qualified accountants are needed are:—

(a) *In the Senior Policy and Management Group.* In industry qualified accountants play a full role in top management since through their training and experience they can contribute much to the solution of major problems. While the Service differs from industry in a number of important respects, we believe that it should follow this example.

(b) *In purchasing.* The public sector is becoming an increasingly important purchaser of goods and services. The Government has decided that public purchasing shall be used to support its economic and financial policies, including regional policies. It is in the general interest that purchasing by the public sector should be carried out with maximum efficiency. The qualified accountant can offer much to achieve this end, particularly in relation to the problems of pricing.

(c) *In developing accountable and responsible management.* In Chapter 5 we referred to the need to develop costing and control procedures to ensure that management has clear objectives against which performance can be measured. Sound accounting skills will be needed to achieve this purpose.

(d) *In management services.* Again in Chapter 5 we have recommended the expansion of management services throughout the Civil Service. In industry the qualified accountant has a central role in management services including regular efficiency audits. A similar role can be played in the Service.

11. We realise that there is a national shortage of qualified accountants and that it will take time to build up an adequate team of first-class talent. But we urge the Service to push ahead rapidly. Although the best training for an accountant is often to be found in the broader experience of private practice, the Service ought in a period of national shortage to be able to help itself by producing some of its own talent. For example, we should like to see trainee accountants articled to members of the profession within government departments. We also suggest that a number of entrants with " A level " or their equivalent should be encouraged to take professional qualifications in accounting and that success in achieving these qualifications should be rewarded with additional increases in pay. We also suggest that the work now done by qualified accountants already in the Service should be examined to see whether some of it could not be devolved upon less qualified staff, thus freeing qualified accountants for posts of higher responsibility.

12. We propose that accountants should continue to be an identifiable occupational group within the Service. The group should include cost and works accountants. The national institutions representing the accountancy profession and the cost and works accountants are currently discussing a merger. As will be clear from the rest of our report, our thinking is very much in line with the conception of more broadly-based groupings of this kind.

13. In recommending a much wider role and greater responsibility for the qualified accountant, we do not wish to be understood as implying that the accountant should be regarded as having a unique claim to the work of financial management. The much-needed increase in their numbers will be no substitute for the necessity of ensuring that managers at all levels have an appropriate understanding of the importance of sound financial management especially in decision-taking and control.

14. We also wish to emphasise the need for broader training, not only in the accountant's early years (when most of it will take place outside and often before entry to the Service), but also at intervals during his Civil Service career. Our witnesses

have laid great stress on this in oral evidence. Especially in management services new techniques are developing so quickly that a man will become out of date unless he undergoes regular re-training. For the same reason our witnesses thought, and we agree, that this is work for relatively young men; we doubt if qualified accountants (or others) should stay in high-level management services much beyond the age of 50. We think too that accounting is a field in which movement between the Service and other employments can be especially valuable in order to ensure that the methods of the Service remain up to date. Late entry and temporary appointments of the kind discussed in general terms in Chapter 4 should be encouraged.

15. There should be adequate central management of accountants, as of other specialist staff, by the Civil Service Department. Accountants will remain scarce and will continue to be distributed among a number of departments in relatively small numbers. A properly developed system of planned movement and wider career opportunities will be essential to attract the right men.

II. LAWYERS

16. There is a brief account of the Legal Class in Chapter 27 of the Introductory Factual Memorandum (Volume 4, No. 1). Memoranda from the Treasury (Volume 5, No. 10) and from the Civil Service Legal Society (Volume 5, No. 26) are the main written evidence that we have received. We discussed the problems of the legal service with the Treasury Solicitor and with the Civil Service Legal Society.

17. The Legal Class is one of the most long-standing professional groups in the Civil Service. The tasks and responsibilities placed upon it and the contribution it can make to administration are continually increasing. There is a serious shortage of lawyers in the Service. Our proposals are designed to improve the career management of lawyers as an occupational group and to give them the opportunity to make a wider contribution to the work of the Service.

ORGANISATION OF THE LEGAL SERVICE

18. We agree with the idea put forward in paragraph 9 of the Treasury memorandum that there should be a greater degree of central management and a better integration of the legal Civil Service in England and Wales. The need for central management applies to lawyers as much as to any other group of staff. At present, as the Treasury memorandum shows, legal staff are irregularly distributed among a large number of departments. The opportunities for promotion vary between them. We should like to see more lawyers moving between departments and more branching out from the strict field of their specialisation to take a full part in the work of policy-making and administration.

19. We have considered what form the central management should take. At present the Treasury Solicitor, as the head of the department employing the largest numbers of legal staff, is to some extent the unofficial head of the legal profession in the Service, and some small-scale exchanges of staff are effected by his good offices. There is also a management committee under Treasury chairmanship with an overall concern for the problems of the class. We think that the role of the Treasury Solicitor should be expanded and put on to a formal basis as Head of the Legal Service. It is appropriate that this post should be held by a lawyer, and since the management alone of a service of this size would not constitute a job that carried the necessary standing, it should in our view be combined with an active legal post at the top of the profession. The Treasury Solicitor will however need support in this additional task; he cannot be expected, in addition to his heavy legal duties, to devote a great deal of time to managing the service. We suggest therefore that the management committee should continue to function and that consideration should be given to including a representative of the legal service (as of other specialist groups—see Chapter 7) in the staff of the Civil Service Department, with any necessary supporting staff.

20. This proposal does not mean that all departmental legal branches should be brought into the Treasury Solicitor's Office or that he should assume responsibility for their work. Departments should have normal control over their legal branches. The central management of the legal service should, however, have a general concern with

all questions of staff, including recruitment, training and career development, and it should be responsible for thinking constructively about improvements in organisation and methods of work. In short, in the balance of responsibility between departments and central management, the general principles laid down in Chapter 7 should be applied in this particular case.

21. Both the Treasury (paragraph 17 of their memorandum) and the Civil Service Legal Society (paragraph 13 of their memorandum) have proposed that certain kinds of legal work, such as conveyancing and litigation, should be centralised. This would mean that the remaining legal branches in other departments would consist largely of lawyers engaged in giving legal advice on the policy of the department. We agree with this proposal, which should improve efficiency and the economic use of staff, in particular by permitting greater devolution of work to sub-professional staff and making possible better career opportunities (see paragraph 25 below).

22. The legal service that we propose in the preceding paragraphs would be for England and Wales. Scotland should clearly continue to have a separate legal service organised on similar lines. The supplementary note of the Civil Service Legal Society draws attention to the problems of the legal service in Scotland. Many of them are similar to those of England and Wales and should be similarly dealt with, with suitable adaptations to meet circumstances in Scotland.

RECRUITMENT

23. The Treasury (paragraph 4 of their memorandum) and the Civil Service Legal Society (paragraphs 7 and 8 of their memorandum) set out the recruitment position. The figures are worrying in themselves and more so when account is taken of the age-structure of the class, with a high proportion reaching retirement in the next ten years. The witnesses have indicated that there is also cause for concern about the quality of recruits. The Treasury say that there is a special problem of recruiting very able lawyers for advisory work. The background to the problem of recruitment is a national shortage of lawyers. As with the other classes of the Service, we have not examined whether the Service offers competitive rates of pay for lawyers. We have however received evidence about the career opportunities. We accept the Treasury's argument (paragraph 11 of their memorandum) that higher-grade posts are only justified by higher-grade work. In our view the right approach is to devolve as much work as possible to staff who are not fully qualified lawyers; this should help to limit the demand within the Service for these scarce qualifications. Career opportunities should then be widened by stimulating movement between departments and by ensuring that lawyers who have the aptitude and inclination to move into more general policy and management work are given the opportunity and the necessary training. We hope that a bigger flow of young lawyers will thus be attracted to the Service.

24. We think too that the Service should seek to help itself in overcoming the recruit-ment problem by producing some of its own qualified lawyers. At present all recruits to the legal service have already obtained their qualifications outside the Service. This will always have to be the principal source of lawyers, because the Service needs men and women with general experience of the law. Nevertheless, we think that civil servants with the right aptitudes and interests should have the opportunity to acquire the qualifications to join the legal service. The contribution that this would make to the supply of lawyers would no doubt be limited. But it would be well worth having. We welcome the Treasury's proposal (paragraph 18 of their memorandum) that experienced legal executive staff should be encouraged and assisted to read for the Bar, and, if successful, brought into the professional legal service. We also hope that ways and means can be found of attaching articled clerks to qualified solicitors serving in government departments.

THE USE OF NON-PROFESSIONAL STAFF

25. The Civil Service Legal Society have proposed the creation of a separate class of legal executives (paragraphs 15-17 of their memorandum). We cannot accept this proposal, which is not compatible with our recommendations for the abolition of separate classes. It would not in any case solve what we take to be the essence of the problem, that is, the provision of reasonable career opportunities for legal executives.

153

We are, however, very much in sympathy with the thinking underlying the Society's proposal. We favour more specialisation among executive staff. We are particularly in favour of it among those who work in support of professional staff, because it gives the qualified specialists the reliable, experienced backing they need, enables them to concentrate on the work for which they have been specially trained, and produces a more economic use of skilled manpower and a source of greater job-satisfaction for all concerned. We recommend therefore that legal executive work should be recognised as a specialism and that administrative staff should be encouraged to take it up. They should be given proper training and career development as specialists; and encouragement and reward should be given for the acquisition of sub-professional legal qualifications as well as for the full qualifications we have discussed above. The greater devolution of work to sub-professional staff and the centralisation of certain kinds of legal work that we have recommended should, we hope, enable the Service to provide attractive opportunities for promotion in this field.

THE PLACE OF LAWYERS IN ADMINISTRATION

26. It is most desirable that lawyers should play their full part in the consideration and formulation of policy. We suspect that practice in this matter now varies a good deal between departments. In our view, close co-operation and discussion between lawyers and administrators should be a regular part of policy-making. This should be a mutually enriching process from which the public interest would gain. While administration in this country is less juridical than in many others, there is a legal element in many administrative questions; it needs to be taken fully into account at an early stage. A good lawyer with deep experience of the affairs of his department can therefore make a valuable contribution to the policy-forming work in his department.

27. In so far as this is a matter of structure and organisation, it should be assisted by our proposal in Chapter 6 for a unified Senior Policy and Management Group in departments, of which, of course, the senior lawyers will be members. We hope that a reality will be made of their membership of the group and that they will be regarded as being concerned with the affairs of the Department at large. As the Civil Service Legal Society agreed in discussion with us, this will require some change of attitudes on both sides. While we think too that some, though perhaps not many, lawyers will wish to be considered for jobs of a more general administrative or managerial character, and that it is important that those with the desire and aptitude should be encouraged to do so, we wish to lay special emphasis on the need for a wider concept of the contribution that lawyers can make as lawyers to the problems of modern administration.

III. RESEARCH OFFICERS

28. The Research Officer Class are employed in the collection, analysis, interpretation and appreciation of information mainly in the field of the social sciences; they prepare studies, reports and surveys. They are principally employed in the intelligence branches of the Ministry of Defence, in the Home Office, in the Ministry of Housing and Local Government, in the Ministry of Technology and in the Board of Trade. They are a graduate class, requiring a first or second-class honours degree, or a post-graduate or research degree, in geography, economics, statistics, sociology or other appropriate subject. There is a brief account of the class, its duties, numbers, pay, structure and recruitment in Chapter 39 of the Introductory Factual Memorandum (Volume 4, No. 1).

29. Research Officers were investigated by the Management Consultancy Group; the findings are set out in paragraphs 136-147 of their report (Volume 2). Several serious criticisms were made of the present use made of the Research Officers and it was found that their status and prospects were unduly depressed. This latter point was also made by the Institution of Professional Civil Servants in their memorandum on a Social Scientist Group (Volume 5, No. 39).

30. Research is not the exclusive preserve of the Research Officer Class in the Civil Service. Apart from research in science and technology, which is of course carried out by appropriate specialists, research is from time to time part of the job of economists, statisticians, and other specialists. Much of this research has achieved a high reputation. Nevertheless, research on social and some economic matters has been

relatively neglected; the Service has only recently and slowly begun to fill the gaps. The position of the Research Officer Class reflects this neglect.

31. The main features that illustrate the unsatisfactory position of Research Officers are as follows:—

   (*a*) They are often poorly used and confined to a back-room role too far removed from the main stream of policy decisions.

   (*b*) The work they are asked to do is frequently of a quality below their capabilities.

   (*c*) They are often without routine clerical assistance.

   (*d*) Their career prospects in their class are inferior to those of the Economist Class for which the recruitment requirements are similar and also to those of the Administrative Class (fuller details on this point are given in paragraphs 144-146 of the report of the Management Consultancy Group).

32. We have recommended in Chapter 5 that the policy-planning function of departments should be considerably strengthened and that research should be recognised as an essential component of this work. Thus, we have suggested the creation of Planning Units headed by Senior Policy Advisers. We have considered whether, when the research function is strengthened in the ways we have proposed, there will still be a need to recruit a special group of staff to do research work. It could be argued that this need would disappear in the social and economic areas of the Service. We are recommending that administrators should cease to be untrained " generalists " whose knowledge of the subject-matter of their jobs is limited to what they pick up in the course of a brief tenure. Under our proposals, administrators will be thoroughly trained in appropriate disciplines. Their careers will be planned to enable them to become really familiar with the subjects on which they are working. In the course of their training some of them will acquire an understanding of research methods and techniques. Some of the best will serve for substantial periods at a relatively early stage of their careers in the Planning Units. In short, administrators will have a much better appreciation and understanding of research, of its scope and limitations, its methods, its evaluation; many will have done it. In our view, however, this does not mean that special research staff can be dispensed with. What it does mean is that their contribution can become more effective.

33. We think that there are three reasons why the Service should continue to recruit staff for the purpose of doing research work. First, knowledge and skills. While the trained, professional administrator will be more conversant with research matters, he will not normally have the same degree of skill in the conduct of research as a trained research worker. Secondly, the demands of day-to-day administration. This is the prime job for which administrators are recruited and its pressures must make it difficult for them to remain at the frontiers of new knowledge. Thirdly, qualities. As the Treasury pointed out in their paper on the question of a Social Scientist Group (Volume 5, No. 40), a man may be qualified to make a valuable contribution to research work, but he may not have the qualities required of an administrator. There are men and women who prefer to be researchers rather than administrators or managers. Some of them see their careers not primarily as civil servants but as researchers, moving between universities and research foundations, central government, local government and intergovernmental organisations, industry and so on; the Service should allow for a good deal of this in-and-out movement on the part of its research staff, which is indeed valuable because it refreshes ideas, skills and outlook and helps to maintain contacts with the outside world. For all these reasons, there is advantage in recruiting research staff to a group in which they can be sure of doing this kind of work.

34. Normally Research Officers should be employed within departments, and especially in Planning Units. We would also expect that some of the research projects of the Civil Service College would be carried out by Research Officers. Wherever they are employed, they should not be regarded as there just to serve up commissioned research with no further interest in the matter. They should take part in the process of considering what research should be done and its translation into policy.

35. The introduction of a unified grading structure should do much to provide

better career opportunities both in research itself and in a wider administrative field (age-bars to promotion, here as elsewhere, would disappear). It should also be recognised that their experience in analysis, and in the evaluation and quantification of the effects of policy, their familiarity with methods of systematic research and with the progress of research outside the Service gives them a highly suitable background for high-level administrative posts in the Service. Departments should therefore pay careful attention to the early identification of those with prospective talents for these posts. Their progress into administration, however, should not in most cases take the form of an abrupt transition. We see it as a steady process of moving into jobs of a more administrative character, but, initially at least, into administration closely related to their specific areas of research.

APPENDIX E

RECRUITMENT PROCEDURE

Selection for established posts in the Civil Service is the responsibility of the Civil Service Commission. The procedures the Commission uses vary for the different classes; they are set out in the following paragraphs, mainly taken from the Commission's evidence published in Volume 4, Section III.

PRESENT PROCEDURES

The Administrative Class

2. At Assistant Principal level candidates are selected either by:—

   (*a*) a qualifying written examination in general subjects followed by an interview and then by written papers in optional academic subjects at honours-degree level (Method I);

   (*b*) a qualifying written examination in general subjects followed by tests and interviews at the Civil Service Selection Board lasting two days, and interview before a Final Board (Method II).

In Method I success is determined by the aggregate mark for interview and academic papers; in Method II by the mark awarded by the Final Selection Board. Method II is now the more important method of selection and produces about three-quarters of the successful candidates.

3. Selection for the Administrative Class at Principal level is similar to that described in 2(*b*) above, under Method II; but for one form of recruitment there is no written qualifying examination.

4. Selection for the Administrative Class at Assistant Secretary level (two or three posts a year) is by means of a preliminary interview of those who from their qualifications and experience seem most suitable, and, for those who in the light of these interviews merit further consideration, an interview before the Final Selection Board.

The Executive Class

5. Recruitment to the Executive Class is from among candidates between the ages of 17½ and 28 (recently raised from 24); it is by interview of those with prescribed GCE qualifications including passes at Advanced level, or with equivalent qualifications. Among candidates from Her Majesty's Forces or Her Majesty's Overseas Civil Service selection is by means of a qualifying written examination in general subjects (from which candidates with appropriate qualifications are exempt) together with an interview; success depends on the mark awarded by the selection board.

The Clerical Classes

6. Over most of the clerical field, recruitment has been delegated to departments. Candidates for established posts must have an educational qualification based on the Ordinary level of the GCE or an equivalent educational qualification. Where necessary, departments may engage temporary officers with less than the prescribed educational qualifications; these officers may have a later opportunity of establishment by taking a Civil Service Commission examination.

7. The Commission itself recruits Clerical Officers in various ways. It conducts examinations on a country-wide basis for candidates from HM Forces and HM Overseas Civil Service, on the basis either of GCE qualifications (or equivalent) and interview, or by written examination. It also supplements the efforts of departments by recruiting Clerical Officers for established posts in or near London. This recruitment is partly by interview of candidates with GCE qualifications who are under 20, and partly by written examination of candidates who do not have the prescribed GCE qualifications.

157

8. Recruitment to Clerical Assistant posts is on similar lines but lower educational qualifications are required.

The Specialist Classes

9. Candidates are usually required to have some particular scientific, professional, academic or technical qualification, and sometimes relevant practical experience. Selection is by interview. Scientists, engineers, architects, accountants, lawyers, doctors, psychologists, librarians, and a wide range of other specialists as well as their supporting staff (technicians, draughtsmen, etc.) are selected in this way. Initial recruitment by departments in a temporary capacity, leading to permanent appointment later, is a common feature in these classes.

PROPOSED CHANGES IN RECRUITMENT PROCEDURE

10. We have proposed (in Chapter 3) that the Civil Service Commission should be integrated with the Civil Service Department. We also made general proposals about the recruitment procedure for:—

    (*a*) specialist staff (both graduate and non-graduate);
    (*b*) graduates for the administrative groups;
    (*c*) the non-specialist " A level " and " O level " entry.

Members of selection boards

11. First we recommend changes in the composition of interview boards who recruit staff at 10(*a*) and (*c*) above. At present where the recruitment of these categories is done centrally, the interview boards normally comprise a chairman and at least two and not more than four members. In addition to members drawn from departments, the members are drawn from panels of interviewers maintained by the Commission; the chairman is either a senior member of the Commission or is drawn from one of the panels. For the appointments at 10(*a*) above, the present panel of interviewers consists exclusively of scientists and professional men, most of whom are *retired* civil servants. For the appointments at 10(*c*) above, the panel of interviewers consists in the main of *retired* administrative and senior executive civil servants, headmasters and Inspectors of Schools, and includes a few former members of the Overseas Civil Service and the Armed Forces. In addition to our recommendation that representatives of departments should be in a majority on the boards, we also consider that serious consideration should be given to the age structure of each board, both for central and departmental recruitment. We think it wrong that retired civil servants should play a large part in the selection of young people particularly at a time when the tasks of the Service are changing so rapidly. In our view all boards should be predominantly composed of men and women who are still on the active list with a good many years still to go before retirement. We realise that departments often find it hard to spare good people (and they must be good) for work on selection boards. But we regard it as essential that serving civil servants should play a large part in the recruitment of the next generation. This should be given high priority in allocating the time of those concerned.

Recruitment of graduates for administrative work

12. A majority of us* recommended in Chapter 3 that the recruitment of graduates for the administrative groups should be by modified forms of either the present Method I or Method II. A minority of us recommended recruitment to this category by a modified form of Method II only. We set out in the following paragraphs the general line of these suggested modifications.

Method I

13. In Method I at present papers are set and marked in a wide range of university subjects at honours degree standard. The numbers taking the academic papers in Method I have dwindled steadily in recent years. The reasons for the decline in its popularity must lie to a large extent in the natural reluctance of candidates to take another written examination so soon after final degree examinations, or if they have

---

* See paragraph 82.

left university, to take an examination of this kind when they have been for some time away from academic study. Moreover, the wide variations in the content of first-degree courses, the growth of new specialisations, and the very wide choice of special subjects and optional subjects in university courses have made it increasingly difficult to devise syllabuses for the Commission's examination which adequately reflect all the main degree courses in the universities of the United Kingdom, and so cater fairly and attractively for all potential candidates. There are already over 160 papers in the examination (from which each candidate has to choose between five and seven). But the range of subjects and of papers is now unsatisfactory. A very large expansion in the number of papers would be required to make the examination fair to candidates from all universities by catering for all the options they can take. In fact this is virtually impracticable, and, in any event, hardly seems worth the effort when we consider that last year only 54 candidates sat the examination.

14. Though Method I is clearly unsatisfactory and unfair in its present form, the majority of us consider that it should be retained in a modified form. It should remain primarily as a written examination. The papers set, however, should be limited to those that have an obvious vocational link with the work of one or other of the administrative groups or the further specialisms that may develop within them; the questions should be designed to test the candidate's ability to relate his knowledge to the problems of modern government. It will be for the Civil Service Department to settle the precise subjects a candidate may offer in the examination and also the number of papers a candidate will be required to take. We would expect the papers to offer candidates the opportunity of answering questions related to the problems of modern government in one or other of the following main fields:—economics and business studies, social and administrative studies, science and technology.

Method II
15. In Chapter 3 the Committee unanimously recommended changes in the procedures and staffing of the present Method II. We said that there should be a larger representation of employing departments among the selectors; that their age distribution should be changed to increase the proportion of younger men; and that the part played by the Final Selection Board should be revised. Further, those of us who recommend " preference for relevance " consider that the selectors should be required, in addition to their assessment of aptitude and ability, to give appropriate weight to the relevance of an individual's graduate or post-graduate qualifications to the administrative group in which he wishes to work and to the specific requirements of particular departments. We elaborate these proposals in further detail in the following paragraphs. They are best considered against the present form of Method II.

16. Method II at present is divided into three parts as follows:—
  (a) There is a written qualifying examination in which all candidates have to take the following three written papers:—
      (i) essay (which carries 100 marks),
      (ii) English (which carries 200 marks),
      (iii) general paper (which carries 150 marks).
  (b) Those getting 230 marks or more out of the possible total of 450, together with borderline candidates selected for further consideration in the light of their records and reports, then attend the Civil Service Selection Board in groups of five for a series of tests and interviews extending over two days. The tests for each group are conducted by a chairman, an observer and a psychologist. There are two groups of tests. The first group are each separately marked out of 300 as follows:—
      (iv) a written appreciation,
       (v) a drafting test,
      (vi) a committee exercise: performance as chairman,
      (vii) a committee exercise: performance as member,
     (viii) a group discussion,
      (ix) an interview (40 minutes) with the chairman of the selection board who gives special attention to how a candidate has spent his time since

159

leaving school, to his leisure pursuits and to his reasons for seeking a job in the public service,

(x) an interview (40 minutes) with the observer, mainly to assess the quality of the candidate's mind,

(xi) an interview (40 minutes) with the psychologist, to assess his temperament and personality.

The second group consists of psychological and cognitive tests designed to measure aspects of intellectual ability. They are each separately marked on a seven-point scale as follows:—

(xii) two short intelligence tests which provide evidence of basic mental ability, though they assume a considerable educational sophistication and facility in the language,

(xiii) a statistical-inference test which gives an indication of ability to think numerically,

(xiv) a short exercise testing the range but not the depth of *general information* about current affairs, not too narrowly interpreted.

In addition, close attention is also paid to reports from school and university; and the assessors have to make their best estimate of potential for future development. The marks given for the various tests are not added together to produce an aggregate score, and, as at present devised, are not capable of being so added. The chairman and the observer arrive after discussion at an overall mark (out of 300) which is then put before the Final Selection Board at (c) below.

(c) Those reaching a certain minimum standard in the tests at (b) above then go before the Final Selection Board, whose composition is set out in paragraph 18(b) below. The interview before this board is decisive; it determines whether or not the candidate is offered an appointment in the Service.

17. We have serious doubts about the staffing and methods of work of the Civil Service Selection Board:—

(a) The present age-distribution of the chairmen and observers who conduct the two-day test at 16(b) above is not properly balanced. Twelve out of the twenty chairmen are over the age of 60 (one of them over 65), and these twelve are those most regularly used. Sixteen of the twenty are over 55. Thus very few chairmen are between 35 and 55, and those who fall within this age-span are the least frequently used at present. On the other hand twenty-three of the fourty-four observers are under the age of 35 (two of them under 30) and fifteen are between the ages of 36 and 44. The age-group between 35 and 55 is thus too little represented.

(b) When the tests at 16(b) have been completed the chairman, the observer and the psychologist together consider the candidate's performance and agree on a final mark (out of 300) which is the one which then goes to the Final Selection Board. Naturally, in agreeing this mark they take into account the candidate's marks on each of the separate tests; but their overall mark is their impression of the candidate's general performance (much influenced by the interviews at 16(b) (ix), (x) and (xi) above) rather than the total of the candidate's marks in each of the component parts. In a series of tests that seek to be as objective as possible, it is disturbing that the final assessment is made in a way in which subjective impressions inevitably play a large part in determining the candidate's final mark.

18. We also have serious doubts about the role, composition and method of work of the Final Selection Board:—

(a) It makes the final choice of those to be offered an appointment in the Service. Though it naturally pays great attention to the mark given to a candidate by the Civil Service Selection Board (C.S.S.B.) and to the reports of the chairman, observer and psychologist, it is not bound by the C.S.S.B.'s findings. The effect of this seems to be to give too much weight to the general (and necessarily impressionistic) interview by the Final Selection Board which lasts less than forty minutes, and too little weight to the tests at C.S.S.B. which last two days and which, notwithstanding our doubts at 17(*b*) above, provide the basis for a searching and objective assessment.

(*b*) The composition of the Final Selection Board is in our view open to question. At present the Commission's aim is to assemble, whenever practicable, a board that consists of the First Civil Service Commissioner (as chairman), two university representatives, two serving civil servants (one of whom is a Principal Establishment Officer), one woman and one representative from industry or the trade unions. When one of these cannot be obtained, a retired civil servant is often called upon. If, as is frequently the case, one of the candidates being interviewed is also being considered for the Diplomatic Service or for a Clerkship in the House of Commons, then one of the serving civil servants will be from the Diplomatic Service or a Clerk of the House. Thus, on these occasions, apart from the First Civil Service Commissioner, there may be only one serving civil servant from the Home Civil Service on the board making the final decision on a candidate's suitability for that Service.

(*c*) Although members of the Final Selection Board are expected to rely heavily on the reports on candidates from C.S.S.B., many members of the board have never seen any candidate put through the various C.S.S.B. tests or have any real knowledge of them.

19. The full solution of the problems to which we have drawn attention in paragraphs 17 and 18 above calls for a more searching inquiry than we have been able to undertake. We are clear that employing departments should play a larger part in the selection process than they do at present. We also believe that most, if not all, the chairmen of C.S.S.B. should be drawn from the 35-55 age-group; if there is to be an interview board in addition to the Civil Service Selection Board, the comments we have made on the age of members of selection boards in paragraph 11 also apply to it.

20. For the rest, while we make no detailed recommendations ourselves, our chief concern is that ways should be found of turning Method II into a process that is less subjective in character. This calls for further inquiry. We have considered three possible lines of approach:—

(*a*) The assessment of a candidate should be based on the cumulative total of the marks he has gained at the various stages of the selection process. Methods of marking performance in the various types of test should be devised to make this aggregation possible.

(*b*) The Final Selection Board should be abolished, and the decision to take or reject a candidate should be taken at the end of the C.S.S.B. process. The argument for this would be that the Final Selection Board is bound to rely too much upon personal and social evaluation, and that a three-stage selection process is unnecessarily lengthy (no-one starting from scratch would devise a three-stage system today). The C.S.S.B. would probably need to be reinforced for this purpose, e.g. by attaching representatives from universities, industry and government departments to the C.S.S.B. for the appropriate stage of the proceedings; but it would be important to avoid re-introducing an excessive element of subjective judgement.

(*c*) The final stage of the selection process should still be a subsequent interview by a separate Interview Board, but this board should be limited to giving its own mark for the interview it conducts (as in Method I); the candidate's place in the final list would then be determined by the aggregate of the marks given by the Interview Board (which would thus cease to be a Final Selection Board), by C.S.S.B. and by the examiners at the qualifying written examination.

The Scope of the Further Inquiry

21. We proposed in Chapter 3 (paragraph 70) that a further inquiry should seek means of speeding up recruitment procedures. We think that it should also consider ways of reducing the subjective element in Method II, paying particular attention to the

views we have discussed above. Its object would be to make recommendations, within the framework of our report, for as speedy and objective a selection process as possible.

22. The report of the social survey which we shall publish in Volume 3 also contains a great deal of material that is highly relevant to the problems of recruitment. For unavoidable reasons, this report could not be ready in time for us to give full consideration to its findings. We have drawn attention in Chapter 1 to Dr. Halsey's analysis of the trend of recruitment to the Administrative Class since the war. Dr. Halsey also finds evidence of a decline in the intellectual quality of successful candidates. Certainly, the proportion of *recruits* with first-class degrees has dropped, while the proportion of *candidates* with firsts has not. In our view, the inquiry we have proposed should include a thorough examination of this evidence and of the inferences that should be drawn from it for future methods of selection of all kinds.

23. We suggest that those who carry out this inquiry should include management consultants, who may be able to make a special contribution to the problem of reducing the time taken by the recruitment process, members drawn from the universities and those with expert knowledge of personnel selection both within the Service and outside.

The Application of " Preference for Relevance "

24. Those of us who recommend " preference for relevance " have considered various possible ways to give effect to this principle. One possibility would be for C.S.S.B. to assess the relevance of the studies of the candidate by reference to the actual curricula of the courses he has pursued.* Another would be to include in the C.S.S.B. procedure an interview designed to test the relevance of the candidate's studies. Another would be to give no preference in the selection procedure itself but to encourage self-selection by offering additional increments to those successful candidates whose studies had been most relevant to their future work, and who would thus be expected to make a valuable contribution to it more quickly.

25. On balance, however, most of us who recommend preference for relevance would prefer to give a small but definite advantage to relevance in the selection procedure itself by means of an objective test. One way of doing this might be to include such a test in the written qualifying examination. This is already done to some small extent by the inclusion of a statistical-inference section in the general paper. We suggest that this practice might well be extended to provide in each of the papers alternative sections in which one alternative specifically tests the candidate's ability to deal with modern social, political, economic and scientific problems—similar, in effect, to the questions now set in France for entry to the *Ecole Nationale d'Adminis-tration*. These sections would carry rather higher marks than the "traditional" sections; a candidate who was able to make profitable use of this option would carry his advantage, under a cumulative marking system of the kind we have discussed, through to the final stage of the selection process. We leave the size of the advantage in terms of numbers of marks for consideration by the Civil Service Department. It should be sufficiently large to indicate clearly the Service's special interest in recruiting those whose studies have already partially equipped them to handle the problems of modern government. At the same time, however, it should not be so great as to discourage the candidature of outstandingly able men and women who have studied other, " irrelevant " disciplines.

26. It may well be that after consultation with the universities the Civil Service Department may propose a better way of introducing an element of " preference for relevance" in Method II. Our proposal at paragraph 25 is no more than an illustration of one possible way. We should be content with any detailed scheme the Civil Service Department might subsequently propose provided that it maintained the spirit of our intentions.

---

*Sir Edward Boyle, Sir William Cook and Mr. Robert Sheldon think that this course should be adopted.

APPENDIX F

THE RECRUITMENT OF GRADUATES

In proposing the merger of the Administrative and Executive Classes (Volume 5, No. 1) the Treasury put forward two main reasons. One was that the character of Civil Service work had changed in the last 20 to 30 years; in consequence the existing division of this part of the Service into these two classes now hindered the most advantageous deployment of staff. We have dealt with this point in Chapter 6.

2. The second was that the pattern of recruitment to the Administrative and Executive Classes no longer fits the changing pattern of the country's educational system. Thus the good 18-year-old who before the war entered the Service after taking his Higher School Certificate now tends to go on to higher education and is thus lost to the Service for entry at that level. At the same time, at the graduate level only a tiny minority are potential recruits for the highly selective Administrative Class, while the Executive Class is not attractive to the rest. Therefore, the Treasury proposed the merger of the Administrative and Executive Classes with an enlarged graduate recruitment to the new combined class. All graduates in future, they suggested, should enter at the same grade; but, in order not to deter the graduate of outstanding ability, the Treasury recommended that he should be " starred " and after entry to the Service should be treated like the present Assistant Principal entry.

3. In our view this second argument and the proposals that flow from it are not well-founded. For one thing the projections of the future output of the educational system supplied to us by the Department of Education and Science which we reproduce in Volume 4, Section II, suggest that the supply of 18-year-olds with two or more " A levels " (the current requirement for entry to the Executive Class) will in fact continue to increase for the foreseeable future, though not steadily and at a slower rate than the output of graduates. With a steadily enlarging 18-year-old output on to the labour market there is no certain evidence that the quality of this output will be lower than it has been in the past; only if the national pool of ability were *both* fully tapped by the universities and other institutions of higher education *and* static would there be reason to suppose that the quality of the 18-year-old output would decline. Thus, in our view the case is not established that the graduate intake into the Civil Service ought to be increased on the sole grounds that the supply of good non-graduates is drying up.

4. Any proposal to increase the graduate intake must, therefore, be based on different grounds. In fact, we think that the Service is likely in the future to seek to employ a larger proportion of graduates than at present. The changing nature of the tasks of the Service and the development of more advanced and sophisticated management techniques increasingly require more highly qualified manpower. Further, the Service does not succeed now in recruiting all the graduates it needs. It manages to meet most of its requirements for graduates with the higher classes of degree, for example, those recruited to the Administrative and Scientific Officer Classes. It is not successful in recruiting enough graduates of less outstanding academic attainments. This is because under the existing system of classes these other graduates are recruited mainly to work in a class and grade deemed appropriate for the " A level " entry. In the light of these considerations and in view of the larger graduate output from the universities, it would be surprising if the Service did not in the future employ an increased proportion of graduates. In any event, our general proposals for recruitment and training must allow for this.

5. If there is a larger graduate entry, the problem arises of making clear that the Service is offering the outstandingly able graduate an attractive career. The Treasury proposal for this was that a proportion of graduates, roughly equivalent to the size of the present Assistant Principal intake, should be " starred " or otherwise identified on the strength of their academic records and their performance at the selection

163

stage. It proposed that these graduates should enter one or two increments higher up the scale and should have a career in their first years close to that of the present Assistant Principal. The remainder of the graduate entry was expected to enter at the present Executive Officer grade (i.e. the grade and level of responsibility to which an " A level " school-leaver is posted at present), and remain there for five years before being promoted to the equivalent of Higher Executive Officer level (i.e. two ranks below the starred graduate after the same period). We recognise that the Service needs to attract graduates of the highest calibre, but we feel unable to accept " starring " on entry. Our reasons are:—

(a) The proposal would to all intents and purposes involve the perpetuation of the present division between the Administrative and Executive Classes.

(b) Because the " starred " graduates were to have different, and better, training facilities immediately after entry as compared with the " unstarred ", it would be clear to the latter that their prospects in the Service were likely to be inferior to those of the " starred " graduates. Thus able graduates of a kind greatly needed by the Service would be reluctant to come in on an " unstarred " basis.

(c) We do not consider that academic performance at university and performance at the selection stage are a reliable enough means of distinguishing between those graduates who from the start should be groomed for the Service's top jobs and those who should not. Actual performance on the job during the first few years in the Service should be the determining factor.

(d) We cannot believe that the majority of graduates would be content to do a job at the present Executive Officer level of responsibility for their first five years in the Service. If this were the extent of the initial offer, they would not come in.

6. The Treasury's " starring " proposals to attract outstandingly able graduates were concerned only with recruitment to the merged Administrative and Executive Classes. There was no similar proposal for the graduate intake into the specialist classes, where no merger was proposed. However, the short-term forecast by the Treasury which we publish in Volume 4 shows that the demand for graduates with certain kinds of specialist qualifications will increase over the next few years. Our recommendations for the reform of the Service will open a wider role for the specialists than they have had in the past. It is therefore, in our view just as important to make it clear to candidates for the various specialist groups as it is to the graduates covered by the Treasury's " starring " proposal, that the Service is offering the best of them an attractive career.

7. Accordingly, we have proposed in Chapter 3 that, though all graduates should enter the same training grade, those judged outstandingly able and well-qualified on entry should be offered a starting salary two or three increments above the basic for the grade. This should apply equally to those recruited for specialist work as to those brought in for the new administrative groups. The more detailed application of these proposals would in our view mean that:—

(a) All graduates should initially be placed in posts thought appropriate to their ability and to the experience they need.

(b) The post-entry training given to graduates should be determined by an assessment of how they have performed and the aptitudes they have shown in one or more jobs, and not by whether they were judged worth extra increments at the selection stage.

(c) A graduate should be posted from the training grade to a job at the level of responsibility appropriate to his ability when:—

(i) The Service is satisfied that it has assessed his ability and, as far as possible, his potential, on the basis of his actual performance in the Service;

(ii) his post-entry training is completed.

At this point (which would not be later than five years after entering the Service), graduates should leave the training grade and the extra increments which some of them had to start with should disappear. We think it important that the best graduates should be promoted to posts in the new grade equivalent to the present Principal, Principal Scientific Officer or Senior Grade Engineer no less quickly than Assistant Principals are promoted to Principal today.

8. We cannot predict the size of the likely increase in the numbers of graduates recruited direct into the Service after the completion of their formal education. At present the Service recruits around 1,900 graduates and equivalents each year, including about 90 Assistant Principals, 100 Executive Officers and 50 Tax Inspectors and Ministry of Labour cadets; and about 350 scientists, 400 engineers and over 150 in other Works Group grades (mainly architects, valuers and surveyors) among a large variety of others from specialist disciplines. Information however is not available to show what proportion of the total enter at stages later than the completion of their formal education. It varies by class and is substantial in some specialist disciplines. The Treasury have estimated that this figure of 1,900 will rise to about 2,100 by 1970 (see Volume 4, Section II). Within this total, they foresee an increased demand for certain kinds of specialist graduates. Over a rather longer period they believe that a substantial addition will be needed to the graduate entry for administrative work. The rate of increase and the pattern of entry as between different disciplines will depend upon the extent to which new tasks are imposed upon the Service and the levels and kinds of skill they require. Our own proposals, if accepted, will also affect the pattern: a substantially larger late entry will reduce the demand for graduates direct from university; wider opportunities for specialists will affect the distribution between disciplines. We are not able to assess the probable quality (as opposed to quantity) of the 18-year-old entry into the Service in the years immediately ahead. The rate of increase in different categories must therefore be a matter for pragmatic decision over the years. We believe that our proposals for recruitment and training will enable the Service to handle whatever increase is likely to be required, and whatever pattern it may need to take. The Service should not however seek to employ more graduates than a rigorous analysis of the work shows to be necessary.

APPENDIX G

INTERCHANGE OF STAFF WITH OTHER EMPLOYMENTS

In Chapter 4 we recommended much more determined efforts to promote short-term interchanges of staff with other employments. We acknowledge the undoubted difficulties. But the value of interchange, both to the Service and the other employments concerned, is so great that energetic efforts should be made to overcome them. We think that a considerable expansion of interchange is feasible.

2. The evidence presented to us is nearly unanimous in supporting the desirability of such expansion. It comes from organisations in private industry and commerce, local government, nationalised industries and other public bodies, trade unions, professional associations and many individuals. The idea commands wide support within the Service from management, staff associations and individuals alike.

3. The idea is not new, but it has never got very far in the past. This has not been for lack of advocacy; but general goodwill has quickly run into the sands of practical difficulty. What has encouraged us on this occasion is the attitude of the Service's potential partners in a programme of interchange. They have expressed support in clear terms; some of them have made practical proposals. The Service should take them at their word.

4. Programmes of interchange involve certain risks for both sides. Some loaned staff may be drawn to stay with their temporary employer; there are risks of embarrassment, of the leakage of confidential information, of the wrong use of personal contacts. We believe that these are risks that should be taken; when the Service and the outside world are so deeply involved in each other's affairs, the dangers of isolation are much more serious than the risks we have referred to.

5. The difficulties are real enough but we believe that many of them can be overcome by concentrating on what will be most useful to both sides. We are particularly grateful here to the Confederation of British Industry whose supplementary evidence (Volume 5, No. 69) identifies many of the main problems and suggests how they might be solved.

6. Interchange is relatively easier to promote for specialists than it is for administrators. Their work in the Service is generally more nearly akin to that of specialists outside. The value of interchange in their case lies in the fact that the Civil Service specialist cannot always acquire within the Service the knowledge and, still more, the practical experience that his work requires. The engineer whose work consists mainly of monitoring the work of other engineers outside the Service is an example. He needs a period of attachment to an outside employment in which he can practise and refresh his professional skill—a period, therefore, long enough to enable him to do a fully responsible job.

7. The case of the administrator is usually different. Sometimes he too needs a long attachment of, say, two years. This arises when the pattern of his career makes it especially important that he should acquire knowledge in depth of a kind that can come only from a working experience of another sphere of activity. One field which seems to us to offer considerable opportunities here is local government. Mutual involvement is increasing all the time; it is most desirable that these two branches of the public service should have a real knowledge and understanding of each other and should share their skills and experience. In the past this has been difficult to arrange; local government, with its large number of small units, has not employed administrators of the Civil Service kind. But as local government comes increasingly to recognise administration as a professional skill in its own right (and possibly moves to larger units of administration), and as the Civil Service for its part comes to produce administrators who have specialised in various fields that are of concern to local government, we hope that this situation will change. We

welcome the recommendation of the Committee on the Staffing of Local Government[1] for a central staff organisation which could handle the mechanics of interchange; and the evidence submitted to us by the Association of Municipal Councils (Volume 5, No. 56), the County Councils Association (Volume 5, No. 73) and the Greater London Council (Volume 5, No. 79), all of whom are in favour of making a start.

8. More often, however, the best arrangement where administrators are concerned is likely to be a shorter attachment or study-visit. Partly this is because long attachments are often uneconomic: in many parts of industry, for example, the work is so different from that of the Civil Service administrator, and it therefore takes so long for him to become able to carry real responsibility, that the numbers of those who go for long attachments must be relatively small. But the main reason why we recommend greater emphasis on shorter attachments is that we wish as many administrators as possible to gain this experience. For example, the number of administrators who in the course of their work are involved with industry and commerce is very large. They need a direct knowledge they seldom acquire at present. We agree with the Confederation of British Industry that the right time for this is often early in a civil servant's career—hence our recommendation for outside attachments during the graduate's training period. But study-visits can also be valuable later, especially when a man moves into a new post and needs a direct insight into the field with which he will have to deal. We recommend that programmes of visits of this kind should be arranged with local government, the nationalised industries, private industry and commerce on the widest practicable scale.

9. Visits of this kind should be related as far as possible to a civil servant's future field of work. The Confederation of British Industry put this well in their supplementary evidence: " We regard systematic career-planning as essential if joint training experiences and secondments are to make a real contribution to a man's career and not simply be a more or less interesting break from his normal work ." Attachments will lose the greater part of their value if they are not carefully related to the development of the individual's career.

10. So far we have discussed only one side of the coin—outward attachments and visits for civil servants. We believe that the traffic should be two-way. There is no need to insist that interchange should be on a head-for-head basis: this would be far too restrictive. But there should be a reasonable balance. Experience shows that " outsiders " can settle down quickly in the Service and make a real contribution: the 1965 scheme, discussed in the Treasury's paper published in Volume 4, Section IV, has been a success. We believe that such inward movement can be no less valuable to those who come into the Service and to their employers. We would point out also that the lack of knowledge and understanding of the outside world for which we have criticised the Service has its mirror-image in the outside world. The public interest requires that active steps should be taken to reduce it.

11. It is for the Service and its partners outside to devise ways and means of putting these proposals into effect. We believe, however, that a systematic effort is needed and that co-ordinating machinery will be required to organise and give the necessary impetus to it. We suggest that joint working parties with local government and with industry, private and nationalised, should be set up to agree on a method of approach and organise the practical details of a programme of interchange.

[1]Published by H.M.S.O., December, 1967.

APPENDIX H

PENSION ARRANGEMENTS AND EARLY RETIREMENT

In this appendix we develop a number of the recommendations on this subject made in Chapter 4:—

    (a) the extension of the pension scheme to cover temporary staff,

    (b) the preservation of pension rights on voluntarily leaving the Service for any other employment,

    (c) improvements in the arrangements for compulsory early retirement,

    (d) improved pensions for certain late entrants.

We also discuss three other topics:—

    (e) the question of a contributory pension scheme,

    (f) the age of retirement,

    (g) the statutory basis of the pension scheme.

PENSIONS FOR TEMPORARY STAFF

2. The Civil Service pension scheme, as embodied in the Superannuation Act 1965, only provides pensions for established staff; temporary staff receive gratuities. Some temporary staff are nevertheless pensionable under other schemes. Certain categories, notably temporary members of the scientific classes, are in the Federated Superannuation System for Universities, and there are a number of other schemes covering small numbers of civil servants. But the majority of the 124,000 temporary civil servants are not pensionable.

3. The reason for this is the historical link between establishment (i.e. the granting of permanent status) and pensionability. This may well have been appropriate when the "fringe" of temporary staff was small and when few, if any, of them served for any length of time. We think, however, that this link between permanence and pensionability has now ceased to be appropriate. While we accept the need to employ staff on a temporary basis, it seems to us that a man or woman who has served for five years or more in the Civil Service ought to earn a pension for his or her service. Steps have already been taken to deal with those temporaries (and there are not a few) who give long service; those who are still serving at the age of 60 and have 20 years of service behind them are automatically nominated for establishment and so made pensionable. We think, however, that this is not a satisfactory way of dealing with the problem and we have therefore recommended in Chapter 4 that all civil servants who have served for the necessary qualifying period should be equal in this respect.

4. Extending the scheme to cover temporary staff would involve certain technical problems. It would presumably be necessary to make sure that their physical health at entry was not such as to impose an undue burden on the finances of the scheme. It would certainly be necessary to adjust the arrangements for redundancy, since it would be unreasonable to pay the generous redundancy terms that are now provided for members of the pension scheme to those who had expressly been engaged on a temporary basis. There is also the question of the reckoning of temporary service rendered before the date of the change. We are, however, satisfied that these problems can be solved, and that they are matters that it is right for us to leave for settlement by subsequent negotiation.

PRESERVATION OF PENSION RIGHTS ON VOLUNTARY LEAVING

5. We recommended in Chapter 4 that all civil servants who have served for an appropriate qualifying period should be able to transfer or preserve their pension rights on voluntarily leaving the Civil Service.

6. There are already a number of arrangements permitting preservation in these circumstances. They include the following:—

(a) There is a widespread system of transfer throughout the public sector. A civil servant who moves, for example, to local government may take with him a transfer value which ensures that his pensionable service in the Civil Service counts in full as pensionable service in local government.

(b) Any civil servant over 50 may retire prematurely and receive the pension and lump sum that he had earned prior to leaving when he reaches his official retiring age (this is generally known as a " frozen " pension).

(c) There is also a system of " approved employment ", whereby a civil servant who leaves for such employment may similarly freeze his pension rights and receive them on retirement from that employment (or from a subsequent approved employment). Approval is generally limited to public or quasi-public employments at home or abroad, but since 1964 civil servants of Assistant Secretary rank (or equivalent) and above have been allowed to leave on approved employment terms for any occupation they may choose.

This amounts to quite a wide area of freedom. But it is far from complete. Most moves into private employment are not covered. Civil Servants under 50 and below the rank of Assistant Secretary cannot have their pension rights frozen on moving to industry or commerce, and there are no transfer arrangements at any level with the private sector.

7. The overwhelming weight of the evidence submitted to us was in favour of full freedom in respect of pension rights. Informed opinion generally in this country has come to regard a pension not as a reward for a life-time of faithful service, but as a kind of additional remuneration which should be attached to any period of employment of a reasonable length, whether it ends in retirement on the ground of age or not. The Minister of Labour's National Joint Advisory Council has recommended in favour of the general preservation of pension rights on voluntary leaving. The National Insurance retirement pension scheme has preservation built into it—a point which will have added importance when earnings-related benefits bring larger National Insurance pensions for higher-paid workers. We have no doubt that preservation is the right principle for the public service. This is partly in order to promote mobility. More generally, we think that the idea of a tied pension nowadays reduces the attractiveness of the Civil Service for the potential recruit, not so much because he is actively concerned about his ultimate pension while still in his early twenties, as because it contributes to a more general feeling that to enter the Civil Service is to commit yourself to it for life. One of the findings of the survey of student attitudes which we reproduce in Volume 3, No. 9, was that transferability was regarded as the most important feature of pension schemes by 71 per cent of the students who had accepted or intended to accept offers of employment. We recommend therefore that civil servants of all ranks should in future be able to preserve their pension rights on leaving for other employment of any kind.

8. We have used two terms, " transferability " (meaning the transfer of pension rights to a new pension scheme) and " preservation " (meaning their storage towards an ultimate pension from the original pension scheme). The distinction involves a point of substance. The majority of pension schemes (and all public sector schemes) relate the level of the pension in one way or another to the salary earned immediately before retirement; the Civil Service pension for example is one-eightieth of the average salary over the last three years of service for each year of reckonable service (with a lump sum calculated on a similar basis). If therefore a man's pension rights are transferred to a new scheme so that his separate periods of service are aggregated for the purpose of calculating his final pension, those rights will grow in accordance with his subsequent earnings in his new employment. The combined effects of promotion and inflation are such as to make these rights much more valuable than they would have been if they had simply been frozen in the old scheme.

9. We therefore recommend that the Civil Service should adopt the principle of making full transfer arrangements with private pension schemes wherever this is practicable. We also regard this as an important aid to movement into the Civil Service, for the reasons set out in Chapter 4, paragraph 134. We recognise, however,

that this will be a slow business. Because pension schemes vary widely in their rates of benefit and accrual, no short cuts have yet been devised that might make it unnecessary to negotiate separate transfer arrangements with each individual pension scheme. In addition, therefore, we recommend that in general a frozen pension should be awarded on voluntary leaving in cases where a more satisfactory transfer arrangement had not yet been made.

10. There are two further aspects of preservation that need examination: the period of service necessary to qualify for a pension and whether preservation should be as of right. The present qualifying period in the Civil Service is ten years (though a transfer value may be paid after only one year). It would be cumbersome and absurd to have to provide for very large numbers of tiny frozen pensions for one or two years' service, which in many cases would not amount to more than a few pounds, and we think that the concept of a qualifying period is sound. There is, however, a strong case for reducing it from ten years to five. We think that in a number of cases the optimum length of a man's employment in the Civil Service may well fall between five and ten years, and that if periods of this length remain unpensionable they will not be attractive. We recommend accordingly that five years should be substituted as the qualifying period both for a frozen pension and (because they are inseparable) for a pension on final retirement.

11. Preservation as of right is more difficult. Under the pension legislation as it stands, no civil servant has a legal right to his pension; he cannot sue the Crown for it. The legislation is therefore couched in discretionary rather than in mandatory terms, but it has long been the policy that pensions should not be stopped or reduced below the maximum payable unless there is specific provision for this. In this sense Civil Service pensions are paid automatically. " Approved employment ", however, is subject to the decision of management and transfer values are occasionally refused, e.g. where the civil servant transfers simply in order to avoid an uncongenial posting. Similarly, cases could arise under full preservation in which a civil servant left " voluntarily " in order to anticipate dismissal for culpable misconduct. We think therefore that the management should retain reserve powers to deal with such cases, though they should be used very sparingly and not, for example, as a penalty because resignation causes inconvenience to the department.

12. It has been represented to us that there are two risks. The first is that our proposals may lead to an exodus of scarce, skilled staff, especially perhaps of those who have acquired in the Service a professional skill that is readily marketable outside. The area of risk however is limited, because senior civil servants and all those over 50 can preserve their pension rights already. More important, we are clear that the staffing problems of the Civil Service should be overcome not by imposing restrictions upon pension rights but by positive steps that will make people willing to enter and remain in the Service. The second risk is that if the Civil Service runs too far ahead of commerce and industry in providing for preservation, it will handicap itself in the labour market: civil servants who can preserve their pension rights will go to business but businessmen who cannot will not come into the Civil Service. This argument does not apply to transfer arrangements, which have so far been and should remain reciprocal. There is something in it as regards frozen pensions. But it cannot be regarded as decisive. The general tide is running in the direction of preservation, and this is an area in which the government as employer should be prepared to give a lead. The terms we have suggested are what seem to us appropriate in the light of the practice of the best employers today. They should be kept up to date as conditions change.

COMPULSORY EARLY RETIREMENT

13. We have recommended that there should be wider powers to retire on pension those who have ceased to give satisfactory performance and who ought to leave before their time in the interests of the Service. In the Civil Service, as in all employments, occasions arise when it is necessary for management to cause to retire early those who are inefficient or otherwise not up to standard. When the inefficiency is culpable, for example when it arises from persistent laziness or misconduct meriting dismissal, no special problems arise. But those cases in which downright dismissal with the total

or partial loss of pension rights is too severe a penalty, and still more those in which no particular blame attaches to the individual, e.g. if he has prematurely " run out of steam ", produce problems for management in all walks of life.

14. In the Civil Service the problem is made more acute by two factors. First, the permanent civil servant has in practice a considerable security of tenure. We discussed this in Chapter 4; in general, there are good reasons for it. But it makes it more difficult, because more conspicuous, to remove those whose performance is unsatisfactory. Secondly, as we have said in Chapter 1, the pace of change in the work of the Civil Service has been fast in recent years and this is likely to continue. The pressure of work, especially on senior civil servants, has been and seems likely to continue to be very severe. Particularly at such a time, it must be expected that some will lose their " cutting edge " before they reach the age of 60. It is sometimes possible quite properly to find them another job within the Service where the demands for speed and adaptability are not so great. But there remain cases, where none of these expedients is open, in which it is necessary in the public interest to retire men and women before their time.

15. The Superannuation Act contains a number of powers to deal with this situation. Under section 10 of the Act a civil servant over the age of 50 may be prematurely retired for inefficiency with the immediate payment of the pension earned by his service. Under section 9 an immediate pension may also be awarded if he is under the age of 50, but in that event the Treasury must lay a Minute before Parliament setting out the reasons for the award. Finally, section 45, which applies only to the Diplomatic Service, provides that an officer may be retired prematurely with an immediate pension if this is considered desirable in the public interest, having regard to his qualifications and the conditions existing in the Service. Section 45 permits early retirement whether or not the officer concerned is personally inefficient; it also empowers the Treasury to grant an enhanced pension in suitable cases. The numbers retired under sections 9, 10 and 45 over the last 15 years are shown in Volume 4, Section IV.

16. We think that these arrangements need to be improved in two respects. First, there is now in our view no good reason for the distinction between section 10 and section 9. We should like to see section 10 extended to all civil servants and section 9 abolished. If a Minute has to be laid before Parliament setting out the name of the person concerned and the reasons why, despite his shortcomings, the Treasury feel able to grant him a pension, this inevitably attaches a public stigma to the retirement, and we suspect that departments go to greater lengths than they should to keep inefficient employees rather than put them to this humiliation; the relatively small numbers of retirements in this category may bear this out. The procedures which have been established for the operation of section 10 seem to us perfectly adequate for the proper protection of individuals under 50 as well as those who have passed that age, and we recommend that the age limitation to section 10 should be removed. We note, incidentally, that this age limitation is the same as that which has hitherto limited the right to retire with a frozen pension, and it seems wholly appropriate that both should disappear together.

17. Secondly, however, we are not satisfied that section 10, as it is now operated, is adequate in modern conditions to deal with those officers who, though not technically " inefficient ", have ceased to be able to give a satisfactory performance. As it is drafted, section 10 covers much the same ground as section 45 and implies the use of very similar criteria. If anything, the words " in the interests of efficiency " in section 10 are wider in scope than those in section 45 " desirable in the public interest, having regard to [an officer's] qualifications and the conditions existing in the Service ". In practice, however, section 10 has not been used in the Home Civil Service for the same purpose as section 45 in the Diplomatic Service. It was apparently never intended that it should be used except in cases of proved personal inefficiency, and assurances have been given to the National Staff Side to that effect. It seems to us that this interpretation is too narrow, and that as a result the Home Civil Service is in a worse position than the Diplomatic Service, which is able to remove those who have failed to develop their potential or whose powers have fallen away unexpectedly early.

18. We do not think however that it is either necessary or practicable to apply

section 45 to the whole of the Home Civil Service. It is unnecessary because these more extensive powers are not needed for management purposes at all levels of the Civil Service. At less senior levels there is enough variety of work for it to be possible to find useful employment for those of limited capacity without detriment to the efficiency of the Service as a whole. It is impracticable because the Service is too large to ensure a common standard of administration throughout all its many establishments. By the nature of the case, what is involved here is not a measure of personal inefficiency that is plainly recognisable as impairing the effective working of the department or branch. It is something a good deal more subtle, and those at the top of a department who are to take action upon it need to know the person concerned and his limitations well if they are to act both justly towards him and wisely in the public interest.

19. We recommend therefore that a procedure analogous to that provided for in section 45 should be introduced for the senior ranks of the Service only, i.e. for those whose pay is above the maximum of the Administrative Class Principal.

20. We leave the exact procedure to be settled later. We think however that there should be adequate safeguards against unfair treatment; it should not become possible to get rid of a man simply because he is an awkward colleague or subordinate. We suggest therefore that there should be provision for appeal to a board, on which the chairman and some of the members should be independent " outsiders " of standing. It is also important in our view that the person concerned should be given the maximum amount of warning. He should be told privately as far ahead as possible that he is being considered for retirement under this procedure, which will be invoked if his performance does not improve. As soon as it is decided to invoke it, he should be informed. When the decision to retire him is reached, he should except in cases of real urgency be given a long period of notice (say nine months to a year) in which to make his arrangements and prepare the ground for his forthcoming retirement.

21. We have considered whether there should be provision for enhancing the pension or lump sum in these circumstances, as there is in the Diplomatic Service. There are arguments against it. Enhancement would mean providing a larger award than is granted in cases of ill health, and it is not clear that a person who *ex hypothesi* has not performed entirely satisfactorily should receive more than a person whose retirement owes nothing to this cause. On balance, however, we have concluded that a measure of enhancement would be right. Unlike the retirement for ill health, this is a deliberate act of management. It may well be that no blame of any kind attaches to the individual; on the contrary he may have worn himself out in the work of the Service. It seems fair that if, as we propose, the most senior civil servants are to be more liable to removal than their juniors, there should be provision for compensation. The form and level of this compensation we leave to be settled later.

22. We draw attention to one other matter in this general field. Occasions may arise, perhaps especially at the lower levels of the Service, when it is preferable to demote a person rather than retire him, especially if he is nearing the end of his working life and unlikely to be able to get another job, but departments may be reluctant to do so because of the reduction of his pension that will follow. Similar considerations may arise if a man has to be moved down because he no longer satisfies the physical requirements of a specialist job, e.g. in air traffic control. Such cases might be met more easily if the pensions were based not on the average salary over the last three years of service, but on the average salary over the last three years during which his salary was at its highest (for convenience in record-keeping, this might be made the best three years in the last ten). Normally this will be the last three years, but where it is not, it seems reasonable that the retiring civil servant should have the benefit of his peak earnings. We recommend that this possibility should be examined.

THE QUESTION OF A CONTRIBUTORY PENSION SCHEME

23. The present Civil Service pension scheme is non-contributory. We have considered whether it should be put on to a contributory basis. This was recommended by the Tomlin Commission, 1929-31, but has never been proceeded with.

24. It would make a marginal contribution to mobility. The full preservation

which we have recommended is practicable whether the pension scheme is contributory or not, and the importance of a contributory basis in this connection is therefore subsidiary. It could however produce two additional benefits:—

(*a*) the option of a return of contributions instead of transfer or preservation for those who left before reaching the retiring age but after serving for long enough to qualify for a pension (five years, as we propose);

(*b*) the return of their contributions to those who had not served for long enough to qualify for a pension.

There is no strong reason to encourage (*a*). The object of pension schemes is to provide against final retirement, not to produce lump sums in mid-career; and the return of an employee's contributions, even with interest, is much less valuable than even a frozen pension, which includes the much larger contributions made by the employer. On the other hand we see no reason why the State should behave more paternally towards its employees than other good employers by maintaining a pension scheme that does not permit voluntary leavers to encash their pension rights if they wish; and we do not therefore wish to preserve the non-contributory basis as a means of protecting civil servants against their own wrong decisions. The main point however is that at (*b*) above. While we think that a minimum qualifying period of five years is reasonable, and necessary for the economical running of the pension scheme, it is undesirable that no provision at all should be made for those who serve for shorter periods. Some, perhaps a high proportion, of those who come into the Service for short periods may stay for less than five years. Not all of them will be able to transfer pension rights in and out or maintain their membership of previous schemes. This problem could be dealt with in a non-contributory scheme by a system of short-service gratuities on the lines of that which now applies to temporary staff. If this solution were adopted, we think that such gratuities should be paid to all staff (temporary or permanent), for whom other pension arrangements had not been made, leaving after two completed years of service. We are however inclined to think that this purpose could be better served by making the scheme contributory, and giving those who left without qualifying for a pension a right to the return of their own contributions.

25. This is because we attach importance to the less tangible advantages of a contributory scheme. First, if a man pays contributions towards the cost of his pension, this helps him to feel that he is a partner in the process of providing for his retirement, and hence that he is more in control of his future. He may recognise that if he left the Service it would not pay him to take a return of his own contributions, but he may nevertheless feel a sense of satisfaction that this is his own decision and not that of a paternal employer. Secondly, a contributory scheme can help to build the right relationship between management and staff over the rules and provisions of the scheme. We have no criticism to make of the consultation that now takes place on these matters. But we think it would be better if the position of the staff in these consultations were based on the fact that they were contributing to the cost, and might have to help to finance improvements. This is already true of the Civil Service Widows' and Children's Scheme, which is contributory. We note moreover that the majority of private sector schemes are contributory, and that the same is true of the nationalised industries and most other public services. It would in our view be surprising if the reasons for this general practice did not equally apply to the Civil Service.

26. We are therefore greatly in favour of a change to a contributory basis. We are not however in a position to examine the practical implications of such a change at the present time. It may be that the additional administrative effort involved in collecting and recording contributions would be heavy, especially if the forthcoming introduction of National Insurance pensions related to earnings necessitated new and more complicated arrangements to combine National Insurance and Civil Service pensions. We recommend that the feasibility of the change should be examined as quickly as possible, and that the scheme should be put on to a contributory basis unless the practical difficulties prove to be over-riding.

Appendix H

IMPROVED PENSIONS FOR SHORT SERVICE

27. The Civil Service pension scheme, like many others, provides a full pension after 40 years' service; the pension accrues in the way described in paragraph 8 above and shorter periods earn smaller pensions *pro rata*. We have no quarrel with this as a general principle; if a man, for example, serves two employers for 20 years each, it is right that each should make provision for his pension. As a nation-wide system of preservation and transfer of pensions develops, it should eventually be possible for a man who changes his job to accumulate as good a total income in retirement as he would have earned by remaining with one employer all his life. This situation however does not exist yet, and a man or woman who enters the Service in middle age and is unable to transfer his pension rights, or perhaps has none to transfer, may end up with an inadequate pension. Private employers have at their disposal a number of expedients for dealing with this problem. The Inland Revenue permit full pension to accrue after 20 years; many pension schemes permit an employee who enters late to purchase " added years " for pension; and " top-hat " schemes are increasingly used to improve the pensions of highly placed individuals. In our view, the Civil Service is badly placed to compete for high talent in this regard. The Super-annuation Act provides one method of granting " added years ", but it is too inflexible and only rarely used.

28. We consider therefore that the existing " added years " provision should be replaced by a power that can be flexibly applied to provide late entrants with a pension that accrues at whatever rate is appropriate in each individual case (any existing pension provision from his previous employment being taken into account) up to a maximum rate falling within the rules set by the Inland Revenue. The appropriate arrangements should be made when the individual first enters the Service and should constitute part of the offer of employment made to him. It is not, however, in our view, necessary or desirable that arrangements of this kind, which are expensive, should apply to all who enter the Service too late to do a full 40 years' work; they should be restricted to those individuals of high quality whom the Service wishes to recruit directly to positions of responsibility and who could not be attracted unless special provisions for pensions were made.

THE RETIRING AGE

29. Formally, the minimum age of retirement is 60 (exceptions are made to allow certain classes, e.g. prison officers, to retire on immediate pension at an earlier age). In practice the highest ranks normally retire at 60; but the majority of civil servants work on after reaching 60, many to 65 and a substantial number beyond that age. There are widely used arrangements under which officers can retire formally at 60 but work on in a temporary capacity, often in a lower grade. We have not received evidence on this matter, and make no recommendation for change. We think however that determining the right retiring age is an important and complex problem to which the Service should pay continuing attention in the light of current research and national policies towards retirement.

THE STATUTORY BASIS OF THE PENSION SCHEME

30. The details of Civil Service superannuation are embodied in Acts of Parliament and in statutory regulations made under the Acts. This means that all changes in the scheme require legislation and that many quite small changes involve not subordinate legislation but a separate Bill. As a result, these changes have to wait for parliamentary time. In consequence, it may be several years before an agreed change can be introduced. We think this to be an unnecessary complication, besides wasting parliamentary time. We do not dispute that Parliament should exercise a proper control over this large element of staff expenditure. But it seems to us that ways could be found of ensuring this that would yet enable changes in the pension scheme to be made more promptly and with less fuss. We recommend that they should be looked for.

174

APPENDIX I

THE WORKING ENVIRONMENT

We mean by " working environment " first, the physical conditions in which civil servants work, and secondly, the office services on which they can draw to deal with their work quickly and efficiently. We have received a paper from the Ministry of Public Building and Works (Volume 4, Section VIII) on government office accommodation and a paper from the Treasury on the adequacy of the provision of office machines (Volume 4, Section VIII). The report of the Management Consultancy Group also commented on these things (Volume 2, paragraphs 277-279).

2. In our view, the Civil Service tends to under-estimate the importance of the working environment. Thrift in these matters is wholly creditable, but parsimony is damaging. We have formed the impression that the Civil Service makes too much of a virtue of austerity, and in some ways has allowed it to develop to the point at which the reputation and efficiency of the Service suffers from it.

PHYSICAL CONDITIONS

3. Several outside witnesses have commented on the generally shabby impression given by many government offices. We agree with them that the effect is often dispiriting, and we find it hard to believe that it has no effect both on potential recruits to the Service and on those who do their daily work in these surroundings.

4. Clearly, there can be no early solution to the problem of old buildings, discussed in the paper submitted by the Ministry of Public Building and Works. A programme of replacing those that are no longer adequate is under way. We have not attempted to form a judgment on whether it is going ahead with the greatest justifiable speed. We do not, however, think that enough is done on the maintenance of the older buildings. More could be done by better cleaning and more frequent painting to make them reasonably pleasant to work in.

5. In particular, it is essential to provide better lavatories and washroom facilities. Some of those which we have used ourselves in the course of the last two years have been below any tolerable standard, and we note without surprise that the same thing struck our Management Consultancy Group (paragraph 277 of their report). Lavatories and washrooms are frequently dirty and without towels and soap. This is unhygienic. It is also absurd to see officials (including sometimes Permanent Secretaries) keeping their personal towels and soap in a drawer of their desk and walking the corridors with them. Responsible management includes good housekeeping.

SECRETARIAL SERVICES

6. Inadequate services waste skilled manpower higher up. If highly-paid staff have to spend time getting their own telephone calls or cannot get urgent work typed quickly, the Service incurs serious costs in frustration and inefficiency. The top levels of the Service are well served. But the secretarial and other services on which the middle ranks can call are often seriously inadequate. We realise that there is a serious shortage of typists in London and that it will probably continue to be necessary to send much typing work to typing pools in the provinces. But we think that the situation could be improved by the more systematic use of dictating machines and by experimenting with different systems for the pay of typists. The Civil Service puts itself at an unnecessary disadvantage in the competition for typists by basing their pay on long salary-scales, which are appropriate to a person who is starting a lifetime's career in the Civil Service, but much less so to people whose turnover is expected to be rapid. We are aware that efforts have been made to improve the position. But the basic typist Grade II, for example, is recruited on a pay-scale which is too long— no less than fourteen annual steps. The top rate is reasonable. But because the scale is so long, the starting rate is unattractive. We have not examined the problems involved in combining pay-scales that are suitable for girls who want a career in the

175

Civil Service with scales appropriate for those who would prefer a short-term contract. But we are clear that something on these lines is needed.

7. Staff at the level of Assistant Secretary and above have personal secretaries. But those below generally do not, and many, especially among the specialists, find that their work is seriously held up by the lack of clerical support and routine office help. This wastes their time. The provision of personal assistants is not necessarily the right solution; it can be very wasteful where they are not fully employed. But shared and central facilities could be extended with great advantage. Their availability should not necessarily be determined by reference to rank; the criterion should be the needs of the work at any level.

8. We have seen that the Service is by no means backward in trying out and providing the most modern office machines. It is, however, less good at making their existence and advantages known to those who could make good use of them. We think also that there is a good deal of scope for the wider use of the simpler aids such as ready-reckoners and adding machines. Too many calculations are still done in longhand. Our Management Consultancy Group also found that complicated procedures were needed to acquire such small items as pens and erasers. We hope that the expanded management services units which we have proposed in Chapter 5 will, as a minor by-product, ensure that such simple obstacles to efficiency are speedily removed.

APPENDIX J

THE SUPPORTING GRADES

The majority of civil servants are in the supporting grades which fall predominantly at the lower end of the pay structure. They are of the greatest importance to the efficient discharge of the tasks of the Service. There are about 112,000 in the general and departmental Clerical Classes, 67,000 in the Clerical Assistant Class, 28,000 in the Typing grades, 26,000 in the Officer Keeper, Messenger and analogous grades and 48,000 in the Ancillary Technical grades—a total of 280,000 which represents over 60 per cent of the whole non-industrial Civil Service.

2. We recommended in Chapter 6 that all classes should be abolished and replaced by a single, unified grading structure covering the whole Service. In the course of the examination that led us to this conclusion we considered whether the problems of the supporting grades were such that we ought to recommend for them a different and special solution. We concluded, however, that the case for a unified grading structure applied to these as well as to the other levels of the Service.

3. In these areas of the Service, as elsewhere, there are a great number of separate classes, again divided both horizontally and vertically. For example, there are upper and lower Reproduction Classes, 'A' comprising craftsmen and 'B' semi-skilled workers. There are separate classes side by side for reproduction (maps), photo-printers, duplicator operators (stencils, offset-litho, etc.) and machine operators (calculating machines, punched cards, etc.). There are separate classes again for office keepers, paperkeepers and messengers, and there are also separate classes for Clerical Officers and Clerical Assistants. The problems posed by this large number of separate classes, many with their own separate career structures, are as we have set out in Chapter 6.

4. We received evidence from the Treasury (Volume 5, No. 11) and from the Civil Service Union, the Civil Service Clerical Association, the Society of Technical Civil Servants, the Association of Government Supervisors and Radio Operators, the Inland Revenue Staff Federation, the Customs and Excise Launch Service Association and the Ministry of Labour Staff Association on the classes they represent within this area of the Service (Volume 5, Nos. 27, 22, 49, 19, 35, 32 and 46). Among the main points they severally put to us were:—

    (a) Promotion prospects should be improved by:—

        (i) the creation of higher posts within the fields now covered by these classes. In particular new supervisory grades for Tracers and Drawing Office Assistants should be created to provide a career for those who are unlikely to rise above their present field; higher supervisory grades should be introduced for the specialised management of stores and reproduction work; and a new grade of Employment Officer should be introduced in the Ministry of Labour.

        (ii) larger promotion outlets to higher classes.

    (b) The Reproduction Classes should be merged and there should also be a merger between the Radio Technicians (who are represented by the CSU and AGSRO) and the Telecommunications Technical Officers (who are represented by the Institution of Professional Civil Servants).

    (c) Many jobs at present graded as industrial should be regraded as non-industrial: and a new class should be created to make possible a continuous grading structure for those who work in electronics.

    (d) There should be a review of the structure of the Typing, Duplicating and Machine Operator classes; as regards the latter it was suggested that the Machine Assistant should become a training grade, and Machine Operator the main working grade, with pay geared to proficiency.

(e) Incremental scales should be shortened to enable the new entrant to reach his maximum sooner, while long-service increments at periodic intervals should be introduced for unpromoted officers who have reached their salary maximum.

5. In our view the main problems exposed by this evidence spring from the rigidities and inflexibilities associated with the structure of classes which we have condemned in Chapter 6. They cannot, therefore, be solved without the abolition of these separate classes and their incorporation within the unified grading structure we have recommended. This will provide the essential framework for the greater flexibility in organisation and deployment that is vital to managerial efficiency in this area of work. It will also provide better career opportunities; we believe these to be unduly restricted by the present arrangements.

6. At the same time, the supporting grades pose a special problem. We would expect the development of mechanisation and especially of computers greatly to change the nature of their work in the coming years. This change will not come suddenly. But its effect will be to make personnel management much more important at these levels. The main need, as the evidence shows, is that there should be an open route to promotion to work of higher responsibility.

7. Departments will accordingly need to give more attention to this. It is not only a question of selecting those men and women who are capable of filling posts of greater responsibility within their own fields; it also means that departments should make special efforts to select and train those who wish and have the aptitude to move to other types of work that offer new prospects and opportunities.

8. In paragraph 243 of Chapter 6 we recommend as a first priority that the Civil Service Department should mount a major study to work out the precise details of a unified grading structure to be applied throughout the Service. We would expect this study to pay particular attention to the likely impact of much more extensive mechanisation of the work at these levels in the Service.

APPENDIX K

MAIN EVIDENCE ON IMPORTANT TOPICS

We refer briefly in this Appendix to those pieces of written evidence, published in Volume 5, that made an especially positive contribution to our work. We have perforce been highly selective. On some questions, for example the structure of the Service, a few papers have dealt thoroughly with the subject while others have referred to it much more briefly; here we refer to the former only. On others, there has been a great deal of evidence, no part of which however stands out as a full-scale treatment of the subject. An example of this is the need for greater mobility between the Service and the outside world, and the case for preserving pension rights on voluntary leaving—a point made very widely indeed. In these cases, we give a few examples, simply to illustrate the general scope and weight of the opinion put to us.

2. We have included no references to oral evidence. As we explain in Appendix L, we decided to take all oral evidence in confidence. A list of those who came to talk with us is at Annex II to that appendix.

3. We have also confined our references to those papers that contained proposals and comments, i.e. those published in Volume 5. We have also been greatly influenced by the reports of investigations and the factual material contained in Volumes 2, 3 and 4, but their scope is too wide for us to attempt to summarise them here.

STRUCTURE OF THE CIVIL SERVICE

4. The Treasury (Volume 5, No. 1) proposed the merger of the Administrative and Executive Classes and the formation of an integrated structure at the top of the Service down to the salary level of the maximum of the Assistant Secretary scale. The main papers on structure took this as their starting-point. As was no doubt to be expected, the main evidence came from inside the Service; outside organisations and individuals for the most part made only brief references to it. The Civil Service Clerical Association (No. 22) proposed the addition of the Clerical Classes to the merger proposed by the Treasury; the Treasury (No. 2) agreed. The Institution of Professional Civil Servants (No. 38) proposed similar mergers of the Scientific and of the Professional (Works Group) and Technical Classes into a Science Group and a Technology Group respectively; and later (No. 39) the creation of a Social Scientist Group. The Treasury disagreed (Nos. 5 to 8 and 40). The IPCS also proposed that the integrated structure at the top of the Service should be extended downwards to the maximum of the Principal scale. The First Division Association (No. 15) supported the merger of the Administrative and Executive Classes, but opposed the integrated top structure. Other staff associations made proposals relating to their particular parts of the Service. Those representing departmental classes were for the most part strongly in favour of their preservation. The Treasury, the Ministry of Public Building and Works and the Ministry of Technology exposed the problems that arise from the present groupings of scientists and engineers in separate classes (No. 7).

RECRUITMENT

5. The Treasury proposed a wider graduate entry to administrative work (Volume 5, No. 1). The Civil Service Commission described present procedures and suggested a method of selection for a wider graduate entry (Volume 4, Section III). Mr. J. H. T. Goldsmith proposed an alternative (Volume 5, No. 126). Other papers which discussed administrative recruitment at some length were submitted by the First Division Association (No. 15), the Society of Civil Servants (No. 47), Professor B. Crick and Mr. W. Thornhill (No. 120), Mr. N. Johnson (No. 133), Mr. J. H. Robertson (No. 143) and Mr. F. Stacey (No. 151). Problems of recruitment to the Clerical Classes were discussed by the Civil Service Clerical Association (No. 22).

6. Recruitment to the specialist classes was discussed by the Treasury in its papers about the Scientific Classes (No. 5), the Works Group (No. 6), the Economist, Statistician and Research Officer Classes (No. 8), Accountants (No. 9) and the Legal Class (No. 10). The Institution of Professional Civil Servants (No. 38), the First Division Association (No. 15), the Society of Technical Civil Servants (No. 49) and the Civil Service Legal Society (No. 26) commented on recruitment to the classes they represent. We were also assisted by papers contributed by the Council of Engineering Institutions (No. 72) and the Engineers Guild Ltd. (No. 77) about engineers; and by the Accountants Joint Parliamentary Committee (Nos. 51 and 52) and the Institute of Cost and Works Accountants about accountants (No. 89). General problems of recruitment were discussed in papers by schools (No. 110) and by Youth Employment Officers (No. 117).

TRAINING

7. Detailed proposals on management training were made in the Report of a Working Party under the chairmanship of Mr. S. P. Osmond (Volume 5, No. 13). Vocational training for specialists was discussed by the Treasury (No. 6) and the Institution of Professional Civil Servants (No. 38). Professor P. J. O. Self (No. 147) discussed in some detail the idea of a Civil Service College. This was also proposed by the Labour Party (No. 97) and Mr. T. Smith (No. 150). Management training for both administrators and specialists was also discussed by many staff associations and in a number of papers submitted by organisations and individuals outside the Service, notably by the Labour Party (No. 97), the Liberal Party (No. 98), the Council of Engineering Institutions (No. 72), the Royal Institute of Public Administration (No. 107), Professor B. Crick and Mr. W. Thornhill (No. 120), Mr. N. Johnson (No. 133), Mr. E. M'Ewen (No. 135), Professor Self (No. 147) and Mr. F. Stacey (No. 151).

CAREER MANAGEMENT

8. The greater specialisation of administrative staff was discussed by the Labour Party (Volume 5, No. 97), the Royal Institute of Public Administration (No. 107), Mr. N. Johnson (No. 133), Professor Self (No. 147), Mr. Deakin, Mr. Mayall and Mr. Plowden (No. 139) and a group of members of the First Division Association (No. 128). The career management of staff in their early years occupied a substantial part of the evidence of several staff associations, notably the Society of Civil Servants (No. 47) and the Civil Service Clerical Association (No. 22). Many papers discussed movement between jobs and between departments, for example those of the National Coal Board (No. 100), several Hospital Boards (Nos. 81-86), the British Railways Board (No. 63), the Confederation of British Industry (No. 67) and Dr. A. F. Earle (No. 123). The need for the better career management of specialists was discussed by the Institution of Professional Civil Servants (No. 38); many papers dealt with the need to give them experience of management work, for example those of the Council of Engineering Institutions (No. 72), the Royal Institute of British Architects (No. 104), the Royal Society (No. 108) and the British Institute of Management (No. 60). Several took the view that personnel work generally was in need of improvement and should be given a higher status within the Service. They included the Royal Institute of Public Administration (No. 107), the Confederation of British Industry (No. 67) and the Institute of Personnel Management (No. 92).

THE NATURE AND ORGANISATION OF CIVIL SERVICE WORK

9. The need for clear allocation of responsibility and authority was discussed by the Society of British Aerospace Companies (Volume 5, No. 113), the Confederation of British Industry (No. 67) and the Association of Municipal Corporations (No. 56). Much of the evidence favoured the setting up of integrated hierarchies and mixed teams. Examples are the papers submitted by the First Division Association (No. 15), the Institution of Professional Civil Servants (No. 38), the Liberal Party (No 98), the Council of Engineering Institutions (No. 72) and the Engineers Guild (No. 77). Stress was also laid on new management techniques, e.g. by the British Institute of Management (No. 60), the Electricity Council (No. 76), and on the need for internal efficiency audit, e.g. by Dr. A. F. Earle (No. 123). Problems of interdepartmental consultation were mentioned in a number of these papers, and also by Mr. P. Jay

(No. 132), Mr. W. S. Ryrie (No. 144) and Mr. J. H. Robertson (No. 143). Mr. Ryrie and Mr. Robertson also discussed the changing nature of Civil Service work. Mr. Robertson advocated the setting up of planning units, as did also Professor Self (No. 147) and Mr. D. Seers (No. 145). The role of the Permanent Secretary came in for a good deal of attention: the papers by the Institution of Professional Civil Servants (No. 38), the Greater London Council (No. 79), Sir Donald Gibson (No. 125) and Mr. N. Johnson (No. 133) are examples. Some discussed the question of hiving off executive functions to autonomous bodies; they included the Confederation of British Industry (No. 67), The Guardian (No. 80) and British European Airways (No. 59).

A CAREER SERVICE AND MOBILITY

10. There have been very few suggestions that the Civil Service should cease to be a career service; very many that there should be more mobility and better contacts between the Service and the outside world. Some, e.g. the Confederation of British Industry (Volume 5, No. 69), Sir Frank Turnbull (No. 152) and Sir Donald Gibson (No. 125), suggested that scientists and engineers in particular should have more mobile careers. The importance of better contacts was stressed, for example, by the Trades Union Congress (No. 115), the Electricity Council (No. 76), ICT Ltd. (No. 95) and the Greater London Council (No. 79). More late entry was widely recommended: examples are the Confederation of British Industry (No. 67), the Royal Society (No. 108), the British Institute of Management (No. 60) and Professor B. Crick and Mr. W. Thornhill (No. 120). Interchange of staff is dealt with in Appendix G. This too attracted very wide support from organisations and individuals in many different walks of life. Joint training courses (whether inside or outside the Service) were also favoured, e.g. by ICT Ltd. (No. 95), the British Railways Board (No. 63) and the Trades Union Congress (No. 115). As regards pension arrangements, there was very wide support for, and no opposition to, preservation on voluntary leaving. Several staff associations, the Royal Institute of Public Administration (No. 107) and the Institute of Personnel Management (No. 92) suggested pensions for temporary staff.

CENTRAL MANAGEMENT OF THE CIVIL SERVICE

11. Sir Laurence Helsby (now Lord Helsby), then Head of the Civil Service, put in a personal paper (Volume 5, No. 14). The general, but not unanimous, weight of opinion was in favour of a change, either to a Public Service Commission or to a new department. Examples are the papers by the Labour Party (No. 97), the Liberal Party (No. 98), the majority of staff associations (but not the Institution of Professional Civil Servants), the Royal Institute of Public Administration (No. 107) and the Trades Union Congress (No. 115). Some of these also proposed the closer association of the Civil Service Commission with the central management; so also, for example, did the Institute of Personal Management (No. 92) and Dr. A. F. Earle (No. 123).

RELATIONS WITH MINISTERS, MINISTERIAL APPOINTMENTS AND CIVIL SERVICE ANONYMITY

12. Relations with Ministers were not widely discussed, but were dealt with by the Labour Party (Volume 5, No. 97), Mr. D. Seers (No. 145) and Sir A. Percival (No. 137). The Labour Party were also in favour of a Ministerial " cabinet " on the French model. A greater number preferred a looser system of ad hoc personal appointments. The fullest treatment of this was in the paper by the Fabian Society (No. 78). It was also discussed by the Liberal Party (No. 98), the Trades Union Congress (No. 115), the Institution of Professional Civil Servants (No. 38) and Mr. T. Smith (No. 150). Comment on the convention that civil servants should be anonymous has been widespread. Most thought it should be relaxed, for example the Liberal Party, the Consumer Council (No. 71), Shell (No. 112), the First Division Association (No. 16), the Inland Revenue Staff Federation (No. 35), Mr. N. Johnson (No. 133), Dr. A. F. Earle (No. 123) and Professor Crick and Mr. Thornhill (No. 120). Some of these warned of the difficulties; so did Sir H. Poynton (No. 140).

GENERAL

13. On most points, there have been dissenting voices. But reviewing the evidence as a whole, we have been struck by a remarkable consensus of opinion. Many tributes have been paid to the strong qualities of the Civil Service. At the same time, there is a large measure of agreement on the major problems that now need to be solved and on some of the reforms that should be introduced for this purpose.

APPENDIX L

PROCEDURE AND ACKNOWLEDGEMENTS

INVESTIGATION AND RESEARCH

We commissioned six investigations. We wish to record our deep debt of gratitude to those who conducted them, many of whom devoted a very great deal of time and trouble to this work, to those who assisted them in various ways and to the individuals who co-operated so willingly by taking part in interviews and replying to question-naires. They have made a most important contribution to our work and, we believe, to a general understanding of the Civil Service.

(a) Management Consultancy Investigation

2. This was an investigation on the ground of a number of blocks of work in government departments, selected to provide as good a cross-section of the main kinds of work done by civil servants in the general service classes as could be examined by a small team in a reasonably short time. The investigation was carried out by a mixed group. It was headed by a member of the Committee, Dr. Norman Hunt. The other members of the team were Mr. John Garrett (in association successively with Mr. D. Morley-Fletcher and Dr. R. Ferguson) of Associated Industrial Consultants Limited, Mr. E. K. Ferguson of the British Petroleum Company Limited, whose services were made available to the Committee without charge over a long period, and Mr. S. D. Walker of the Organisation and Methods I Division of the Treasury. Twelve depart-ments provided facilities for the examination of their work, the staff associations concerned encouraged their members to co-operate, and nearly 600 individual civil servants took part in interviews and helped in other ways. The report of the team is published simultaneously with our report in Volume 2.

(b) Social Survey

3. This was a survey by questionnaire designed to provide the outline of a sociological portrait of the main general service classes of the Civil Service. It was conducted by Dr. A. H. Halsey, Head of the Department of Social and Administrative Studies at the University of Oxford, and Mr. I. M. Crewe, Assistant Lecturer in Politics at the University of Lancaster. The time available was too short to allow for a pilot inquiry or any study by the interview method of opinions or attitude to work, and the survey had therefore to be confined to factual information about the social and educational background of the sample. It will be published later in Volume 3.

4. Others who took part in this survey were the Government Social Survey, especially Mr. Louis Moss and Miss H. B. Lewin, who devoted much time and labour to the preparation of the material; the Treasury, which prepared the sample and gave other help; Dr. M. Knott of the London School of Economics who helped with the statistical side of the survey; Professor R. K. Kelsall of Sheffield University, who helped to design the shape of the survey; Professor Asa Briggs, Lord Heyworth, Professor W. J. M. Mackenzie, Sir Peter Runge, Sir Henry Wilson Smith, Dr. A. T. M. Wilson, Dr. E. G. Woodroofe and Mr. M. Zinkin, who read and commented on early drafts; and the individual civil servants who responded in overwhelming majority to the questionnaire.

(c) Entrants to the Administrative Class in 1956

5. Dr. R. A. Chapman of Liverpool University conducted a survey by questionnaire and interview of those men and women who entered the Administrative Class as Assistant Principals in 1956. His survey is also published in Volume 3 under the title " Profile of a Profession ".

(d) *Unsuccessful Candidates for the Administrative Class in 1951*

6. Dr. J. F. Pickering of Sussex University conducted a survey by questionnaire designed to examine the subsequent careers of candidates who had been unsuccessful in the open competitions for the Administrative Class fifteen years before our own inquiry. His report is also published under the title " The Civil Service Unsuccessfuls " in Volume 3.

(e) *Administrative Class Follow-up*

7. Dr. E. Anstey of the Civil Service Commission, assisted by departments, conducted a follow-up survey of members of the Administrative Class to compare the relative progress and performance of different types of entrant and to check the validity of the selection procedure. His report also is published in Volume 3.

(f) *Reports on the Civil Service since Northcote-Trevelyan*

8. Mr. J. B. Bourn of the Ministry of Defence made a study of the work of the main Royal Commissions and committees that have examined the Civil Service. His account is also published in Volume 3.

9. We also publish in Volume 3 reports resulting from other inquiries which were not commissioned by us, and in the design of which we took little or no part, but the results of which were made available to us by their authors. They are the following:—

    (i) Recruitment of graduates to the Civil Service.—The report of a survey conducted by the Psychological Research Centre.

    (ii) Executive Officers and Clerical Officers: a study of factors affecting ability, efficiency and job satisfaction.—The report of a survey conducted by the Treasury.

    (iii) Wastage of Executive and Clerical Officers.—Interim report of a survey conducted by the Treasury.

    (iv) Executive Class follow-up.—Interim report of a survey conducted by the Civil Service Commission and departments.

    (v) Evidence submitted to the Public Schools Commission.—Note by the Treasury for the Commission comparing members of the Administrative Class by school background.

These reports have been of great assistance to us.

FACTUAL AND STATISTICAL MATERIAL

10. We have received a great volume of factual and statistical material from the Treasury, the Civil Service Commission and other departments. This material has been an invaluable basis for our work. We are publishing much the greater part of it in Volume 4 simultaneously with our report, not only in order to show the facts on which we have based our conclusions, but also in the belief that this information should be made public for its intrinsic interest and value. We wish to record our appreciation of the time and trouble that went into preparing it for us.

VISITS ABROAD

11. Groups of us visited France (November, 1966) and Sweden (February, 1967). The Chairman and one other member also visited the United States (September, 1966). Our impressions of these visits are recorded in Appendix C. We cannot here record the names of all those who did so much to help us, but we are deeply grateful to each government which acted as our host and took great trouble to make our visit to their country interesting and profitable.

WRITTEN EVIDENCE

12. We have received a great deal of written evidence. It came from many sources: from the Treasury and other departments, from the Civil Service staff associations, from organisations outside the Civil Service (political parties, professional and learned bodies, nationalised and private industry, local authority associations and others), and from individuals both inside and outside the Civil Service. We think it right to

publish much the greater part of this evidence, and it is appearing simultaneously with our report in Volume 5. A list of the organisations and individuals whose evidence is being published is at Annex I to this appendix.

ORAL EVIDENCE

13. Many of our 89 meetings were devoted to taking oral evidence. We took the decision to take it all in confidence. We did so in the belief that we should best discharge our duty if we based our report on exchanges of views that were as frank and informal as possible, and not upon open statements of formal positions, which must necessarily be more reserved. In consequence we are precluded from publishing this evidence. A list of the organisations and individuals who came to talk with us is at Annex II to this appendix.

ESTIMATES COMMITTEE

14. We gratefully acknowledge the report of the Estimates Committee, which laid the foundations for our work in its Sixth Report to Parliament (1964-1965).

OTHER ACKNOWLEDGEMENTS

15. Our thanks are also due:—

To the governing body of Exeter College, Oxford, who released Dr. Norman Hunt from his many college duties for over a year so that he could devote his whole time to our work.

To Shell International Petroleum Company Limited, Imperial Chemical Industries Limited, Unilever Limited and Marks and Spencer Limited for information on their personnel management practice.

To Barclays Bank Limited, Courtaulds Limited, Electric and Musical Industries Limited, Electricity Council, Elliot Automation Limited, Fisons Limited, C. A. Parsons and Company Limited, Pilkington Brothers Limited, Prudential Assurance Company Limited, Rolls Royce Limited, Rover Company Limited, Tate and Lyle Refineries Limited and Tube Investments Limited for information on the turnover of staff in their employment.

16. We are also most grateful for the help of the typing and duplicating services of the Treasury. They met the heavy demands we placed upon them with impressive speed and efficiency.

GENERAL

17. The reports, the material and the evidence we are publishing give some indication of the amount of help we have received in the course of our inquiry. We mention in Appendix K those contributions that influenced our thinking on particular topics. Here we wish to record our gratitude to those on whom we imposed the greatest labours, especially the Management Consultancy Group, and Dr. Halsey and Mr. Crewe.

18. We have also received a great deal of help, official and private, from many civil servants in many departments. We may perhaps most suitably thank them all, and particularly the Pay and Management Group of the Treasury, in the person of Sir Laurence Helsby (now Lord Helsby). He put at our disposal all the knowledge, wisdom and experience gathered in the course of his distinguished career in the Civil Service, particularly over the last five years as its Head. We are very conscious of the load that our work has placed on him and on his colleagues, and are most grateful for all they have done.

We are publishing written evidence submitted by the following:—

GOVERNMENT DEPARTMENTS

HM Treasury*
Ministry of Agriculture, Fisheries and Food
Civil Service Commission*
Department of Education and Science
Home Office
Ministry of Housing and Local Government
Ministry of Labour*
Ministry of Power
Ministry of Public Building and Works
Ministry of Technology
Scottish Education Department

STAFF ASSOCIATIONS

Association of First Division Civil Servants*
Association of Government Supervisors and Radio Officers*
Association of Her Majesty's Inspectors of Taxes*
Association of Officers of the Ministry of Labour*

Civil Service Clerical Association*
Civil Service Legal Society*
Civil Service Union*
County Court Officers Association*
Customs and Excise Controlling Grade Association*
Customs and Excise Federation*
Customs and Excise Launch Service Association*
Customs and Excise Preventive Staff Association*
Customs and Excise Surveyors' Association*

Inland Revenue Staff Federation*
Institution of Professional Civil Servants*

Ministry of Labour Staff Association*

Society of Civil Servants*
Society of Technical Civil Servants*

ORGANISATIONS

Accepting Houses Committee jointly with Issuing Houses Association
Accountants Joint Parliamentary Committee*
Association of Child Care Officers
Association of Education Committees
Association of Family Caseworkers
Association of Municipal Corporations
Association of Unit Trust Managers

British Electrical and Allied Manufacturers Association
British European Airways
British Institute of Management
British Insurance Association
British National Export Council
British Railways Board
Building Societies Association

Chartered Land Societies Committee
Committee of Directors of Research Associations

* Also gave oral evidence.

185

Confederation of British Industry*
Conference of the Electronics Industry
Consumer Council
Council of Engineering Institutions*
County Councils Association

Educational Institute of Scotland (and comment by Scottish Education Department)
Electricity Council
Engineers Guild Limited

Fabian Society

Greater London Council
The Guardian

Hospital Boards:—
    Eastern Regional Hospital Board (Scotland)
    Manchester Regional Hospital Board
    North-East Metropolitan Regional Hospital Board
    Oxford Regional Hospital Board
    Sheffield Regional Hospital Board
    Welsh Hospital Board

Incorporated Society of Auctioneers and Landed Property Agents
Institute of Biology
Institute of Cost and Works Accountants
Institute of Landscape Architects
Institute of Municipal Treasurers and Accountants
Institute of Personnel Management
Institute of Physics and Physical Society
Institution of Heating and Ventilating Engineers
International Computers and Tabulators Limited
International Publishing Corporation

Labour Party
Liberal Party

National Citizens' Advice Bureaux Council*
National Coal Board
National Council of Social Service

Operational Research Society

Rating and Valuation Association
Royal Institute of British Architects
Royal Institute of Chemistry
Royal Institute of Public Administration
Royal Society
Royal Statistical Society

Science Research Council
Shell International Petroleum Company Limited
Society of British Aerospace Companies Limited
Stock Exchange

Trades Union Congress*

United Kingdom Atomic Energy Authority*

Youth Employment Officers

SCHOOLS AND COLLEGES
Apsley Grammar School, Hemel Hempstead

* Also gave oral evidence.

Ardwyn Grammar School, Aberystwyth
Boroughmuir Secondary School, Edinburgh
Bradford Girls Grammar School
Cardiff High School for Boys
Cathays High School for Girls, Cardiff
Colfe's Grammar School, Lee
The Grammar School, Llandysul
The High School, Kidderminster
Inverurie Academy, Aberdeenshire
Kesteven and Grantham Girls School
King Edward VI Grammar School, Stourbridge
King's College School, Wimbledon
King's Norton Grammar School for Boys, Birmingham
Peterhead Academy
Royal High School, Edinburgh
St. Albans Grammar School for Girls
Thomas Bennett School, Crawley
Tulse Hill School
Wandsworth School
Watford Grammar School
Wath-upon-Dearne Grammar School
Welwyn Garden City Grammar School

INDIVIDUALS

Group of Members of the Association of First Division Civil Servants
Mr. R. G. S. Brown
Mr. J. W. P. Chidell
Dr. T. L. Cottrell
Professor B. Crick, jointly with Mr. W. Thornhill
Mr. N. D. Deakin jointly with Mr. J. B. L. Mayall and Mr. W. J. L. Plowden
Sir George Dunnett, K.B.E., C.B.
Dr. A. F. Earle
Sir Donald Gibson, C.B.E.
Mr. J. H. T. Goldsmith, C.B.E.
Mr. L. J. Harris
Sir Laurence Helsby, G.C.B., K.B.E. (now Lord Helsby)*
Mr. C. E. Horton, C.B.E.
Sir Herbert Hutchinson, K.B.E., C.B.
Mr. P. Jay
Mr. N. Johnson
Mr. E. M'Ewen*
Mr. D. L. Munby
Sir Anthony Percival, K.C.B.
Sir Edward Playfair, K.C.B.
Sir Hilton Poynton, G.C.M.G.
Dr. R. Pryce
Mr. J. H. Robertson*
Mr. W. S. Ryrie
Mr. D. Seers
Professor P. J. O. Self*
Mr. I. S. T. Senior jointly with Mr. E. A. French and Mr. A. Axon
A Senior Executive Officer
Mr. T. Smith on behalf of the Action Society Trust
Mr. F. Stacey
Sir Frank Turnbull, K.B.E., C.B., C.I.E., jointly with Dr. A. V. Cohen and Dr. H. T. Hookway
Mr. R. Turvey

*Also gave oral evidence.

Appendix L

ANNEX II

The following gave oral evidence:—

GOVERNMENT DEPARTMENTS

HM Treasury

Sir Laurence Helsby, G.C.B., K.B.E. (now Lord Helsby)
Sir Louis Petch, K.C.B.
Dame Elsie Abbot, D.B.E.
Mr. S. P. Osmond, C.B.
Mr. P. Rogers, C.B., C.M.G.
Mr. M. E. Johnston
Mr. C. D. E. Keeling
Mr. S. L. Lees, M.V.O.
Mr. N. G. Morrison
Mr. H. Pitchforth
Mr. J. J. S. Shaw
Mr. F. R. Barratt
Mr. T. H. Caulcott
Mr. P. S. Ross
Mr. P. L. Burton (from the Civil Service Pay Research Unit)

Civil Service Commission

Sir George Abell, K.C.I.E., O.B.E.
Sir Frederick Brundrett, K.C.B., K.B.E.
Mr. K. A. G. Murray
Mr. K. M. Reader

Customs and Excise Department

Sir Wilfred Morton, K.C.B.
Mr. G. Imms, C.B.

Diplomatic Service Administration Office

Sir Colin Crowe, K.C.M.G.
Mr. J. Heath
Mr. P. H. Laurence

Ministry of Health

Sir Arnold France, K.C.B.
Sir George Godber, K.C.B.

Inland Revenue Department

Sir Alexander Johnston, G.C.B., K.B.E.
Sir Leonard Barford

Ministry of Labour

Mr. C. H. Sisson

STAFF ASSOCIATIONS AND THE NATIONAL STAFF SIDE

Association of First Division Civil Servants

Mr. J. A. Battersby
Mr. R. B. M. King
Mr. T. S. Pilling
Mr. G. W. Watson

Association of Government Supervisors and Radio Officers

Mr. P. L. Avery
Mr. W. Fenn
Mr. R. Hadlow
Mr. G. Keen

188

Association of Her Majesty's Inspectors of Taxes
Mr. A. D. M. Brown
Mr. E. Cropper
Mr. A. B. Scott

Association of Officers of the Ministry of Labour
Mr. M. J. Booth
Mr. J. J. Brennan
Mr. K. V. Powell

Civil Service Clerical Association
Mr. W. L. Kendall
Mr. L. A. Wines

Civil Service Legal Society
Mr. E. M. Cockburn, M.B.E.
Mr. J. R. B. Hodgetts
Mr. B. M. F. O'Brien
Mr. R. F. N. Thoyts

Civil Service Union
Mr. L. H. Moody
Mr. E. Roberts
Mr. M. J. Rose
Mr. J. O. N. Vickers

County Court Officers Association
Mr. R. Hacham
Mr. F. Humphries
Mr. D. F. Martin

Customs and Excise Controlling Grade Association
Mr. E. F. Elfick
Mr. F. R. Frost

Customs and Excise Federation
Mr. H. E. Buckingham
Mr. S. Cramp

Customs and Excise Launch Service Association
Mr. L. E. Anderson
Mr. N. J. H. Canning

Customs and Excise Preventive Staff Association
Mr. J. F. Douglas
Mr. H. G. Farren
Mr. F. Gray
Mr. J. N. S. Moore, M.B.E.
Mr. J. E. Morrish

Customs and Excise Surveyors' Association
Mr. E. J. Hoskin
Mr. J. R. Knipe

Inland Revenue Staff Federation
Mr. W. G. Lloyd
Mr. C. T. H. Plant, O.B.E.
Mr. F. D. Swift

Appendix L

Institution of Professional Civil Servants
Mr. W. A. T. Dorey
Mr. R. G. Fall
Mr. W. McCall

Ministry of Labour Staff Association
Mr. C. Bocock
Mr. G. Pearce
Mr. J. L. Tindall

Society of Civil Servants
Mr. J. R. M. Dryden
Mr. V. T. Morgan
Mr. L. Williams
Mr. V. A. C. Willis

Society of Technical Civil Servants
Mr. E. W. Baldwin
Mr. A. C. Carter
Mr. C. Cooper

Civil Service National Whitley Council (*Staff Side*)
Lord Delacourt-Smith
Mr. J. R. M. Dryden
Mr. T. Jackson
Mr. P. D. Jones
Mr. W. Kendall
Mr. W. McCall
Mr. C. T. H. Plant, O.B.E.
Mr. L. Williams

ORGANISATIONS

Accountants Joint Parliamentary Committee
Sir Henry Benson, C.B.E., F.C.A.
Mr. R. G. Leach, C.B.E., F.C.A.
Mr. J. M. Renshall
Sir William Slimmings, C.B.E.

British Petroleum Company Limited
Mr. P. D. Ince
Mr. B. W. R. Mooring

Confederation of British Industry
Mr. A. Cadbury
Miss R. Clay
Mr. J. Whitehorn

Council of Engineering Institutions
Brigadier J. R. G. Finch, O.B.E.
Lord Hinton of Bankside, K.B.E., F.R.S.
Mr. Ewen M'Ewen
Mr. H. N. Pemberton
Sir Robert Wynne-Edwards, C.B.E., D.S.O., M.C.

Trades Union Congress
Sir Harry Douglass
Mr. V. Feather, C.B.E.
Mr. D. E. Lea
Mr. L. Murray, O.B.E.
Mr. C. T. H. Plant, O.B.E.

National Citizens Advice Bureaux Council
   Mr. M. Bowers
   Mrs. C. Davis
   Mr. C. Hemming
   Miss J. Pridham

United Kingdom Atomic Energy Authority
   Mr. J. Charles
   Sir Charles Cunningham, K.C.B., K.B.E., C.V.O.
   Lord Penney, K.B.E., F.R.S.

INDIVIDUALS OUTSIDE THE CIVIL SERVICE (INCLUDING EX-CIVIL SERVANTS)
   Sir Henry Benson, C.B.E., F.C.A.
   Mr. M. H. Bernstein
   Mr. F. A. Bishop, C.B., C.V.O.
   Dr. J. Bray, M.P.
   Rt. Hon. Lord Bridges, K.G., G.C.B., G.C.V.O., M.C.
   Mrs. E. M. Chilver
   Sir Edmund Compton, K.C.B., K.B.E.
   Rt. Hon. A. Crosland, M.P.
   Rt. Hon. R. H. S. Crossman, O.B.E., M.P.
   Professor A. Day
   Professor D. Donnison
   Professor Sir Ronald Edwards, K.B.E.
   Rt. Hon. Lord Franks, G.C.M.G., K.C.B., C.B.E.
   Rt. Hon. J. Grimond, M.P.
   Sir Arnold Hall, F.R.S.
   Mr. R. A. Hayward, C.B.E.
   Rt. Hon. D. Healey, M.P.
   Rt. Hon. A. Jones
   Lord Kings Norton
   Professor M. J. Lighthill
   Sir Arnold Lindley
   Professor W. J. M. Mackenzie, C.B.E.
   Sir George Mallaby, K.C.M.G., O.B.E.
   Rt. Hon. R. Maudling, M.P.
   Sir Philip Morris, K.C.M.G., C.B.E.
   Mr. R. Morrison
   Rt. Hon. Lord Normanbrook, G.C.B.
   Sir Leslie O'Brien, G.B.E.
   Lord Penney, K.B.E., F.R.S.
   Rt. Hon. J. E. Powell, M.P.
   Sir Gordon Radley, K.C.B., C.B.E.
   Lord Redcliffe-Maud, G.C.B., C.B.E.
   Mr. J. H. Robertson
   Mr. W. Rodgers, M.P.
   Sir Leslie Rowan, K.C.B., C.V.O.
   Professor P. J. O. Self
   Baroness Sharp, G.B.E.
   Professor M. Titmuss
   Mrs. E. White, M.P.
   Mr. W. Whitelaw, M.P.
   Sir Henry Wilson Smith, K.C.B., K.B.E.

INDIVIDUALS WHO ARE, OR WERE AT THE TIME, CIVIL SERVANTS
   Sir George Abell, K.C.I.E., O.B.E.
   Mr. J. Allcock
   Sir Douglas Allen, K.C.B.
   Sir Herbert Andrew, K.C.M.G., C.B.
   Sir William Armstrong, G.C.B., M.V.O.

Dr. T. Balogh
Mr. H. R. Barnell
Mr. R. A. Bell
Mr. J. N. C. Benstead
Professor P. M. S. Blackett, C.H., P.R.S.
Mr. L. R. A. Bradshaw
Mr. A. R. Bunker, C.B.
Mr. D. B. Cahill
Sir Alec Cairncross, K.C.M.G.
Sir Harry Campion, C.B., C.B.E.
Mr. J. H. Cawthra
Mr. M. Clipsham
Sir Andrew Cohen, K.C.M.G., K.C.V.O., O.B.E.
Mr. E. C. Cornford
Sir Charles Cunningham, K.C.B., K.B.E., C.V.O.
Mr. D. Curtis
Mr. H. Davies, C.B.
Mr. P. Davies
Mr. R. Davy
Sir Maurice Dean, K.C.B., K.C.M.G.
Mr. I. A. Deane
Mr. F. J. Doggett, C.B.
Sir Harvey Druitt, K.C.B.
Mr. E. N. Eden
Mr. R. G. Elkington
Mr. J. D. Farmer
Mr. L. T. Foster, C.B.
Mr. L. G. Gale, C.B., O.B.E.
Sir Paul Gore-Booth, G.C.M.G., K.C.V.O.
Mr. R. J. H. Grieves
Sir Douglas Haddow, K.C.B.
Mr. W. G. Harris, C.B.
Sir Laurence Helsby, G.C.B., K.B.E. (now Lord Helsby)
Mr. P. D. Henderson
Mr. A. Hodgson
Mr. A. C. Hopkinson
Mr. M. C. Inglis
Mr. J. R. James
Sir Alexander Johnston, G.C.B., K.B.E.
Mr. G. F. Jones
Professor N. Kaldor
Mr. M. Kogan
Mr. W. D. Lacey
Mr. F. J. M. Laver
Mr. I. Maddock
Mr. F. R. Martin
Mr. J. M. McKeever
Mr. M. B. Morgan, C.B.
Professor C. A. Moser
Mr. J. Newton
Sir Thomas Padmore, G.C.B.
Miss L. Parry
Sir Antony Part, K.C.B., M.B.E.
Mr. G. A. H. Pearce
Mr. J. Plastow
Mr. R. D. Potter
Sir Richard Powell, K.C.B., K.B.E., C.M.G.
Mr. C. J. Pulham
Mr. J. G. Quinton
Sir Eric Roll, K.C.M.G., C.B.
Mr. R. E. Sainsbury, C.B.E.

Mr. M. Shanks
Mr. A. H. Spengler
Mr. J. P. Spens
Mr. M. Spiers
Mr. R. S. C. Stewart
Mr. L. J. F. Stone
Sir Burke Trend, G.C.B., C.V.O.
Mr. E. W. Tucker
Sir Richard Way, K.C.B., C.B.E.
Mr. D. F. Weatherup
Mr. I. Young
Sir Solly Zuckerman, O.M., K.C.B., F.R.S.

LIST OF RECOMMENDATIONS

THE TASKS OF THE MODERN CIVIL SERVICE
AND THE MEN AND WOMEN THEY DEMAND (CHAPTER 2)

The Service should act more quickly to identify and recruit new specialist skills that are needed. It should allow specialists to carry more responsibility than they do at present; the obstacles preventing them from reaching top management should be removed; there should be a deliberate policy of training in administration and management for specialists who are to carry these greater responsibilities (paragraphs 36 and 39).

2. New principles should be applied to the selection, training and deployment of administrators; they must possess the basic concepts and knowledge relevant to their area of administration (paragraph 41).

3. The administrator should specialise, particularly in his early years, in an area of administration (paragraph 42).

4. Administrative specialisation should be based on categorisation by subject-matter rather than by departments or groups of departments (paragraph 44).

5. We propose as a starting-point two broad groups of administrative jobs which provide a field for specialisation on the basis of their subject-matter: economic and financial, and social, each with its own internal specialisms; this pattern should be reflected in the training and deployment of administrators (paragraphs 45-47).

6. Economic and financial administrators should, in addition to their skill in administration, have appropriate qualifications, experience and training in such subjects as economics, finance, business administration and statistics, especially as applied to government work; to their basic knowledge of their field they should add any further specialisation that particular areas of government work require (paragraph 49).

7. The deployment of economic and financial administrators should not be limited to the main economic departments; they should be deployed in any department in posts that are mainly financial or concerned with economic administration and management (paragraph 49).

8. There will be a continuing need in some departments for economic and financial administrators who have been specially trained to apply their skills to work of a high scientific and technological content (paragraph 50).

9. Social administrators should have training and experience, in addition to their administrative skills, in the social studies relevant to modern government; the emphasis should vary depending on the social area of government concerned (paragraph 51).

10. Most social administrators should be concentrated in the main social departments, but many should be employed throughout the Service; there will be jobs in the economic departments for which social administrators are needed (paragraph 51).

11. Administrators should not replace those specialists whose primary concern is the practice of their specialism (paragraph 52).

12. It should be the task of the Civil Service Department to develop and refine these groups and keep them up to date (paragraph 55).

13. Some, both administrators and specialists, should be encouraged to specialise and make their careers in the kinds of work for which many different kinds of background and experience can be appropriate, such as contracts, computers, O & M, personnel (paragraph 56).

194

THE RESPONSIBILITY FOR RECRUITMENT

14. Recruitment, training and career management should be as closely integrated as possible; recruitment should be in the hands of those who also share a direct responsibility for the individual's subsequent training, deployment and development (paragraph 62).

15. The Civil Service Commission should cease to be a separate and independent organisation; it should become part of a new Civil Service Department and its staff should be integrated with it; some of its functions should be shared with the employing departments (paragraph 63).

16. The selection of recruits should be, and should be seen to be, independent of any form of patronage (paragraph 64).

17. Recruitment should be for specific ranges of jobs (paragraph 66).

18. Departments should have a greater influence on the selection of individuals; a higher proportion of staff should be recruited direct by departments; the employing departments should be better represented in the central recruitment of staff (paragraph 67).

RECRUITMENT PROCEDURES AND THE PROBLEMS OF DELAY

19. The procedures of formal competition should be restricted to posts for which there are many well-qualified candidates for a small number of posts, and even then it should be made possible to offer outstanding candidates rapid appointment; where it is in practice certain that there will be posts for all suitable candidates; they should be brought in without delay once it is clear that they are up to the required standard (paragraph 69).

THE PRINCIPLES AND METHODS OF RECRUITMENT

20. Specialist staff should normally be recruited direct by the department or establishment that is to employ them; recruitment should be by interview before a board, consisting of a majority from the employing department or establishment but including a kindred specialist from outside the Service and a representative of the Civil Service Department (paragraph 73).

21. Non-graduate specialists should be recruited by similar procedures to those recommended for graduate specialists (paragraph 88).

22. Of the non-specialist entry:—
   (a) School-leavers with " A levels " should continue for the most part to be recruited by the Civil Service Department, but departments should be associated closely with the process.
   (b) School-leavers with " O levels " should continue to be recruited by individual departments (paragraph 88).

23. Representatives of departments should be in a majority on selection boards, both central and departmental; they should be primarily composed of men and women with a good many years to go before retirement (Appendix E, paragraph 11).

24. In the recruitment of graduates, etc., for administrative work the Service should aim to recruit those with the best qualifications, aptitudes, qualities and experience for the jobs falling into one of the broad categories of administration. In the view of a majority of the Committee this means that the relevance of graduates' university studies to their future work should be an important qualification for recruitment to administrative posts (paragraphs 71 and 75). Those appointed without relevant qualifications should be required to take either a special, additional training course at the Civil Service College or a relevant post-graduate degree or course of study at a university (paragraph 79).

25. Over the years an increasing importance should be attached to the requirement that undergraduates seeking appointment to administrative posts should understand the use of numerical techniques and be able to apply quantitative methods to the solution of their problems (paragraph 81).

195

26. Non-specialist graduates should be recruited centrally by the Civil Service Department (paragraph 82).

27. There should be two main methods of entry for non-specialist graduates:—

    (a) In the view of a majority, Method I should be retained in a modified form on a trial basis only. The papers should be restricted entirely to those with a direct relevance to the problems of modern government.

    (b) Method II should involve a procedure based on that of the present Civil Service Selection Board, but with changes in the procedure and staffing of the selection process (paragraph 82).

28. There should be an inquiry into the methods of selection to consider ways of making the process of selection more objective in character, the problem of reducing the time taken by the selection process, and the evidence of trends in recruitment (paragraphs 70 and 83, Appendix E, paragraphs 20-23).

29. Separate entry competitions should continue to be held for such groups as Tax Inspectors and Ministry of Labour Cadets, wherever they are found to be appropriate (paragraph 83).

30. Graduate recruits to both administrative and specialist posts who are judged outstandingly able and well-qualified on entry should be offered a starting salary two or three increments above the basic for the entry grade (paragraph 86).

31. The Service should not seek to employ more graduates than a rigorous analysis of the work shows to be necessary (Appendix F, paragraph 8).

32. Recruits with such qualifications as the H.N.C. or with " A levels " in scientific or technical subjects should normally be posted to jobs for which their qualifications are relevant. For administrative staff recruited at this level their " A level " qualifications may be pointers to the direction in which they should specialise (paragraph 87).

LATE ENTRANTS AND RECRUITMENT FOR SHORT-TERM APPOINTMENTS

33. The prime factor in the appointment of late entrants should be the relevance of the skills, qualifications and experience they already possess for the job or range of jobs in which it is proposed to employ them (paragraph 89).

THE MANAGEMENT OF NEW ENTRANTS

34. There should be a complete review of grading at the levels of Clerical Assistant, Clerical Officer and Executive Officer to separate the jobs appropriate to the older civil servant from those appropriate to the young entrant who with training and experience should be capable of rising in the Service (paragraph 93).

35. School-leaver recruits should be regarded as under training for the first three or four years; they should receive substantial induction training; they all should be carefully watched by personnel management; more specialised training should be provided as aptitudes and potential begin to emerge (paragraph 94).

36. A training grade should be introduced for the graduate entry and for those of the non-graduates who have shown the highest ability (paragraph 95).

37. When they leave the training grade trainees should go straight to the level justified by their performance, without regard to the claims of seniority (paragraph 96).

TRAINING

38. A Civil Service College should be created (paragraph 99).

39. The College should provide major training courses in administration and management:—

    (a) Courses for specialists who need training in administration and management;

    (b) Post-entry training for graduates recruited for administrative work;

    (c) Additional courses in management for those in their thirties and forties moving into top management;

    (d) Refresher courses in the latest management techniques;

    (e) Courses for the best of the school-leaver entry.

Some of these courses should be wholly or partly residential (paragraph 100).

40. The College should provide a wide range of shorter courses in both general management and vocational subjects, for all levels of staff and particularly for the more junior; there should be a review of the balance between central and departmental training (paragraph 101).

41. The College should have research functions (paragraph 102).

42. Major courses should be concentrated in a single establishment close to London; a non-residential centre in London will also be needed (paragraph 104).

43. Graduate trainees in the administrative groups should, after an induction course, spend up to two years in their departments in jobs selected to test their ability and aptitudes and develop their capacity to take responsibility. As many as possible should get the experience of working at the places and at the levels at which the Service meets and deals with individual members of the public (paragraph 106).

44. Their main formal training should last up to one year, and should consist mainly of:—
   (a) Further training in the subject-matter of the various administrative groups;
   (b) The techniques of modern management;
   (c) Advanced and specialised training in the application of an individual's specialism to his field of activity.
   (d) The machinery and practice of government and administration.
The trainee should spend some further time in his department undertaking more responsible work. As many as possible should gain experience of work outside the Service. All should have some practical experience in the supervision and control of staff. The whole process should take up to five years (paragraph 106).

45. Many specialist graduates should go to management courses at the Civil Service College after a few years in the Service. Many should also be selected to return to the College at an appropriate stage for longer and more general courses in administration and management (paragraph 108).

46. The 18-year-old entry should be encouraged to take additional qualifications appropriate to their work; training and further education facilities outside the Service should be supplemented as necessary within the Service itself; bursaries and paid leave should be made available. Those going into management work will require training; the best should be picked out to join the graduates on major training courses (paragraph 109).

47. The College should put in hand a rapid and large-scale programme for the further training of the present generation of civil servants (paragraph 110).

48. Courses at the Civil Service College should not be restricted to civil servants; on many courses a proportion should be set aside for men and women from other spheres (paragraph 111).

49. The Civil Service College should not attempt to provide the total amount of training required by civil servants; departments should continue to run their own courses; more civil servants should attend courses at universities and business schools (paragraph 112).

50. The College will need its own full-time staff but should also employ on a part-time or *ad hoc* basis civil servants, and teachers and instructors drawn from universities, business schools, industry and commerce, nationalised industry and local government (paragraph 113).

51. The Civil Service College should be under the general direction of the Civil Service Department, but it should have its own governing body consisting of civil servants and men and women from outside (paragraph 114).

CAREER MANAGEMENT

52. During the early years of a man's career he should remain within the specialism or group for which he is trained; he should move between jobs and perhaps between departments, but usually within the area of his specialism, and, in the case of the administrator, at much less frequent intervals than now; the basic principle of career management should be a progressive development within a specialism and between related fields of activity; the personal interests and wishes of the individual should be taken into account more positively (paragraph 115).

53. Increased attention to personnel management and individual career planning should apply to specialists no less than to administrative staff (paragraph 115).

54. Personnel and organisation branches should be expanded to meet much greater demands (paragraph 115).

55. Seniority should count for promotion when it reflects experience of value for higher posts; but there should be more opportunity for the really able to move rapidly up. In the assessment of staff more weight should be given to performance on the job measured against set objectives (paragraph 117).

56. It should be evident to all that a man's performance before a promotion board is not the decisive factor in determining fitness for promotion; the primary job of the board should be to produce a fair and uniform judgement of individuals' promise and potentiality based primarily on their superiors' assessment of their performance in their present job (paragraph 119).

57. For promotions to posts at the level of Assistant Secretary, Under Secretary, etc. the Permanent Secretary should be assisted by a small committee (a " paper board "); there should be specialists on the committee, and, for promotion to Under Secretary level, a representative of the Civil Service Department (paragraph 120).

58. The terms " establishments division " and " establishments work " should be used no longer (paragraph 121).

59. Personnel management and organisation work will call for higher expertise and greater specialisation. Those specialising in it should from time to time get experience of work in the field outside the Service; they should have had experience of working in an operating division (paragraph 122).

MOBILITY, PENSIONS AND A CAREER SERVICE
(CHAPTER 4, APPENDIX G AND APPENDIX H)

LATE ENTRY

60. Late entry should be considerably expanded; there should be no restriction on the levels to which suitably qualified and experienced people from outside the Service can be directly appointed (paragraph 124).

TEMPORARY APPOINTMENTS

61. There should be more temporary appointments on short-term contracts, particularly of specialists (paragraph 125).

62. The Service should find means of reducing the proportion of other temporary staff and should examine ways of ensuring that civil servants do not continue to serve on a temporary basis for unduly long periods (paragraph 127).

INTERCHANGE OF STAFF WITH OTHER EMPLOYMENTS

63. Determined efforts should be made to bring about, as a two-way process, the temporary interchange of staff, both administrative and specialist, with other employments on a much larger scale; the Service should set up joint working parties with local government and with industry to agree on a method and organise the practical details of a programme (paragraph 128; Appendix G, paragraph 11).

PERSONAL APPOINTMENTS BY MINISTERS

64. A Minister should be able to employ on a temporary basis such small numbers of professional experts as he personally considers he needs to help and advise him; this practice should be put on to a regular and clearly understood basis (paragraph 129).

MOVEMENT OUT OF THE SERVICE

65. All civil servants who have served for an appropriate qualifying period should be able to transfer or preserve their pension rights on voluntarily leaving the Service (paragraph 136).

66. The Service should take the system of probation much more seriously (paragraph 132).

67. The Service should have wider powers to retire on pension those who have ceased to earn their keep, and should use them with more determination (paragraph 133).

THE CIVIL SERVICE AS A CAREER

68. The Civil Service should remain a career service in the sense that most civil servants should enter at young ages with the expectation, but not the guarantee, of a life-time's employment; and that the great majority of those who come to occupy top jobs will be career civil servants (paragraph 134).

PENSION ARRANGEMENTS

69. Full transfer arrangements should be made with private pension schemes wherever this is practicable; a frozen pension should be awarded on voluntary leaving in cases where a more satisfactory transfer arrangement has not yet been made (paragraph 136; Appendix H, paragraph 9).

70. Every civil servant—subject to having served for the appropriate qualifying period—should be entitled to a pension related to the length of his service; the pension scheme should be extended to cover temporary staff (paragraph 137).

71. Five years should be substituted as the qualifying period both for a frozen pension and for a pension on final retirement (Appendix H, paragraph 10).

72. The management should retain reserve powers to withhold the preservation of pension rights, but they should be used very sparingly (Appendix H, paragraph 11).

73. The possibility of basing retirement pensions not on the average salary over the last three years of service, but on the average salary over the best three years, should be considered (Appendix H, paragraph 22).

74. The feasibility of a change to a contributory pension scheme should be examined as quickly as possible (Appendix H, paragraph 26).

75. The existing " added years " provision should be replaced by a wider power that can be more flexibly applied (Appendix H, paragraph 28).

76. The need to legislate in order to make changes in the pension scheme is an unnecessary complication; another method should be looked for (Appendix H, paragraph 30).

TERMS OF EMPLOYMENT

77. " Establishment " should be abolished (paragraph 142). The new terms of employment should be:—

    (a) For all appointments except temporary staff, there should be a two-year period of probation.

    (b) On successful completion of probation, an individual should be informed and offered indefinite employment subject to a reasonably long period of notice; we suggest up to six months on each side. The Service should be able to end the employment only on one of the following grounds:—

        (i) redundancy,

        (ii) ill-health,

        (iii) disciplinary reasons,

        (iv) culpable inefficiency,

        (v) early retirement in the interests of the Service.

    In each case there should be appropriate safeguards for the person concerned.

    (c) Temporary staff should whenever possible be offered short-term appointments for a specified number of years (paragraph 143).

78. The process of confirming a civil servant in his appointment should be handled in a way that reduces the administrative complications involved in the process. It should be deferred until successful completion of probation. There should be considerable delegation of authority, subject to appropriate checks by the Civil Service Department (paragraph 144).

79. Section 9 of the Superannuation Act should be abolished and section 10 should be extended to all civil servants so that a civil servant over the age of 50 may be prematurely retired for inefficiency with the immediate payment of the pension earned by his service (Appendix H, paragraphs 15-16).

80. A new procedure should be introduced for the senior ranks of the Home Civil Service to deal with those officers whose retirement is " desirable in the public interest "; the procedure should include provision for an appeal to an independent board; the person concerned should be given the maximum amount of warning at all stages of the procedure. There should be some enhancement of pension in the case of officers retired prematurely under this procedure (Appendix H, paragraphs 17-21).

RETIRING AGE

81. The Service should pay continuing attention to the problem of determining the right retiring age in the light of current research and national policies towards retirement. (Appendix H, paragraph 29.)

THE STRUCTURE OF DEPARTMENTS AND THE PROMOTION OF EFFICIENCY (CHAPTER 5, APPENDIX I).

ACCOUNTABLE AND EFFICIENT MANAGEMENT

82. The principles of accountable management should be applied to the work of departments. Where measures of achievement can be established in quantitative or financial terms and individuals held responsible for output and costs, accountable units should be set up; work of this kind should be organised into separate " commands "; the manager of each command should be given clear-cut responsibilities and commensurate authority and should be held accountable for performance against budgets, standards of achievement and other tests; within his unit he should set up sub-systems of responsibility and delegated authority (paragraphs 153-154).

83. In much administrative work, measurable output cannot always be made the criterion for assessing performance; the principle to be applied is management by objective; the objectives and priorities of the branch should be clearly established; individuals at all levels should know what they are responsible for and what authority they have (paragraphs 155-156).

84. The establishment of accountable units must involve an addition to the Service's traditional accounting to supplement the formal Parliamentary accounts with cost data (paragraph 151).

85. When several departments, or several branches within a department, have a substantial interest in the same problem, methods should be devised of concentrating in one man or group the responsibility for organising the material and putting forward a solution; departments should make opportunities for adopting the problem-solving approach whenever they can (paragraph 158).

86. The Service should make experiments in reducing the number of working levels in the organisation of the flow of business (paragraph 159).

87. Where administrators and specialists are jointly engaged on a common task, there should be a single integrated structure under a single head, who should be the man with the most appropriate qualifications for the job. Below him administrators and specialists should be integrated in teams or unified hierarchies, in which the individual posts are filled by administrators or specialists according to the requirements of the task (paragraphs 160-162).

THE DEPARTMENTAL MANAGEMENT SERVICES UNIT

88. Each major department should contain a management services unit with wider responsibilities and functions than are given to O and M divisions at present and, in particular, with the following changes:—

(a) There should be efficiency audits involving all aspects of the department's work at all levels, with special attention to studies designed to improve organisational efficiency.

(b) The management services unit should be made responsible for promoting the use of the best management techniques.

(c) O and M should be equipped to operate effectively at all levels in a department.

(d) The functions of O and M and staff inspection should be combined in the same unit, which would mount operations of varying scale and depth according to the problem (paragraph 165).

89. The staff of the management services unit should be drawn from administrators, appropriate specialists, including accountants, and those with experience of similar work outside the Service; many should spend long periods in this type of work; many should have a relevant degree or professional qualification and experience as a manager or administrator in an operating division, followed by more specialised training in management techniques and subsequent refresher training (paragraphs 166-167).

90. Departments should continue to bring in outside consultants for special assignments (paragraph 168).

91. Management services units themselves should be periodically subjected to external efficiency audit (paragraph 170).

THE WORKING ENVIRONMENT

92. Much more needs to be done to improve the physical surroundings in which civil servants work (paragraph 171). In particular, lavatories and washroom facilities should be improved (Appendix I, paragraph 5).

93. The pay of typists should be examined in order to combine scales suitable for girls who want a career in the Civil Service with scales appropriate for those who would prefer a short-term contract (Appendix I, paragraph 6).

94. Shared and central secretarial assistance should be extended; the criterion should be the needs of the work at any level (Appendix I, paragraph 7).

POLICY PLANNING WORK

95. A department's responsibility for major long-term policy planning should be clearly allocated to a planning and research unit (paragraph 173).

96. Planning Units should be staffed by comparatively young men and women who should not normally remain in them beyond their mid-forties (paragraphs 175-176).

THE OVERALL DIRECTION OF DEPARTMENTS

97. There should be a Senior Policy Adviser or Advisers in most, if not all, departments to assist the Minister; he should be the head of the Planning Unit; his prime job would be to look to, and prepare for, the future and to ensure that day-to-day policy decisions are taken with a full recognition of likely future developments; he should have direct and unrestricted access to the Minister and should be free to determine, after consultation with the Permanent Secretary but subject only to the approval of the Minister, what problems his Planning Unit should tackle; he should not have responsibility for the day-to-day operations of the department; his rank should not normally be below that of Deputy Secretary (paragraphs 182-184).

98. In some big technical departments, it may be right to appoint a chief scientist, engineer, etc., to take charge of the department's technical work (paragraph 185).

99. One man, the Permanent Secretary, should continue to have overall responsibility for all the affairs of the department; he should be head of the office under the Minister (paragraph 186).

THE DELEGATION OF RESPONSIBILITY TO AUTONOMOUS PUBLIC BOARDS

100. We recommend an early and thorough review of the question of " hiving off " (paragraph 180).

101. The structure of the Service should be based on the following principles:—

(a) Both the grading of a post and the selection of the man to fill it should be based on an evaluation of the job.

(b) Management should appoint to each post the person it considers best fitted to fill it.

(c) No posts should be the preserve of any group except in so far as the individuals comprising the group may be uniquely qualified for them.

(d) It should be the right and duty of management to determine the new qualifications and experience required for particular posts from time to time.

(e) In filling individual posts, management should promote the right man even if he is not the next in the order of seniority, or bring him in from outside the Service if he cannot be found within it or if it believes that an appointment from outside would bring a valuable reinforcement of skill and experience.

(f) The pay for posts should continue to reflect the rate for the job on the basis of fair comparison with market rates for jobs of comparable responsibility and authority outside the Service.

(g) The structure should permit work to be organised in such a way that chains of command reflect the demands of the task and, where necessary, cut across any groupings by discipline or type of skill (paragraph 214).

102. To give full effect to our proposals, the present multitude of classes and their separate career structures should be replaced by a classless, uniformly graded structure (paragraph 218).

103. The salary range or scale for each grade should be relatively broad and there should be overlapping of salaries between grades (paragraph 219).

104. All the jobs now performed by the many different classes should be fitted into the appropriate grade by a process of job evaluation (paragraph 220).

105. The structure proposed is essentially a pay structure; it should not be used to determine the actual organisation of work (paragraph 221).

106. At all levels where the work requires civil servants to specialise, occupational groups will be needed and civil servants should generally be recruited and trained as members of them; they should include the administrative groups, the present specialist disciplines and the supporting grades (paragraph 223).

107. Occupational groups will tend to develop their own career patterns, and it should be established that it is normal to skip grades on promotion (paragraph 225).

108. The principle of " fair comparison with the current remuneration of outside staffs employed on broadly comparable work," established by the Royal Commission on the Civil Service 1953-55, remains valid. Outside comparisons should be made as part of the process of job evaluation, assessing the importance of the job to the work of the Service and establishing the rate for jobs of similar responsibility outside the Service (paragraph 226).

109. Negotiation and arbitration in the settling of pay claims should be preserved (paragraph 227).

110. Each grade should carry a range of pay except (in the view of a majority) the grade equivalent to that of Permanent Secretary, which should be paid at a flat rate (paragraph 228).

111. Progression through the pay-scale of each grade should be more flexible; annual increments should continue up to the level of Under Secretary, but:—

(a) Additional increments should be granted for especially good work and for success in gaining relevant qualifications;

(b) Increments should be withheld when they have not been earned.

Above this level the range of pay for each grade should become a " band " of pay; the progress of each officer through the band should not be on a regular incremental basis but determined by an annual review of his performance (paragraph 229).

112. The case for a unified grading structure applies to the supporting grades as well as to the other levels of the Service (Appendix J, paragraph 2).

113. Departments should make special efforts to select and train those in the supporting grades who wish and have the aptitude to move to other types of work (Appendix J, paragraph 7).

PRIORITIES IN THE ESTABLISHMENT OF A UNIFIED GRADING STRUCTURE

114. The Civil Service Department should mount a major study to work out the details (including the number of grades and the system of job evaluation appropriate to the Service) of a scheme for a unified grading structure together with the time-scale for its application (paragraph 243).

THE CENTRAL MANAGEMENT OF THE CIVIL SERVICE AND RELATIONS WITH STAFF ASSOCIATIONS (CHAPTER 7)

115. The role of central management should be changed and enlarged; its primary role should be to ensure that the Service is continuously governed by the principle outlined in Chapter 1 (paragraphs 247 and 248).

116. Central management should have the appropriate degree of ultimate authority in those questions that affect the interests of the public service as a whole (paragraph 248).

117. The expanded and unified central management of the Service should be made the responsibility of a new department created specifically for that purpose; the first main step to be taken in the reform of the Service should be the setting up of a new Civil Service Department which should absorb the functions of the Civil Service Commission, and carry the responsibilities for central management (paragraphs 248 and 254).

118. The new department should be staffed by a mixture of long-term and short-term appointments; departments should release some of their best men for a period of service in it, and some should be appointed from outside the Service (paragraph 255).

119. The department should include specialists; there should be an appropriate measure of central management for all the major occupational groups (paragraph 256).

120. The new department should include a Planning Unit (paragraph 257).

121. The official head of the Civil Service Department should be designated Head of the Home Civil Service; he should receive a lead in pay over the other official heads of departments in the Home Civil Service (paragraph 258).

122. We hope that the Prime Minister will remain directly responsible for senior appointments as well as for the machinery of government and security (paragraph 259). In putting forward names for top appointments to the Prime Minister, the Head of the Civil Service should be assisted by a committee of variable composition drawn from a panel with a rotating membership consisting of Permanent Secretaries, scientists and other specialists and one or two eminent people from outside the Service (paragraph 260).

123. The Prime Minister may wish to delegate day-to-day responsibility, outside the area for which he is directly responsible, to a non-departmental Minister of appropriate seniority who is also a member of the Cabinet (paragraph 261).

RELATIONS BETWEEN THE CIVIL SERVICE DEPARTMENT AND OTHER DEPARTMENTS

124. The principle should be to delegate to individual departments the maximum authority in staff and organisation matters compatible with the requirements of the Service as a whole (paragraph 263).

125. On questions of departmental efficiency and organisation, the main role of the Civil Service Department should be to encourage the use of the most modern techniques; it may have a special part to play in assisting reorganisation at the higher levels of other departments; in the last analysis it should be in a position to call departments to

account for failure to use the recommended techniques, to carry out investigations of departmental organisation and to recommend improvements (paragraph 263 (c)).

126. In the management of staff, especially the planning of careers, the main responsibility must remain with the employing departments; but the Civil Service Department should play a larger part than the Treasury does today and should have more ultimate authority; it should be responsible for informing itself about those civil servants who are identified as capable of filling the highest posts, should consult with the employing departments about their training and development and should take the initiative in proposing appropriate moves; it should have a voice, especially during the early years of the new system, in promotions to the Senior Policy and Management Group and should be represented on all the departmental boards for promotions within the group (paragraph 263(d)).

RELATIONS WITH THE TREASURY

127. The functions now exercised by the " Pay and Management " group of the Treasury should be transferred to the Civil Service Department, including:—

(a) responsibility for advising the Prime Minister on machinery of government questions;

(b) general supervision of departmental organisation;

(c) the development and dissemination of administrative and managerial techniques

—in addition to the broad responsibility for the management of the Civil Service; the division should be based on the principle that all the functions that belong to the Treasury in its role as " employer " should be transferred (paragraphs 265-266).

128. The Civil Service Department should be solely responsible for applying the Government's incomes policy to the public service; within the normal rules of collective Cabinet responsibility, it should have the final authority on any given pay settlement (paragraph 267(a)).

129. The central responsibility for ensuring that departments are efficiently and economically staffed should rest solely with the Civil Service Department; it should be its task to determine the scales of the staffs necessary for the efficient discharge of the tasks of departments (paragraph 267(b)).

130. Working procedures between spending departments and the two central departments, and between the central departments themselves, should be devised in order to reduce administrative complications to the minimum; arrangements should be based upon the clearest possible distinction between the functions and responsibilities of the two departments (paragraph 268).

WHITLEY COUNCIL MACHINERY AND THE ROLE OF STAFF ASSOCIATIONS

131. The staff associations and the Civil Service Department should jointly take part in a review to determine the new pattern of joint consultation appropriate in the light of the Government's decisions on our report; the pattern of joint consultation should reflect, not determine, the results of the changes we propose (paragraphs 273-274).

THE CIVIL SERVICE AND THE COMMUNITY (CHAPTER 8)

CONSULTATION AND SECRECY

132. Consultation with the interests concerned should be as wide as possible and should form part of the normal processes of decision-making (paragraph 278).

133. The Government should set up an inquiry to make recommendations for getting rid of unnecessary secrecy; the Official Secrets Acts should be included in such a review (paragraph 280).

THE ANONYMITY OF CIVIL SERVANTS

134. The convention of anonymity should be modified and civil servants, as professional administrators, should be able to go further than now in explaining what their departments are doing, at any rate so far as concerns managing existing policies and implementing legislation (paragraph 283).

135. There should be no obstacle in the way of the Minister's selecting within the department, or on occasion more widely within the Service, as his Private Secretary the individual best suited to his ways of working, and no stigma should attach to a person who is moved out of this job (paragraph 286).

136. We expect that Ministers will not normally wish to replace their Senior Policy Advisers; this must however be possible when a new Minister finds the current holder of this office too closely identified with, or wedded to, policies that he wishes to change (paragraph 286).

137. It should be more exceptional for a Minister to change his Permanent Secretary, but Ministers should not be stuck with Permanent Secretaries who are too rigid or tired (paragraph 286).

MANPOWER

138. We attach considerable importance to the developing practice whereby new policy proposals are accompanied by detailed estimates of manpower costs; these, no less than other costs, should be the subject of parliamentary and public debate (paragraph 301).

THE IMPLEMENTATION OF OUR PROPOSALS

139. We hope that the Government will take steps to review the progress made in implementing our proposals (paragraph 304).

PROBLEMS OF THREE SPECIALIST GROUPS:
ACCOUNTANTS, RESEARCH OFFICERS AND LAWYERS (APPENDIX D)

ACCOUNTANTS

140. The practice of bringing in accountants from outside for major jobs outside the normal routine should continue (paragraph 9).

141. A strong force of highly-qualified professional accountants within the Service is also needed; more qualified accountants are needed:—

    (a) in the Senior Policy and Management Group;

    (b) in purchasing;

    (c) in developing accountable and responsible management;

    (d) in management services (paragraphs 9-10).

142. Trainee accountants should be articled to members of the profession within government departments; some entrants with 'A levels' should be encouraged to take professional qualifications in accounting for which they should be rewarded with additional increases of pay (paragraph 11).

143. The work now done by qualified accountants already in the Service should be examined to see whether some of it could not be devolved upon less qualified staff (paragraph 11).

144. Accountants should continue to be an identifiable occupational group within the Service; the group should include cost and works accountants (paragraph 12).

145. The accountant needs broader training in his early years and also at intervals during his career (paragraph 14).

146. Late entry and temporary appointments should be encouraged (paragraph 14).

147. There should be adequate central management of accountants by the Civil Service Department (paragraph 15).

LAWYERS

148. The role of the Treasury Solicitor should be expanded and put on to a formal basis as Head of the Legal Service; the management committee should continue to function; consideration should be given to including a representative of the legal service in the staff of the Civil Service Department (paragraph 19).

149. Departments should have normal control over their legal branches; but the central management of the legal service should have a general concern for all questions of staff, and should be responsible for thinking constructively about improvements in organisation and methods of work (paragraph 20).

150. Certain kinds of legal work, such as conveyancing and litigation, should be centralised; legal branches in other departments should consist largely of lawyers engaged in giving legal advice on the policy of the department (paragraph 21).

151. Scotland should have a separate legal service organised on similar lines (paragraph 22).

152. Civil servants with the right aptitudes and interests should be given the opportunity to acquire professional qualifications in order to join the legal service (paragraph 24).

153. Legal executive work should be recognised as a specialism, and administrative staff encouraged to take it up (paragraph 25).

154. Lawyers should play their full part in the consideration and formulation of policy. Senior lawyers, as members of the Senior Policy and Management Group, should be regarded as being concerned with the affairs of the department at large (paragraph 26).

155. Lawyers with the desire and aptitude should be considered for jobs of a more general administrative or managerial character (paragraph 27).

RESEARCH OFFICERS

156. The Service should continue to recruit staff for doing research work (paragraph 33).

157. Research Officers should normally be employed within departments, and especially in Planning Units. We should also expect them to be employed by the Civil Service College. They should take part in the process of considering what research should be done and its translation into policy (paragraph 34).

158. Departments should pay careful attention to the early identification of those Research Officers capable of filling administrative posts (paragraph 35).

Printed in England for HM Stationery Office by Keliher, Hudson & Kearns
C1023   Dd142490   K240   6/68   51-8546